A TOUR TO THE HEBRIDES

Scale
English Statute Miles

0   10   20   30   40   50

MAP OF THE TOUR
through
SCOTLAND AND THE HEBRIDES
by Samuel Johnson LL.D and James Boswell Esq
in 1773.

THE JOURNAL OF
A TOUR TO THE HEBRIDES
WITH SAMUEL JOHNSON

by

JAMES BOSWELL

THOMAS NELSON AND SONS LTD
LONDON EDINBURGH PARIS MELBOURNE
TORONTO AND NEW YORK

James Boswell, Laird of Auchinleck, was born at Edinburgh, October 18, 1740, educated at Edinburgh High School and the Universities of Edinburgh and Glasgow, was called to the English Bar in 1786, and died in London on May 19, 1795.

He is remembered chiefly for his great " Life of Samuel Johnson," an abridged version of which appears in this series : " A Shorter Boswell," edited, with an introduction, by John Bailey, and with twelve illustrations.

This " Journal of a Tour to the Hebrides " first appeared in 1785.

DEDICATION

TO

EDMOND MALONE, Esq.

My dear Sir,

    In every narrative, whether historical or biographical, authenticity is of the utmost consequence. Of this I have ever been so firmly persuaded, that I inscribed a former work to that person who was the best judge of its truth. I need not tell you I mean General Paoli; who, after his great, though unsuccessful, efforts to preserve the liberties of his country, has found an honourable asylum in Britain, where he has now lived many years the object of Royal regard and private respect; and whom I cannot name without expressing my very grateful sense of the uniform kindness which he has been pleased to shew me.

    The friends of Doctor Johnson can best judge, from internal evidence, whether the numerous conversations which form the most valuable part of the ensuing pages, are correctly related. To them, therefore, I wish to appeal, for the accuracy of the portrait here exhibited to the world.

    As one of those who were intimately acquainted with him, you have a title to this address. You have obligingly taken the trouble to peruse the original manuscript of this Tour, and can vouch for the strict fidelity of the present publication. Your literary alliance with our much lamented friend, in consequence of having undertaken to render one of his labours more complete, by your edition of Shakspeare, a work which I am confident will not disappoint the expectations of the publick, gives you another claim. But I have a still more powerful inducement to prefix your name to this volume, as it gives me an opportunity of letting the world know that I enjoy the honour and happiness of your friendship; and of thus publickly testifying the sincere regard with which I am,

My dear Sir,

Your very faithful

And obedient servant,

JAMES BOSWELL.

LONDON,
20th September, 1785.

CONTENTS

CONTENTS

CONTENTS

HE WAS OF AN ADMIRABLE PREGNANCY OF WIT, AND THAT
PREGNANCY MUCH IMPROVED BY CONTINUAL STUDY FROM
HIS CHILDHOOD; BY WHICH HE HAD GOTTEN SUCH A
PROMPTNESS IN EXPRESSING HIS MIND, THAT HIS EXTEM-
PORAL SPEECHES WERE LITTLE INFERIOR TO HIS PRE-
MEDITATED WRITINGS. MANY, NO DOUBT, HAD READ AS
MUCH, AND PERHAPS MORE THAN HE; BUT SCARCE EVER
ANY CONCOCTED HIS READING INTO JUDGEMENT AS HE
DID.—*Baker's Chronicle.*

THE JOURNAL OF A
TOUR TO THE HEBRIDES

WITH

SAMUEL JOHNSON, LL.D.

DR. JOHNSON had for many years given me hopes that we should go together, and visit the Hebrides. Martin's Account of those islands had impressed us with a notion that we might there contemplate a system of life almost totally different from what we had been accustomed to see; and, to find simplicity and wildness, and all the circumstances of remote time or place, so near to our native great island, was an object within the reach of reasonable curiosity. Dr. Johnson has said in his *Journey*, "that he scarcely remembered how the wish to visit the Hebrides was excited;" but he told me, in summer, 1763, that his father put Martin's Account into his hands when he was very young, and that he was much pleased with it. We reckoned there would be some inconveniencies and hardships, and perhaps a little danger; but these we were persuaded were magnified in the imagination of every body. When I was at Ferney, in 1764, I mentioned our design to Voltaire. He looked at me, as if I had talked of going to the North Pole, and said, "You do not insist on my accompanying you?"—"No, sir."—"Then I am very willing you should go." I was not afraid that our curious expedition would be prevented by such appre-

hensions ; but I doubted that it would not be possible
to prevail on Dr. Johnson to relinquish, for some time,
the felicity of a London life, which, to a man who can
enjoy it with full intellectual relish, is apt to make
existence in any narrower sphere seem insipid or irksome. I doubted that he would not be willing to
come down from his elevated state of philosophical
dignity ; from a superiority of wisdom among the wise,
and of learning among the learned ; and from flashing
his wit upon minds bright enough to reflect it.

He had disappointed my expectations so long, that
I began to despair ; but in spring, 1773, he talked of
coming to Scotland that year with so much firmness,
that I hoped he was at last in earnest. I knew that,
if he were once launched from the metropolis, he would
go forward very well ; and I got our common friends
there to assist in setting him afloat. To Mrs. Thrale
in particular, whose enchantment over him seldom
failed, I was much obliged. It was, " *I'll give thee a
wind.*"—" *Thou art kind.*"—To *attract* him, we had
invitations from the chiefs Macdonald and Macleod ;
and, for additional aid, I wrote to Lord Elibank, Dr.
William Robertson, and Dr. Beattie.

To Dr. Robertson, so far as my letter concerned the
present subject, I wrote as follows :

" Our friend, Mr. Samuel Johnson, is in great health
and spirits ; and, I do think, has a serious resolution
to visit Scotland this year. The more attraction, however, the better ; and therefore, though I know he will
be happy to meet you there, it will forward the scheme,
if, in your answer to this, you express yourself concerning it with that power of which you are so happily
possessed, and which may be so directed as to operate
strongly upon him."

His answer to that part of my letter was quite as I
could have wished. It was written with the address
and persuasion of the historian of America.

"When I saw you last, you gave us some hopes that you might prevail with Mr. Johnson to make out that excursion to Scotland, with the expectation of which we have long flattered ourselves. If he could order matters so, as to pass some time in Edinburgh, about the close of the summer session, and then visit some of the Highland scenes, I am confident he would be pleased with the grand features of nature in many parts of this country : he will meet with many persons here who respect him, and some whom I am persuaded he will think not unworthy of his esteem. I wish he would make the experiment. He sometimes cracks his jokes upon us ; but he will find that we can distinguish between the stabs of malevolence, and *the rebukes of the righteous, which are like excellent oil, and break not the head.* Offer my best compliments to him, and assure him that I shall be happy to have the satisfaction of seeing him under my roof."

To Dr. Beattie I wrote, "The chief intention of this letter is to inform you, that I now seriously believe Mr. Samuel Johnson will visit Scotland this year : but I wish that every power of attraction may be employed to secure our having so valuable an acquisition, and therefore I hope you will without delay write to me what I know you think, that I may read it to the mighty sage, with proper emphasis, before I leave London, which I must do soon. He talks of you with the same warmth that he did last year. We are to see as much of Scotland as we can, in the months of August and September. We shall not be long of being at Marischal College. He is particularly desirous of seeing some of the Western Islands."

Dr. Beattie did better : *ipse venit.* He was, however, so polite as to wave his privilege of *nil mihi rescribas*, and wrote from Edinburgh, as follows :

"Your very kind and agreeable favour of the 20th of April overtook me here yesterday, after having gone to Aberdeen, which place I left about a week ago. I am to set out this day for London, and hope to have the honour of paying my respects to Mr. Johnson and you, about a week or ten days hence. I shall then do what I can, to enforce the topick you mention ; but at present I cannot enter upon it, as I am in a very great hurry ; for I intend to begin my journey within an hour or two."

He was as good as his word, and threw some pleasing motives into the northern scale. But, indeed, Mr. Johnson loved all that he heard, from one whom he tells us, in his *Lives of the Poets*, Gray found " a poet, a philosopher, and a good man."

My Lord Elibank did not answer my letter to his lordship for some time. The reason will appear, when we come to the isle of Sky. I shall then insert my letter, with letters from his lordship, both to myself and Mr. Johnson. I beg it may be understood, that I insert my own letters, as I relate my own sayings, rather as keys to what is valuable belonging to others, than for their own sake.

Luckily Mr. Justice (now Sir Robert) Chambers, who was about to sail for the East-Indies, was going to take leave of his relations at Newcastle, and he conducted Dr. Johnson to that town. Mr. Scott, of University College, Oxford, (now Dr. Scott, of the Commons,) accompanied him from thence to Edinburgh. With such propitious convoys did he proceed to my native city. But, lest metaphor should make it be supposed he actually went by sea, I choose to mention that he travelled in post-chaises, of which the rapid motion was one of his most favourite amusements.

Dr. Samuel Johnson's character, religious, moral, political, and literary, nay his figure and manner, are, I believe, more generally known than those of almost any man ; yet it may not be superfluous here to attempt a sketch of him. Let my readers then remember that he was a sincere and zealous christian, of high church of England and monarchical principles, which he would not tamely suffer to be questioned ; steady and inflexible in maintaining the obligations of piety and virtue, both from a regard to the order of society, and from a veneration for the Great Source of all order ; correct, nay stern in his taste ; hard to please, and easily offended, impetuous and irritable in his temper, but of a most humane and benevolent heart ; having a mind stored with a vast and various collection of learning and knowledge, which he communicated with peculiar perspicuity and force, in rich and choice expression. He united a most logical head with a most fertile imagination, which gave him an extraordinary advantage in arguing ; for he could reason close or wide, as he saw best for the moment. He could, when he chose it, be the greatest sophist that ever wielded a weapon in the schools of declamation ; but he indulged this only in conversation ; for he owned he sometimes talked for victory ; he was too conscientious to make errour permanent and pernicious, by deliberately writing it. He was conscious of his superiority. He loved praise when it was brought to him ; but was too proud to seek for it. He was somewhat susceptible of flattery. His mind was so full of imagery, that he might have been perpetually a poet. It has been often remarked, that in his poetical pieces, which it is to be regretted are so few, because so excellent, his style is easier than in his prose. There is deception in this : it is not easier, but better suited to the dignity of verse ; as one may dance with grace, whose motions, in ordinary walking,—in the common step, are awkward. He had a constitutional melancholy, the clouds of which darkened the brightness of his fancy, and gave a gloomy cast to his whole course of thinking : yet, though grave and awful in his deportment, when he thought it necessary or proper,— he frequently indulged himself in pleasantry and sportive sallies. He was prone to superstition, but not to credulity. Though his imagination might incline him to a belief of the marvellous, and the mysterious, his vigorous reason examined the evidence with jealousy. He had a loud voice, and a slow deliberate utterance, which no doubt gave some additional weight to the sterling metal of his conversation. Lord Pembroke said once to me at Wilton, with a happy pleasantry, and some truth, that " Dr. Johnson's sayings would not appear so extraordinary, were it not for his *bow-wow way:* " but I admit the truth of this only on some occasions. The *Messiah*, played upon the *Canterbury organ*, is more sublime than when played upon an inferior instrument : but very slight musick will seem grand, when conveyed to the ear through that majestick medium. *While therefore Doctor Johnson's sayings are read, let his manner be taken along with them.* Let it however be observed, that the sayings themselves are generally great ; that, though he might be an ordinary composer at times, he was for the most part a Handel. —His person was large, robust, I may say approaching to the gigantick, and grown unwieldy from corpulency. His countenance was naturally of the cast of an ancient statue, but somewhat disfigured by the scars of that *evil*, which, it was formerly imagined, the *royal touch* could cure. He was now in his sixty-fourth year, and was become a little dull of hearing. His sight had always been somewhat weak ; yet, so much does mind govern, and even supply the deficiency of organs, that his perceptions were uncommonly quick and accurate. His head, and sometimes also his body, shook with a kind of motion like the effect of a palsy : he appeared to be frequently disturbed by cramps, or convulsive contractions, of the nature of that distemper called *St. Vitus's* dance. He wore a full suit of plain brown clothes, with twisted-hair-buttons of the same colour, a large bushy greyish wig, a plain shirt, black worsted stockings, and silver buckles.   Upon this tour, when journeying, he wore boots, and a very wide brown cloth great coat, with pockets which might have almost held the two volumes of his folio dictionary ; and he carried in his hand a large English oak stick.   Let me not be censured for mentioning such minute particulars. Every thing relative to so great a man is worth observing.   I remember Dr. Adam Smith, in his rhetorical lectures at Glasgow, told us he was glad to know that Milton wore latchets in his shoes, instead of buckles. When I mention the oak stick, it is but letting *Hercules* have his club ; and, by-and-by, my readers will find this stick will bud, and produce a good joke.

This imperfect sketch of " the COMBINATION and the *form* " of that Wonderful Man, whom I venerated and loved while in this world, and after whom I gaze with humble hope, now that it has pleased ALMIGHTY GOD to call him to a better world, will serve to introduce to the fancy of my readers the capital object of the following journal, in the course of which I trust they will attain to a considerable degree of acquaintance with him.

His prejudice against Scotland was announced almost as soon as he began to appear in the world of letters. In his *London*, a poem, are the following nervous lines :

> " For who would leave, unbrib'd, Hibernia's land ?
> Or change the rocks of Scotland for the Strand ?
> There none are swept by sudden fate away ;
> But all, whom hunger spares, with age decay."

The truth is, like the ancient Greeks and Romans, he allowed himself to look upon all nations but his own as barbarians : not only Hibernia, and Scotland, but Spain, Italy, and France, are attacked in the same poem.   If he was particularly prejudiced against the Scots, it was because they were more in his way ; because he thought their success in England rather

exceeded the due proportion of their real merit ; and
because he could not but see in them that nationality
which I believe no liberal-minded Scotsman will deny.
He was indeed, if I may be allowed the phrase, at
bottom much of a *John Bull ;* much of a blunt *true
born Englishman.* There was a stratum of common
clay under the rock of marble. He was voraciously
fond of good eating ; and he had a great deal of that
quality called *humour,* which gives an oiliness and a
gloss to every other quality.

I am, I flatter myself, completely a citizen of the
world.—In my travels through Holland, Germany,
Switzerland, Italy, Corsica, France, I never felt myself from home ; and I sincerely love " every kindred
and tongue and people and nation." I subscribe to
what my late truly learned and philosophical friend
Mr. Crosbie said, that the English are better animals
than the Scots ; they are nearer the sun ; their blood
is richer, and more mellow : but when I humour any
of them in an outrageous contempt of Scotland, I fairly
own I treat them as children. And thus I have, at
some moments, found myself obliged to treat even
Dr. Johnson.

To Scotland however he ventured ; and he returned
from it in great good humour, with his prejudices much
lessened, and with very grateful feelings of the hospitality with which he was treated ; as is evident from
that admirable work, his *Journey to the Western Islands
of Scotland,* which, to my utter astonishment, has been
misapprehended, even to rancour, by many of my
countrymen.

To have the company of Chambers and Scott, he
delayed his journey so long, that the court of session,
which rises on the eleventh of August, was broke up
before he got to Edinburgh.

On Saturday the fourteenth of August, 1773, late
in the evening, I received a note from him, that he

was arrived at Boyd's inn, at the head of the Canongate. I went to him directly. He embraced me
cordially ; and I exulted in the thought, that I now
had him actually in Caledonia. Mr. Scott's amiable
manners, and attachment to our *Socrates*, at once united
me to him. He told me that, before I came in, the
Doctor had unluckily had a bad specimen of Scottish
cleanliness. He then drank no fermented liquor. He
asked to have his lemonade made sweeter ; upon which
the waiter, with his greasy fingers, lifted a lump of
sugar, and put it into it. The Doctor, in indignation,
threw it out of the window. Scott said, he was afraid
he would have knocked the waiter down. Mr. Johnson
told me, that such another trick was played him at
the house of a lady in Paris. He was to do me the
honour to lodge under my roof. I regretted sincerely
that I had not also a room for Mr. Scott. Mr. Johnson and I walked arm-in-arm up the High-street, to
my house in James's court : it was a dusky night : I
could not prevent his being assailed by the evening
effluvia of Edinburgh. I heard a late baronet, of some
distinction in the political world in the beginning of
the present reign, observe, that " walking the streets of
Edinburgh at night was pretty perilous, and a good deal
odoriferous." The peril is much abated, by the care
which the magistrates have taken to enforce the city
laws against throwing foul water from the windows ;
but, from the structure of the houses in the old town,
which consist of many stories, in each of which a different family lives, and there being no covered sewers,
the odour still continues. A zealous Scotsman would
have wished Mr. Johnson to be without one of his five
senses upon this occasion. As we marched slowly
along, he grumbled in my ear, " I smell you in the
dark ! " But he acknowledged that the breadth of
the street, and the loftiness of the buildings on each
side, made a noble appearance.

My wife had tea ready for him, which it is well known he delighted to drink at all hours, particularly when sitting up late, and of which his able defence against Mr. Jonas Hanway should have obtained him a magnificent reward from the East-India Company. He showed much complacency upon finding that the mistress of the house was so attentive to his singular habit ; and as no man could be more polite when he chose to be so, his address to her was most courteous and engaging ; and his conversation soon charmed her into a forgetfulness of his external appearance.

I did not begin to keep a regular full journal till some days after we had set out from Edinburgh ; but I have luckily preserved a good many fragments of his *Memorabilia* from his very first evening in Scotland.

We had, a little before this, had a trial for murder, in which the judges had allowed the lapse of twenty years since its commission as a plea in bar, in conformity with the doctrine of prescription in the *civil* law, which Scotland and several other countries in Europe have adopted. He at first disapproved of this ; but then he thought there was something in it, if there had been for twenty years a neglect to prosecute a crime which was *known*. He would not allow that a murder, by not being *discovered* for twenty years, should escape punishment. We talked of the ancient trial by duel. He did not think it so absurd as is generally supposed ; " For (said he) it was only allowed when the question was *in equilibrio*, as when one affirmed and another denied ; and they had a notion that Providence would interfere in favour of him who was in the right. But as it was found that in a duel, he who was in the right had not a better chance than he who was in the wrong, therefore society instituted the present mode of trial, and gave the advantage to him who is in the right."

We sat till near two in the morning, having chatted

a good while after my wife left us. She had insisted, that to show all respect to the Sage, she would give up her own bed-chamber to him, and take a worse. This I cannot but gratefully mention, as one of a thousand obligations which I owe her, since the great obligation of her being pleased to accept of me as her husband.

Sunday, 15th August

Mr. Scott came to breakfast, at which I introduced to Dr. Johnson, and him, my friend Sir William Forbes, now of Pitsligo ; a man of whom too much good cannot be said ; who, with distinguished abilities and application in his profession of a Banker, is at once a good companion, and a good christian ; which I think is saying enough. Yet it is but justice to record, that once, when he was in a dangerous illness, he was watched with the anxious apprehension of a general calamity ; day and night his house was beset with affectionate inquiries ; and, upon his recovery, *Te deum* was the universal chorus from the *hearts* of his countrymen.

Mr. Johnson was pleased with my daughter Veronica, then a child of about four months old. She had the appearance of listening to him. His motions seemed to her to be intended for her amusement ; and when he stopped, she fluttered, and made a little infantine noise, and a kind of signal for him to begin again. She would be held close to him ; which was a proof, from simple nature, that his figure was not horrid. Her fondness for him endeared her still more to me, and I declared she should have five hundred pounds of additional fortune.

We talked of the practice of the law. Sir William Forbes said, he thought an honest lawyer should never undertake a cause which he was satisfied was not a just one. " Sir, (said Mr. Johnson,) a lawyer has no business with the justice or injustice of the cause which he undertakes, unless his client asks his opinion, and then he is bound to give it honestly. The justice or injustice of the cause is to be decided by the judge. Consider, sir ; what is the purpose of courts of justice ? It is, that every man may have his cause fairly tried, by men appointed to try causes. A lawyer is not to tell what he knows to be a lie : he is not to produce what he knows to be a false deed ; but he is not to usurp the province of the jury and of the judge, and determine what shall be the effect of evidence,—what shall be the result of legal argument. As it rarely happens that a man is fit to plead his own cause, lawyers are a class of the community, who, by study and experience, have acquired the art and power of arranging evidence, and of applying to the points at issue what the law has settled. A lawyer is to do for his client all that his client might fairly do for himself, if he could. If, by a superiority of attention, of knowledge, of skill, and a better method of communication, he has the advantage of his adversary, it is an advantage to which he is entitled. There must always be some advantage, on one side or other ; and it is better that advantage should be had by talents, than by chance. If lawyers were to undertake no causes till they were sure they were just, a man might be precluded altogether from a trial of his claim, though, were it judicially examined, it might be found a very just claim."—This was sound practical doctrine, and rationally repressed a too refined scrupulosity of conscience.

Emigration was at this time a common topick of discourse. Dr. Johnson regretted it as hurtful to human happiness : " For (said he) it spreads mankind which weakens the defence of a nation, and lessens the comfort of living. Men, thinly scattered, make a shift, but a bad shift, without many things. A smith is ten miles off : they'll do without a nail or a staple. A taylor is far from them : they'll botch their own clothes. It is being concentrated which produces high convenience."

Sir William Forbes, Mr. Scott, and I, accompanied Mr. Johnson to the chapel, founded by Lord Chief Baron Smith, for the Service of the Church of England. The Reverend Mr. Carre, the senior clergyman, preached from these words, " Because the Lord reigneth, let the earth be glad."—I was sorry to think Mr. Johnson did not attend to the sermon, Mr. Carre's low voice not being strong enough to reach his hearing. A selection of Mr. Carre's sermons has, since his death, been published by Sir William Forbes, and the world has acknowledged their uncommon merit. I am well assured Lord Mansfield has pronounced them to be excellent.

Here I obtained a promise from Lord Chief Baron Orde, that he would dine at my house next day. I presented Mr. Johnson to his Lordship, who politely said to him, " I have not the honour of knowing you ; but I hope for it, and to see you at my house. I am to wait on you to-morrow." This respectable English judge will be long remembered in Scotland, where he built an elegant house, and lived in it magnificently. His own ample fortune, with the addition of his salary, enabled him to be splendidly hospitable. It may be fortunate for an individual amongst ourselves to be Lord Chief Baron ; and a most worthy man now has the office ; but, in my opinion, it is better for Scotland in general, that some of our publick employments should be filled by gentlemen of distinction from the south side of the Tweed, as we have the benefit of promotion in England. Such an interchange would make a beneficial mixture of manners, and render our union more complete. Lord Chief Baron Orde was on good terms with us all, in a narrow country filled with jarring interests

and keen parties ; and, though I well knew his opinion
to be the same with my own, he kept himself aloof at
a very critical period indeed, when the *Douglas cause*
shook the sacred security of *birthright* in Scotland to
its foundation ; a cause, which had it happened before
the Union, when there was no appeal to a British
House of Lords, would have left the great fortress
of honours and of property in ruins.

When we got home, Dr. Johnson desired to see
my books. He took down Ogden's *Sermons on Prayer*,
on which I set a very high value, having been much
edified by them, and he retired with them to his room.
He did not stay long, but soon joined us in the drawing-
room. I presented to him Mr. Robert Arbuthnot, a
relation of the celebrated Dr. Arbuthnot, and a man
of literature and taste. To him we were obliged for a
previous recommendation, which secured us a very agreeable reception at St. Andrews, and which Dr. Johnson,
in his *Journey*, ascribes to " some invisible friend."

Of Dr. Beattie, Mr. Johnson said, " Sir, he has written
like a man conscious of the truth, and feeling his own
strength. Treating your adversary with respect, is
giving him an advantage to which he is not entitled.
The greatest part of men cannot judge of reasoning,
and are impressed by character ; so that, if you allow
your adversary a respectable character, they will think,
that though you differ from him, you may be in the
wrong. Sir, treating your adversary with respect, is
striking soft in a battle. And as to Hume,—a man
who has so much conceit as to tell all mankind that
they have been bubbled for ages, and he is the wise
man who sees better than they,—a man who has so
little scrupulosity as to venture to oppose those principles
which have been thought necessary to human happiness,
—is he to be surprised if another man comes and laughs
at him ? If he is the great man he thinks himself, all
this cannot hurt him : it is like throwing peas against a

rock." He added " *something much too rough*," both
as to Mr. Hume's head and heart, which I suppress.
Violence is, in my opinion, not suitable to the Christian
cause. Besides, I always lived on good terms with
Mr. Hume, though I have frankly told him, I was
not clear that it was right in me to keep company
with him. " But (said I) how much better are you
than your books ! " He was cheerful, obliging, and
instructive ; he was charitable to the poor ; and many
an agreeable hour have I passed with him : I have
preserved some entertaining and interesting memoirs
of him, particularly when he knew himself to be dying,
which I may some time or other communicate to the
world. I shall not, however, extol him so very highly
as Dr. Adam Smith does, who says, in a letter to Mr.
Strahan the Printer (not a confidential letter to his
friend, but a letter which is published with all formality) : " Upon the whole, I have always considered
him, both in his life time and since his death, as approaching as nearly to the idea of a perfectly wise and
virtuous man as perhaps the nature of human frailty
will permit." Let Dr. Smith consider : Was not Mr.
Hume blest with good health, good spirits, good friends,
a competent and increasing fortune ? And had he not
also a perpetual feast of fame ? But, as a learned
friend has observed to me, " What trials did he undergo,
to prove the perfection of his virtue ? Did he ever
experience any great instance of adversity ? "—When
I read this sentence, delivered by my old Professor of
Moral Philosophy, I could not help exclaiming with the
Psalmist, " Surely I have now more understanding than
my teachers ! "

While we were talking, there came a note to me from
Dr. William Robertson.

" DEAR SIR,
        " I have been expecting every day to hear from

you, of Dr. Johnson's arrival. Pray, what do you
know about his motions? I long to take him by the
hand. I write this from the college, where I have
only this scrap of paper. Ever yours,

"W. R."

"Sunday."

It pleased me to find Dr. Robertson thus eager to
meet Dr. Johnson. I was glad I could answer, that
he was come: and I begged Dr. Robertson might be
with us as soon as he could.

Sir William Forbes, Mr. Scott, Mr. Arbuthnot, and
another gentleman dined with us. "Come, Dr. Johnson, (said I,) it is commonly thought that our veal
in Scotland is not good. But here is some which I
believe you will like."—There was no catching him.
—JOHNSON. "Why, sir, what is commonly thought, I
should take to be true. *Your* veal may be good; but
that will only be an exception to the general opinion;
not a proof against it."

Dr. Robertson, according to the custom of Edinburgh at that time, dined in the interval between the
forenoon and afternoon service, which was then later
than now; so we had not the pleasure of his company
till dinner was over, when he came and drank wine
with us. And then began some animated dialogue, of
which here follows a pretty full note.

We talked of Mr. Burke.—Dr. Johnson said, he
had great variety of knowledge, store of imagery,
copiousness of language.—ROBERTSON. "He has wit
too."—JOHNSON. "No, sir; he never succeeds there.
'Tis low; 'tis conceit. I used to say, Burke never
once made a good joke. What I most envy Burke
for, is, his being constantly the same. He is never
what we call hum-drum; never unwilling to begin to
talk, nor in haste to leave off."—BOSWELL. "Yet he
can listen."—JOHNSON. "No; I cannot say he is good

at that. So desirous is he to talk, that, if one is speaking at this end of the table, he'll speak to somebody at the other end. Burke, sir, is such a man, that if you met him for the first time in the street where you were stopped by a drove of oxen, and you and he stepped aside to take shelter but for five minutes, he'd talk to you in such a manner, that, when you parted, you would say, this is an extraordinary man. Now, you may be long enough with me, without finding any thing extraordinary." He said, he believed Burke was intended for the law ; but either had not money enough to follow it, or had not diligence enough. He said, he could not understand how a man could apply to one thing, and not to another. Robertson said, one man had more judgment, another more imagination.— JOHNSON. " No, sir ; it is only, one man has more mind than another. He may direct it differently ; he may, by accident, see the success of one kind of study, and take a desire to excel in it. I am persuaded that, had Sir Isaac Newton applied to poetry, he would have made a very fine epick poem. I could as easily apply to law as to tragick poetry."—BOSWELL. " Yet, sir, you did apply to tragick poetry, not to law."—JOHNSON. " Because, sir, I had not money to study law. Sir, the man who has vigour, may walk to the east, just as well as to the west, if he happens to turn his head that way."—BOSWELL. " But, sir, 'tis like walking up and down a hill ; one man will naturally do the one better than the other. A hare will run up a hill best, from her fore-legs being short ; a dog down."—JOHNSON. " Nay, sir ; that is from mechanical powers. If you make mind mechanical, you may argue in that manner. One mind is a vice, and holds fast ; there's a good memory. Another is a file ; and he is a disputant, a controversialist. Another is a razor ; and he is sarcastical."—We talked of Whitefield. He said, he was at the same college with him, and knew him *before*

2

he began to be better than other people (smiling) ; **that** he believed he sincerely meant well, but had a mixture of politicks and ostentation : whereas Wesley thought of religion only.—Robertson said, Whitefield had strong natural eloquence, which, if cultivated, would have done great things.—JOHNSON. " Why, sir, I take it, he was at the height of what his abilities could do, and was sensible of it. He had the ordinary advantages of education ; but he chose to pursue that oratory which is for the mob."—BOSWELL. " He had great effect on the passions."—JOHNSON. " Why, sir, I don't think so. He could not represent a succession of pathetick images. He vociferated, and made an impression. *There*, again, was a mind like a hammer."—Dr. Johnson now said, a certain eminent political friend of our's was wrong in his maxim of sticking to a certain set of *men* on all occasions. " I can see that a man may do right to stick to a party (said he) ; that is to say, he is a Whig, or he is a Tory, and he thinks one of those parties upon the whole the best, and that to make it prevail, it must be generally supported, though, in particulars, it may be wrong. He takes its faggot of principles, in which there are fewer rotten sticks than in the other, though some rotten sticks to be sure ; and they cannot well be separated. But, to bind one's self to one man, or one set of men, (who may be right to-day and wrong to-morrow,) without any general preference of system, I must disapprove."

He told us of Cooke, who translated Hesiod, and lived twenty years on a translation of Plautus, for which he was always taking subscriptions ; and that he presented Foote to a Club, in the following singular manner : " This is the nephew of the gentleman who was lately hung in chains for murdering his brother."

In the evening I introduced to Mr. Johnson two good friends of mine, Mr. William Nairne, Advocate, and Mr. Hamilton of Sundrum, my neighbour in the country, both of whom supped with us. I have preserved nothing of what passed, except that Dr. Johnson displayed another of his heterodox opinions,—a contempt of tragick acting. He said, " the action of all players in tragedy is bad. It should be a man's study to repress those signs of emotion and passion, as they are called." He was of a directly contrary opinion to that of Fielding, in his *Tom Jones;* who makes Partridge say, of Garrick, " why, I could act as well as he myself. I am sure, if I had seen a ghost, I should have looked in the very same manner, and done just as he did." For, when I asked him, " Would not you, sir, start as Mr. Garrick does, if you saw a ghost ? " He answered, " I hope not. If I did, I should frighten the ghost."

Monday, 16th August

Dr. William Robertson came to breakfast. We talked of *Ogden on Prayer*. Dr. Johnson said, " The same arguments which are used against GOD's hearing prayer, will serve against his rewarding good, and punishing evil. He has resolved, he has declared, in the former case as in the latter." He had last night looked into Lord Hailes's *Remarks on the History of Scotland*." Dr. Robertson and I said, it was a pity Lord Hailes did not write greater things. His lordship had not then published his *Annals of Scotland.*— JOHNSON. " I remember I was once on a visit at the house of a lady for whom I had a high respect. There was a good deal of company in the room. When they were gone, I said to this lady, ' What foolish talking have we had ! '—' Yes, (said she,) but while they talked, you said nothing.'—I was struck with the reproof. How much better is the man who does any thing that is innocent, than he who does nothing.

Besides, I love anecdotes. I fancy mankind may come, in time, to write all aphoristically, except in narrative; grow weary of preparation, and connection, and illustration, and all those arts by which a big book is made. —If a man is to wait till he weaves anecdotes into a system, we may be long in getting them, and get but few, in comparison of what we might get."

Dr. Robertson said, the notions of Eupham Macallan, a fanatick woman, of whom Lord Hailes gives a sketch, were still prevalent among some of the Presbyterians; and therefore it was right in Lord Hailes, a man of known piety, to undeceive them.

We walked out, that Dr. Johnson might see some of the things which we have to shew at Edinburgh. We went to the Parliament-House, where the Parliament of Scotland sat, and where the *Ordinary Lords* of Session hold their courts; and to the New Session-House adjoining to it, where our Court of Fifteen (the fourteen *Ordinaries*, with the Lord President at their head,) sit as a court of Review. We went to the Advocates' Library, of which Dr. Johnson took a cursory view, and then to what is called the *Laigh* (or under) Parliament-House, where the records of Scotland, which has an universal security by register, are deposited, till the great Register Office be finished. I was pleased to behold Dr. Samuel Johnson rolling about in this old magazine of antiquities. There was, by this time, a pretty numerous circle of us attending upon him. Somebody talked of happy moments for composition; and how a man can write at one time, and not at another.—" Nay (said Dr. Johnson) a man may write at any time, if he will set himself *doggedly* to it."

I here began to indulge old Scottish sentiments, and to express a warm regret, that, by our Union with England, we were no more;—our independent kingdom was lost.—JOHNSON. " Sir, never talk of your inde-

pendency, who could let your Queen remain twenty
years in captivity, and then be put to death, without
even a pretence of justice, without your ever attempting to rescue her ; and such a Queen too ! as every
man of any gallantry of spirit would have sacrificed his
life for."—Worthy Mr. JAMES KERR, Keeper of the
Records. " Half our nation was bribed by English
money."—JOHNSON. " Sir, that is no defence : that
makes you worse."—Good Mr. BROWN, Keeper of
the Advocates' Library. " We had better say nothing
about it."—BOSWELL. " You would have been glad,
however, to have had us last war, sir, to fight your
battles ! "—JOHNSON. " We should have had you for
the same price, though there had been no Union, as
we might have had Swiss, or other troops. No, no,
I shall agree to a separation. You have only to *go
home*."—Just as he had said this, I to divert the subject, shewed him the signed assurances of the three
successive Kings of the Hanover family, to maintain
the Presbyterian establishment in Scotland.—" We'll
give you that (said he) into the bargain."

We next went to the great church of St. Giles, which
has lost its original magnificence in the inside, by being
divided into four places of Presbyterian worship. " Come,
(said Dr. Johnson jocularly to Principal Robertson,)
let me see what was once a church ! " We entered
that division which was formerly called the *New Church*,
and of late the *High Church*, so well known by the
eloquence of Dr. Hugh Blair. It is now very elegantly
fitted up ; but it was then shamefully dirty. Dr.
Johnson said nothing at the time ; but when we came
to the great door of the Royal Infirmary, where, upon
a board, was this inscription, " *Clean your feet !* " he
turned about slyly, and said, " There is no occasio.1
for putting this at the doors of your churches ! "

We then conducted him down the Post-house stairs,
Parliament-close, and made him look up from the

Cow-gate to the highest building in Edinburgh, (from which he had just descended,) being thirteen floors or stories from the ground upon the back elevation ; the front wall being built upon the edge of the hill, and the back wall rising from the bottom of the hill several stories before it comes to a level with the front wall. We proceeded to the College, with the Principal at our head. Dr. Adam Fergusson, whose *Essay on the History of Civil Society* gives him a respectable place in the ranks of literature, was with us. As the College buildings are indeed very mean, the Principal said to Dr. Johnson, that he must give them the same epithet that a Jesuit did when shewing a poor college abroad : "*Hæ miseriæ nostræ.*" Dr. Johnson was, however, much pleased with the library, and with the conversation of Dr. James Robertson, Professor of Oriental Languages, the Librarian. We talked of Kennicot's edition of the Hebrew Bible, and hoped it would be quite faithful.—JOHNSON. "Sir, I know not any crime so great that a man could contrive to commit, as poisoning the sources of eternal truth."

I pointed out to him where there formerly stood an old wall enclosing part of the college, which I remember bulged out in a threatening manner, and of which there was a common tradition similar to that concerning Bacon's study at Oxford, that it would fall upon some very learned man. It had some time before this been taken down, that the street might be widened, and a more convenient wall built. Dr. Johnson, glad of an opportunity to have a pleasant hit at Scottish learning, said, "they have been afraid it never would fall."

We shewed him the Royal Infirmary, for which, and for every other exertion of generous publick spirit in his power, that noble-minded citizen of Edinburgh, George Drummond, will be ever held in honourable remembrance. And we were too proud not to carry

him to the Abbey of Holyrood-house, that beautiful
piece of architecture, but, alas! that deserted mansion
of royalty, which Hamilton of Bangour, in one of his
elegant poems, calls

> " A virtuous palace, where no monarch dwells."

I was much entertained while Principal Robertson
fluently harangued to Dr. Johnson, upon the spot, concerning scenes of his celebrated *History of Scotland*.
We surveyed that part of the palace appropriated to the
Duke of Hamilton, as Keeper, in which our beautiful
Queen Mary lived, and in which David Rizzio was
murdered; and also the State Rooms. Dr. Johnson
was a great reciter of all sorts of things serious or
comical. I over-heard him repeating here, in a kind
of muttering tone, a line of the old ballad, *Johnny
Armstrong's Last Good-Night*:

> " And ran him through the fair body ! "

We returned to my house, where there met him,
at dinner, the Duchess of Douglas, Sir Adolphus
Oughton, Lord Chief Baron, Sir William Forbes,
Principal Robertson, Mr. Cullen, advocate. Before
dinner, he told us of a curious conversation between
the famous George Faulkner and him. George said
that England had drained Ireland of fifty thousand
pounds in specie, annually, for fifty years. " How so,
sir! (said Dr. Johnson,) you must have a very great
trade ? " " No trade."—" Very rich mines ? " " No
mines."—" From whence, then, does all this money
come ? " " Come ! why out of the blood and bowels
of the poor people of Ireland ! "
He seemed to me to have an unaccountable prejudice against Swift; for I once took the liberty to ask
him, if Swift had personally offended him, and he told

me, he had not. He said to-day, " Swift is clear, but he is shallow. In coarse humour, he is inferior to Arbuthnot ; in delicate humour, he is inferior to Addison : So he is inferior to his contemporaries ; without putting him against the whole world. I doubt if the *Tale of a Tub* was his : it has so much more thinking, more knowledge, more power, more colour, than any of the works which are indisputably his. If it was his, I shall only say, he was *impar sibi.*"

We gave him as good a dinner as we could. Our Scotch muir-fowl, or growse, were then abundant, and quite in season ; and, so far as wisdom and wit can be aided by administering agreeable sensations to the palate, my wife took care that our great guest should not be deficient.

Sir Adolphus Oughton, then our Deputy Commander in Chief, who was not only an excellent officer, but one of the most universal scholars I ever knew, had learned the Erse language, and expressed his belief in the authenticity of Ossian's Poetry. Dr. Johnson took the opposite side of that perplexed question ; and I was afraid the dispute would have run high between them. But Sir Adolphus, who had a very sweet temper, changed the discourse, grew playful, laughed at Lord Monboddo's notion of men having tails, and called him a Judge, *à posteriori*, which amused Dr. Johnson ; and thus hostilities were prevented.

At supper we had Dr. Cullen, his son the advocate, Dr. Adam Fergusson, and Mr. Crosbie, advocate. Witchcraft was introduced. Mr. Crosbie said, he thought it the greatest blasphemy to suppose evil spirits counteracting the Deity, and raising storms, for instance, to destroy his creatures.—JOHNSON. " Why, sir, if moral evil be consistent with the government of the Deity, why may not physical evil be also consistent with it ? It is not more strange that there should be evil spirits, than evil men : evil unembodied spirits, than evil embodied spirits. And as to storms, we know there are such things; and it is no worse that evil spirits raise them, than that they rise."—CROSBIE. " But it is not credible, that witches should have effected what they are said in stories to have done."—JOHNSON. " Sir, I am not defending their credibility. I am only saying, that your arguments are not good, and will not overturn the belief of witchcraft.—(Dr. Fergusson said to me, aside, ' He is right.')—And then, sir, you have all mankind, rude and civilized, agreeing in the belief of the agency of preternatural powers. You must take evidence: you must consider, that wise and great men have condemned witches to die."—CROSBIE. " But an act of parliament put an end to witchcraft."— JOHNSON. " No, sir; witchcraft had ceased; and there-fore an act of parliament was passed to prevent per-secution for what was not witchcraft. Why it ceased, we cannot tell, as we cannot tell the reason of many other things."—Dr. Cullen, to keep up the gratification of mysterious disquisition, with the grave address for which he is remarkable in his companionable as in his professional hours, talked, in a very entertaining manner, of people walking and conversing in their sleep. I am very sorry I have no note of this. We talked of the Ouran-Outang, and of Lord Monboddo's thinking that he might be taught to speak. Dr. Johnson treated this with ridicule. Mr. Crosbie said, that Lord Mon-boddo believed the existence of every thing possible; in short, that all which is in *posse* might be found in *esse*.—JOHNSON. " But, sir, it is as possible that the Ouran-Outang does not speak, as that he speaks. How-ever, I shall not contest the point. I should have thought it not possible to find a Monboddo; yet *he* exists."—I again mentioned the stage.—JOHNSON. " The appearance of a player, with whom I have drunk tea, counteracts the imagination that he is the character he represents. Nay, you know, nobody imagines that he

is the character he represents. They say, ' See Garrick !
how he looks to-night ! See how he'll clutch the
dagger ! ' That is the buz of the theatre."

Tuesday, 17th August

Sir William Forbes came to breakfast, and brought
with him Dr. Blacklock, whom he introduced to Dr.
Johnson, who received him with a most humane complacency ; " Dear Dr. Blacklock, I am glad to see
you ! "—Blacklock seemed to be much surprized,
when Dr. Johnson said, " it was easier to him to write
poetry than to compose his Dictionary. His mind
was less on the stretch in doing the one than the other.
Besides ; composing a Dictionary requires books and
a desk : you can make a poem walking in the fields, or
lying in bed."—Dr. Blacklock spoke of scepticism in
morals and religion, with apparent uneasiness, as if he
wished for more certainty. Dr. Johnson, who had
thought it all over, and whose vigorous understanding
was fortified by much experience, thus encouraged the
blind Bard to apply to higher speculations what we all
willingly submit to in common life : in short, he gave
him more familiarly the able and fair reasoning of
Butler's *Analogy :* " Why, sir, the greatest concern
we have in this world, the choice of our profession,
must be determined without demonstrative reasoning.
Human life is not yet so well known, as that we can
have it. And take the case of a man who is ill. I
call two physicians : they differ in opinion. I am not
to lie down, and die between them : I must do something."—The conversation then turned on Atheism ;
on that horrible book, *Système de la Nature ;* and on
the supposition of an eternal necessity, without design,
without a governing mind.—JOHNSON. " If it were so,

why has it ceased? Why don't we see men thus produced around us now? Why, at least, does it not keep pace, in some measure, with the progress of time? If it stops because there is now no need of it, then it is plain there is, and ever has been, an all-powerful intelligence. But stay! (said he, with one of his satyrick laughs.) Ha! ha! ha! I shall suppose Scotchmen made necessarily, and Englishmen by choice."

At dinner this day, we had Sir Alexander Dick, whose amiable character, and ingenious and cultivated mind, are so generally known; (he was then on the verge of seventy, and is now (1785) eighty-one, with his faculties entire, his heart warm, and his temper gay;) Sir David Dalrymple Lord Hailes; Mr. Maclaurin, advocate; Dr. Gregory, who now worthily fills his father's medical chair; and my uncle, Dr. Boswell. This was one of Dr. Johnson's best days. He was quite in his element. All was literature and taste, without any interruption. Lord Hailes, who is one of the best philologists in Great Britain, who has written papers in the *World*, and a variety of other works in prose and in verse, both Latin and English, pleased him highly. He told him, he had discovered the Life of Cheynel, in the *Student*, to be his.—JOHNSON. "No one else knows it."—Dr. Johnson had, before this, dictated to me a law-paper, upon a question purely in the law of Scotland, concerning *vicious intromission*, that is to say, intermeddling with the effects of a deceased person, without a regular title; which formerly was understood to subject the intermeddler to payment of all the defunct's debts. The principle has of late been relaxed. Dr. Johnson's argument was, for a renewal of its strictness. The paper was printed, with additions by me, and given into the Court of Session. Lord Hailes knew Dr. Johnson's part not to be mine, and pointed out exactly where it began, and where it ended.

Dr. Johnson said, " It is much, now, that his lordship can distinguish so."

In Dr. Johnson's *Vanity of Human Wishes*, there is the following passage :

> " The teeming mother, anxious for her race,
>   Begs, for each birth, the fortune of a face :
>   Yet *Vane* could tell, what ills from beauty spring ;
>   And *Sedley* curs'd the charms which pleas'd a king."

Lord Hailes told him, he was mistaken in the instances he had given of unfortunate fair ones ; for neither *Vane* nor *Sedley* had a title to that description. His Lordship has since been so obliging as to send me a note of this, for the communication of which I am sure my readers will thank me.

" The lines in the tenth Satire of Juvenal, according to my alteration, should have run thus :

> " Yet *Shore* could tell—— ;
>   And *Valiere* curs'd——.

" The first was a penitent by compulsion, the second by sentiment ; though the truth is, Mademoiselle de la Valiere threw herself (but still from sentiment) in the King's way.

" Our friend chose *Vane*, who was far from being well-looked ; and *Sedley*, who was so ugly, that Charles II. said, his brother had her by way of penance."

Mr. Maclaurin's learning and talents enabled him to do his part very well in Dr. Johnson's company. He produced two epitaphs upon his father, the celebrated mathematician. One was in English, of which Dr. Johnson did not change one word. In the other, which was in Latin, he made several alterations. In place of the very words of Virgil, " *Ubi luctus et pavor et plurima mortis imago*," he wrote " *Ubi luctus regnant et pavor*. He introduced the word *prorsus* into the line " *Mortalibus prorsus non absit solatium,*" and after " *Hujus enim scripta evolve* " he added, " *Mentemque tantarum rerum capacem corpori caduco superstitem crede;*" which is quite applicable to Dr. Johnson himself.

Mr. Murray, advocate, who married a niece of Lord Mansfield's and is now one of the Judges of Scotland, by the title of Lord Henderland, sat with us a part of the evening ; but did not venture to say any thing, that I remember, though he is certainly possessed of talents which would have enabled him to have shewn himself to advantage, if too great anxiety had not prevented him.

At supper we had Dr. Alexander Webster, who, though not learned, had such a knowledge of mankind, such a fund of information and entertainment, so clear a head and such accommodating manners, that Dr. Johnson found him a very agreeable companion.

When Dr. Johnson and I were left by ourselves, I read to him my notes of the Opinions of our Judges upon the questions of Literary Property. He did not like them ; and said, " they make me think of your Judges not with that respect which I should wish to do." To the argument of one of them, that there can be no property in blasphemy or nonsense, he answered, " then your rotten sheep are mine !—By that rule, when a man's house falls into decay, he must lose it." —I mentioned an argument of mine, that literary performances are not taxed.—As Churchill says,

> " No statesman yet has thought it worth his pains
> To tax our labours, or excise our brains ; "

and therefore they are not property.—" Yet, (said he,) we hang a man for stealing a horse, and horses are not taxed."—Mr. Pitt has since put an end to that argument.

Wednesday, 18th August

On this day we set out from Edinburgh. We should gladly have had Mr. Scott to go with us ; but he was obliged to return to England.—I have given a sketch of Dr. Johnson : my readers may wish to know a little of his fellow traveller. Think then, of a gentleman of ancient blood, the pride of which was his predominant passion. He was then in his thirty-third year, and had been about four years happily married. His inclination was to be a soldier ; but his father, a respectable Judge, had pressed him into the profession of the law. He had travelled a good deal, and seen many varieties of human life. He had thought more than any body supposed, and had a pretty good stock of general learning and knowledge. He had all Dr. Johnson's principles, with some degree of relaxation. He had rather too little, than too much prudence ; and, his imagination being lively, he often said things of which the effect was very different from the intention. He resembled sometimes

"The best good man, with the worst natur'd muse."

He cannot deny himself the vanity of finishing with the encomium of Dr. Johnson, whose friendly partiality to the companion of his Tour represents him as one, " whose acuteness would help my inquiry, and whose gaiety of conversation, and civility of manners, are sufficient to counteract the inconveniences of travel, in countries less hospitable than we have passed."

Dr. Johnson thought it unnecessary to put himself to the additional expence of bringing with him Francis Barber, his faithful black servant ; so we were attended only by my man, Joseph Ritter, a Bohemian ; a fine stately fellow above six feet high, who had been over a great part of Europe, and spoke many languages. He was the best servant I ever saw. Let not my readers disdain his introduction ! For Dr. Johnson gave him this character : " Sir, he is a civil man, and a wise man."

From an erroneous apprehension of violence, Dr. Johnson had provided a pair of pistols, some gunpowder, and a quantity of bullets : but upon being assured we should run no risk of meeting any robbers, he left his arms and ammunition in an open drawer, of which he gave my wife the charge. He also left in that drawer one volume of a pretty full and curious Diary of his Life, of which I have a few fragments ; but the book had been destroyed. I wish female curiosity had been strong enough to have had it all transcribed, which might easily have been done ; and I should think the theft, being *pro bono publico*, might have been forgiven. But I may be wrong. My wife told me she never once looked into it.—She did not seem quite easy when we left her : but away we went !

Mr. Nairne, advocate, was to go with us as far as St. Andrews. It gives me pleasure that, by mentioning his *name*, I connect his title to the just and handsome compliment paid him by Dr. Johnson, in his book : " A gentleman who could stay with us only long enough to make us know how much we lost by his leaving us." When we came to Leith, I talked with perhaps too boasting an air, how pretty the Frith of Forth looked ; as indeed, after the prospect from Constantinople, of which I have been told, and that from Naples, which I have seen, I believe the view of that Frith and its environs, from the Castle-hill of Edinburgh, is the finest prospect in Europe. " Ay, (said Dr. Johnson,) that is the state of the world. Water is the same every where.

" Una est injusti cærula forma maris."

I told him the port here was the mouth of the river or water of Leith. "Not *Lethe*," said Mr. Nairne.— "Why, sir, (said Dr. Johnson,) when a Scotchman sets out from this port for England, he forgets his native country."—NAIRNE. "I hope, sir, you will forget England here."—JOHNSON. "Then 'twill be still more *Lethe*." —He observed of the Pier or Quay, "you have no occasion for so large a one : your trade does not require it : but you are like a shopkeeper who takes a shop, not only for what he has to put into it, but that it may be believed he has a great deal to put into it." It is very true, that there is now, comparatively, little trade upon the eastern coast of Scotland. The riches of Glasgow shew how much there is in the west ; and perhaps we shall find trade travel westward on a great scale, as well as a small.

We talked of a man's drowning himself.—JOHNSON. "I should never think it time to make away with myself."—I put the case of Eustace Budgell, who was accused of forging a will, and sunk himself in the Thames, before the trial of its authenticity came on. "Suppose, sir, (said I,) that a man is absolutely sure, that, if he lives a few days longer, he shall be detected in a fraud, the consequence of which will be utter disgrace and expulsion from society."—JOHNSON. "Then, sir, let him go abroad to a distant country ; let him go to some place where he is *not* known. Don't let him go to the devil where he *is* known ! "

He then said, "I see a number of people barefooted here : I suppose you all went so before the Union. Boswell, your ancestors went so, when they had as much land as your family has now. Yet Auchinleck is the Field of Stones : there would be bad going barefooted there. The Lairds, however, did it."—I bought some *speldings*, fish (generally whitings) salted and dried in a particular manner, being dipped in the sea and dried in the sun, and eaten by the Scots by way of a relish. He had never seen them, though they are sold in London. I insisted on *scottifying* his palate; but he was very reluctant. With difficulty I prevailed with him to let a bit of one of them lie in his mouth. He did not like it.

In crossing the Frith, Dr. Johnson determined that we should land upon Inch Keith. On approaching it, we first observed a high rocky shore. We coasted about, and put into a little bay on the North-west. We clambered up a very steep ascent, on which was very good grass, but rather a profusion of thistles. There were sixteen head of black cattle grazing upon the island. Lord Hailes observed to me, that Brantome calls it *L'isle des Chevaux*, and that it was probably " a *safer* stable " than many others in his time. The fort, with an inscription on it, *Maria Re* 1564, is strongly built. Dr. Johnson examined it with much attention. He stalked like a giant among the luxuriant thistles and nettles. There are three wells in the island; but we could not find one in the fort. There must probably have been one, though now filled up, as a garrison could not subsist without it. But I have dwelt too long on this little spot. Dr. Johnson afterwards bade me try to write a description of our discovering Inch Keith, in the usual style of travellers, describing fully every particular; stating the grounds on which we concluded that it must have once been inhabited, and introducing many sage reflections; and we should see how a thing might be covered in words, so as to induce people to come and survey it. All that was told might be true, and yet in reality there might be nothing to see. He said, " I'd have this island. I'd build a house, make a good landing-place, have a garden, and vines, and all sorts of trees. A rich man, of a hospitable turn, here, would have many visitors from Edinburgh." When we had got into our boat again, he called to me, " Come, now, pay a classical

compliment to the island on quitting it." I happened
luckily, in allusion to the beautiful Queen Mary, whose
name is upon the fort, to think of what Virgil makes
Æneas say, on having left the country of his charming
Dido :

> Invitus, regina, tuo de littore cessi.

"Very well hit off!" said he.

We dined at Kinghorn, and then got into a post-
chaise. Mr. Nairne and his servant, and Joseph, rode
by us. We stopped at Cupar, and drank tea. We
talked of parliament ; and I said, I supposed very few
of the members knew much of what was going on, as
indeed very few gentlemen know much of their own
private affairs.—JOHNSON. "Why, sir, if a man is not
of a sluggish mind, he may be his own steward. If he
will look into his affairs, he will soon learn. So it is
as to publick affairs. There must always be a certain
number of men of business in parliament."—BOSWELL.
"But consider, sir ; what is the House of Commons ?
Is not a great part of it chosen by peers ? Do you
think, sir, they ought to have such an influence ? "—
JOHNSON. "Yes, sir. Influence must ever be in proportion to property ; and it is right it should."—
BOSWELL. "But is there not reason to fear that the
common people may be oppressed ? "—JOHNSON. "No,
sir. Our great fear is from want of power in government. Such a storm of vulgar force has broke in."—
BOSWELL. "It has only roared."—JOHNSON. "Sir, it
has roared, till the Judges in Westminster-Hall have
been afraid to pronounce sentence in opposition to the
popular cry. You are frightened by what is no longer
dangerous, like Presbyterians by Popery."—He then
repeated a passage, I think, in Butler's *Remains*, which
ends, "and would cry, Fire! Fire! in Noah's flood."

We had a dreary drive, in a dusky night, to St.
Andrews, where we arrived late. We found a good

supper at Glass's inn, and Dr. Johnson revived agreeably. He said, " the collection called *The Muses'
Welcome to King James*, (first of England, and sixth
of Scotland,) on his return to his native kingdom, shewed
that there was then abundance of learning in Scotland ;
and that the conceits in that collection, with which people
find fault, were mere mode." He added, " we could
not now entertain a sovereign so ; that Buchanan had
spread the spirit of learning amongst us, but we had
lost it during the civil wars." He did not allow the
Latin Poetry of Pitcairne so much merit as has been
usually attributed to it ; though he owned that one of
his pieces, which he mentioned, but which I am sorry
is not specified in my notes, was " very well." It is
not improbable that it was the poem which Prior has
so elegantly translated.

After supper, we made a *procession* to Saint Leonard's
College, the landlord walking before us with a candle,
and the waiter with a lantern. That college had some
time before been dissolved ; and Dr. Watson, a professor here, (the historian of Philip II.) had purchased
the ground, and what buildings remained. When
we entered his court, it seemed quite academical ; and
we found in his house very comfortable and genteel
accommodation.

Thursday, 19th August

We rose much refreshed. I had with me a map of
Scotland, a Bible, which was given me by Lord Mount-
stuart when we were together in Italy, and Ogden's
Sermons on Prayer. Mr. Nairne introduced us to
Dr. Watson, whom we found a well-informed man,
of very amiable manners. Dr. Johnson, after they
were acquainted, said, " I take great delight in him."
—His daughter, a very pleasing young lady, made

breakfast. Dr. Watson observed, that Glasgow University had fewer home-students, since trade increased, as learning was rather incompatible with it.—JOHNSON. " Why, sir, as trade is now carried on by subordinate hands, men in trade have as much leisure as others ; and now learning itself is a trade. A man goes to a bookseller, and gets what he can. We have done with patronage. In the infancy of learning, we find some great man praised for it. This diffused it among others. When it becomes general, an author leaves the great, and applies to the multitude."—BOSWELL. " It is a shame that authors are not now better patronized."— JOHNSON. " No, sir. If learning cannot support a man, if he must sit with his hands across till somebody feeds him, it is as to him a bad thing, and it is better as it is. With patronage, what flattery ! what falsehood ! While a man is in equilibrio, he throws truth among the multitude, and lets them take it as they please : in patronage, he must say what pleases his patron, and it is an equal chance whether that be truth or falsehood." —WATSON. " But is not the case now, that, instead of flattering one person, we flatter the age ? "—JOHNSON. " No, sir. The world always lets a man tell what he thinks, his own way. I wonder however, that so many people have written, who might have let it alone. That people should endeavour to excel in conversation, I do not wonder ; because in conversation praise is instantly reverberated."

We talked of change of manners. Dr. Johnson observed, that our drinking less than our ancestors was owing to the change from ale to wine. " I remember, (said he,) when all the *decent* people in Lichfield got drunk every night, and were not the worse thought of. Ale was cheap, so you pressed strongly. When a man must bring a bottle of wine, he is not in such haste. Smoking has gone out. To be sure, it is a shocking thing, blowing smoke out of our mouths into other people's mouths, eyes, and noses, and having the same thing done to us. Yet I cannot account, why a thing which requires so little exertion, and yet preserves the mind from total vacuity, should have gone out. Every man has something by which he calms himself : beating with his feet, or so. I remember when people in England changed a shirt only once a week ; a Pandour, when he gets a shirt, greases it to make it last. Formerly, good tradesmen had no fire but in the kitchen ; never in the parlour, except on Sunday. My father, who was a magistrate of Lichfield, lived thus. They never began to have a fire in the parlour, but on leaving off business, or some great revolution of their life."—Dr. Watson said, the hall was as a kitchen, in old squires' houses.—JOHNSON. " No, sir. The hall was for great occasions, and never was used for domestick refection."—We talked of the Union, and what money it had brought into Scotland. Dr. Watson observed, that a little money formerly went as far as a great deal now.—JOHNSON. " In speculation, it seems that a smaller quantity of money, equal in value to a larger quantity, if equally divided, should produce the same effect. But it is not so in reality. Many more conveniences and elegancies are enjoyed where money is plentiful, than where it is scarce. Perhaps a great familiarity with it, which arises from plenty, makes us more easily part with it."

After what Dr. Johnson had said of St. Andrews, which he had long wished to see, as our oldest university, and the seat of our Primate in the days of episcopacy, I can say little. Since the publication of Dr. Johnson's book, I find that he has been censured for not seeing here the ancient chapel of St. Rule, a curious piece of sacred architecture. But this was neither his fault nor mine. We were both of us abundantly desirous of surveying such sort of antiquities : but neither of us knew of this. I am afraid the cen-

sure must fall on those who did not tell us of it. In
every place, where there is any thing worthy of observation, there should be a short printed directory for
strangers, such as we find in all the towns of Italy,
and in some of the towns in England. I was told
that there is a manuscript account of St. Andrews, by
Martin, secretary to Archbishop Sharp; and that one
Douglas has published a small account of it. I inquired at a bookseller's, but could not get it. Dr.
Johnson's veneration for the Hierarchy is well known.
There is no wonder then, that he was affected with
a strong indignation, while he beheld the ruins of
religious magnificence. I happened to ask where
John Knox was buried. Dr. Johnson burst out, " I
hope in the high-way. I have been looking at his
reformations."

It was a very fine day. Dr. Johnson seemed quite
wrapt up in the contemplation of the scenes which were
now presented to him. He kept his hat off while he
was upon any part of the ground where the cathedral
had stood. He said well, that " Knox had set on a
mob, without knowing where it would end; and that
differing from a man in doctrine was no reason why
you should pull his house about his ears." As we
walked in the cloisters, there was a solemn echo, while
he talked loudly of a proper retirement from the world.
Mr. Nairne said, he had an inclination to retire. I
called Dr. Johnson's attention to this, that I might
hear his opinion if it was right.—JOHNSON. " Yes,
when he has done his duty to society. In general, as
every man is obliged not only to ' love GOD, but his
neighbour as himself,' he must bear his part in active
life; yet there are exceptions. Those who are exceedingly scrupulous, (which I do not approve, for I
am no friend to scruples,) and find their scrupulosity
invincible, so that they are quite in the dark, and know
not what they shall do,—or those who cannot resist

temptations, and find they make themselves worse by
being in the world, without making it better, may
retire. I never read of a hermit, but in imagination I
kiss his feet ; never of a monastery, but I could fall on
my knees, and kiss the pavement. But I think putting
young people there, who know nothing of life, nothing
of retirement, is dangerous and wicked. It is a saying
as old as Hesiod,

Ἔργα νεῶν, βουλαίτε μέσων, εὐχαίτε γερόντων.

That is a very noble line : not that young men should
not pray, or old men not give counsel, but that every
season of life has its proper duties. I have thought of
retiring, and have talked of it to a friend ; but I find
my vocation is rather to active life." I said, *some*
young monks might be allowed, to shew that it is not
age alone that can retire to pious solitude ; but he
thought this would only shew that they could not
resist temptation.

He wanted to mount the steeples, but it could not
be done. There are no good inscriptions here. Bad
Roman characters he naturally mistook for half Gothick,
half Roman. One of the steeples, which he was told
was in danger, he wished not to be taken down ; " for,
said he, it may fall on some of the posterity of John
Knox ; and no great matter ! "—Dinner was mentioned.——JOHNSON. " Ay, ay ; amidst all these sorrowful scenes, I have no objection to dinner."

We went and looked at the castle, where Cardinal
Beaton was murdered, and then visited Principal Murison
at his college, where is a good library-room ; but the
principal was abundantly vain of it, for he seriously
said to Dr. Johnson, " you have not such a one in
England."

The professors entertained us with a very good
dinner. Present : Murison, Shaw, Cooke, Hill, Haddo,

Watson, Flint, Brown. I observed, that I wondered to see him eat so well, after viewing so many sorrowful scenes of ruined religious magnificence. " Why," said he, " I am not sorry, after seeing these gentlemen ; for they are not sorry."—Murison said, all sorrow was bad, as it was murmuring against the dispensations of Providence.—JOHNSON. " Sir, sorrow is inherent in humanity. As you cannot judge two and two to be either five, or three, but certainly four, so, when comparing a worse present state with a better which is past, you cannot but feel sorrow. It is not cured by reason, but by the incursion of present objects, which wear out the past. You need not murmur, though you are sorry."—MURISON. " But St. Paul says, ' I have learnt, in whatever state I am, therewith to be content.' "—JOHNSON. " Sir, that relates to riches and poverty ; for we see St. Paul, when he had a thorn in the flesh, prayed earnestly to have it removed ; and then he could not be content."—Murison, thus refuted, tried to be smart, and drank to Dr. Johnson, " Long may you lecture ! "—Dr. Johnson afterwards, speaking of his not drinking wine, said, " The Doctor spoke of *lecturing* (looking to him). I give all these lectures on water."

He defended requiring subscription in those admitted to universities, thus : " As all who come into the country must obey the king, so all who come into an university must be of the church."

And here I must do Dr. Johnson the justice to contradict a very absurd and ill-natured story, as to what passed at St. Andrews. It has been circulated, that, after grace was said in English, in the usual manner, he with the greatest marks of contempt, as if he had held it to be no grace in an university, would not sit down till he had said grace aloud in Latin. This would have been an insult indeed to the gentlemen who were entertaining us. But the truth was precisely thus.

In the course of conversation at dinner, Dr. Johnson, in very good humour, said, " I should have expected to have heard a Latin grace, among so many learned men : we had always a Latin grace at Oxford. I believe I can repeat it." Which he did, as giving the learned men in one place a specimen of what was done by the learned men in another place.

We went and saw the church, in which is Archbishop Sharp's monument. I was struck with the same kind of feelings with which the churches of Italy impressed me. I was much pleased, to see Dr. Johnson actually in St. Andrews, of which we had talked so long. Professor Haddo was with us this afternoon, along with Dr. Watson. We looked at St. Salvador's College. The rooms for students seemed very commodious, and Dr. Johnson said, the chapel was the neatest place of worship he had seen. The key of the library could not be found ; for it seems Professor Hill, who was out of town, had taken it with him. Dr. Johnson told a joke he had heard of a monastery abroad, where the key of the library could never be found.

It was somewhat dispiriting, to see this ancient archiepiscopal city now sadly deserted. We saw in one of its streets a remarkable proof of liberal toleration ; a nonjuring clergyman, strutting about in his canonicals, with a jolly countenance and a round belly, like a well-fed monk.

We observed two occupations united in the same person, who had hung out two sign-posts. Upon one was, " James Hood, White Iron Smith " (*i.e.* Tinplate Worker). Upon another, " The Art of Fencing taught, by James Hood."—Upon this last were painted some trees, and two men fencing, one of whom had hit the other in the eye, to shew his great dexterity ; so that the art was well taught.—JOHNSON. " Were I studying here, I should go and take a lesson. I remember Hope, in his book on this art, says, ' the Scotch are very good fencers.' "

We returned to the inn, where we had been entertained at dinner, and drank tea in company with some of the Professors, of whose civilities I beg leave to add my humble and very grateful acknowledgement to the honourable testimony of Dr. Johnson, in his *Journey*.

We talked of composition, which was a favourite topick of Dr. Watson's, who first distinguished himself by lectures on rhetorick.—JOHNSON. " I advised Chambers, and would advise every young man beginning to compose, to do it as fast as he can, to get a habit of having his mind to start promptly ; it is so much more difficult to improve in speed than in accuracy."—WATSON. " I own I am for much attention to accuracy in composing, lest one should get bad habits of doing it in a slovenly manner."—JOHNSON. " Why, sir, you are confounding *doing* inaccurately with the *necessity* of doing inaccurately. A man knows when his composition is inaccurate, and when he thinks fit he'll correct it. But, if a man is accustomed to compose slowly, and with difficulty, upon all occasions, there is danger that he may not compose at all, as we do not like to do that which is not done easily ; and, at any rate, more time is consumed in a small matter than ought to be."—WATSON. " Dr. Hugh Blair has taken a week to compose a sermon."—JOHNSON. " Then, sir, that is for want of the habit of composing quickly, which I am insisting one should acquire."—WATSON. " Blair was not composing all the week, but only such hours as he found himself disposed for composition." —JOHNSON. " Nay, sir, unless you tell me the time he took, you tell me nothing. If I say I took a week to walk a mile, and have had the gout five days, and been ill otherwise another day, I have taken but one day. I myself have composed about forty sermons. I have begun a sermon after dinner, and sent it off by the post that night. I wrote forty-eight of the printed octavo pages of the *Life of Savage* at a sitting ; but then I sat up all night. I have also written six sheets in a day of translation from the French."—BOSWELL. " We have all observed how one man dresses himself slowly, and another fast."—JOHNSON. " Yes, sir ; it is wonderful how much time some people will consume in dressing ; taking up a thing and looking at it, and laying it down, and taking it up again. Every one should get the habit of doing it quickly. I would say to a young divine, ' Here is your text ; let me see how soon you can make a sermon.' Then I'd say, ' Let me see how much better you can make it.' Thus I should see both his powers and his judgement."

We all went to Dr. Watson's to supper. Miss Sharp, great grandchild of Archbishop Sharp, was there ; as was Mr. Craig, the ingenious architect of the new town of Edinburgh, and nephew of Thomson, to whom Dr. Johnson has since done so much justice, in his *Lives of the Poets*.

We talked of memory, and its various modes.— JOHNSON. " Memory will play strange tricks. One sometimes loses a single word. I once lost *fugaces* in the Ode *Posthume, Posthume*." I mentioned to him, that a worthy gentleman of my acquaintance actually forgot his own name.—JOHNSON. " Sir, that was a morbid oblivion."

Friday, 20th August

Dr. Shaw, the professor of divinity, breakfasted with us. I took out my *Ogden on Prayer*, and read some of it to the company. Dr. Johnson praised him. " Abernethy (said he,) allows only of a physical effect of prayer upon the mind, which may be produced many ways, as well as by prayer ; for instance, by meditation.

Ogden goes farther. In truth, we have the consent of all nations for the efficacy of prayer, whether offered up by individuals, or by assemblies ; and Revelation has told us, it will be effectual."—I said, " Leechman seemed to incline to Abernethy's doctrine." Dr. Watson observed, that Leechman meant to shew, that, even admitting no effect to be produced by prayer, respecting the Deity, it was useful to our own minds. He had given only a part of his system : Dr. Johnson thought he should have given the whole.

Dr. Johnson enforced the strict observance of Sunday. " It should be different (he observed) from another day. People may walk, but not throw stones at birds. There may be relaxation, but there should be no levity."

We went and saw Colonel Nairne's garden and grotto. Here was a fine old plane tree. Unluckily the colonel said, there was but this and another large tree in the county. This assertion was an excellent cue for Dr. Johnson, who laughed enormously, calling to me to hear it. He had expatiated to me on the nakedness of that part of Scotland which he had seen. His *Journey* has been violently abused for what he has said upon this subject. But let it be considered, that, when Dr. Johnson talks of trees, he means trees of good size, such as he was accustomed to see in England ; and of these there are certainly very few upon the *eastern coast* of Scotland. Besides, he said, that he meant to give only a map of the road ; and let any traveller observe how many trees, which deserve the name, he can see from the road from Berwick to Aberdeen. Had Dr. Johnson said, " there are *no* trees " upon this line, he would have said what is colloquially true ; because, by no trees, in common speech, we mean few. When he is particular in counting, he may be attacked. I know not how Colonel Nairne came to say there were but *two* large trees in the county of Fife.

I did not perceive that he smiled. There are certainly not a great many ; but I could have shewn him more than two at Balmuto, from whence my ancestors came, and which now belongs to a branch of my family.

The grotto was ingeniously constructed. In the front of it were petrified stocks of fir, plane, and some other tree. Dr. Johnson said, " Scotland has no right to boast of this grotto ; it is owing to personal merit. I never denied personal merit to many of you."— Professor Shaw said to me, as we walked, " This is a wonderful man : he is master of every subject he handles."—Dr. Watson allowed him a very strong understanding, but wondered at his total inattention to established manners, as he came from London.

I have not preserved, in my Journal, any of the conversation which passed between Dr. Johnson and Professor Shaw ; but I recollect Dr. Johnson said to me afterwards, " I took much to Shaw."

We left St. Andrews about noon, and some miles from it observing, at Leuchars, a church with an old tower, we stopped to look at it. The *manse*, as the parsonage-house is called in Scotland, was close by. I waited on the minister, mentioned our names, and begged he would tell us what he knew about it. He was a very civil old man ; but could only inform us, that it was supposed to have stood eight hundred years. He told us, there was a colony of Danes in his parish ; that they had landed at a remote period of time, and still remained a distinct people. Dr. Johnson shrewdly inquired whether they had brought women with them. We were not satisfied as to this colony.

We saw, this day, Dundee and Aberbrothick, the last of which Dr. Johnson has celebrated in his *Journey*. Upon the road we talked of the Roman Catholick faith. He mentioned (I think) Tillotson's argument against transubstantiation : " That we are as sure we

see bread and wine only, as that we read in the Bible
the text on which that false doctrine is founded. We
have only the evidence of our senses for both." "If,
(he added,) GOD had never spoken figuratively, we
might hold that he speaks literally, when he says,
'This is my body.'"—BOSWELL. "But what do you
say, sir, to the ancient and continued tradition of the
church upon this point?"—JOHNSON. "Tradition, sir,
has no place, where the Scriptures are plain; and
tradition cannot persuade a man into a belief of transubstantiation. Able men, indeed, have *said* they
believed it."

This is an awful subject. I did not then press Dr.
Johnson upon it; nor shall I now enter upon a disquisition concerning the import of those words uttered
by our Saviour, which had such an effect upon many
of his disciples, that they "went back, and walked no
more with him." The Catechism and solemn office
for Communion, in the Church of England, maintain
a mysterious belief in more than a mere commemoration
of the death of Christ, by partaking of the elements of
bread and wine.

Dr. Johnson put me in mind that, at St. Andrews,
I had defended my profession very well, when the
question had again been started, Whether a lawyer
might honestly engage with the first side that offers
him a fee. "Sir, (said I,) it was with your arguments
against Sir William Forbes: but it was much that I
could wield the arms of Goliath."

He said, our judges had not gone deep in the question concerning literary property. I mentioned Lord
Monboddo's opinion, that if a man could get a work by
heart, he might print it, as by such an act the mind is
exercised.—JOHNSON. "No, sir; a man's repeating it
no more makes it his property, than a man may sell
a cow which he drives home."—I said, printing an
abridgement of a work was allowed, which was only

cutting the horns and tail off the cow.—JOHNSON. " No, sir ; 'tis making the cow have a calf."

About eleven at night we arrived at Montrose. We found but a sorry inn, where I myself saw another waiter put a lump of sugar with his fingers into Dr. Johnson's lemonade, for which he called him " Rascal ! " It put me in great glee that our landlord was an Englishman. I rallied the Doctor upon this, and he grew quiet. Both Sir John Hawkins's and Dr. Burney's *History of Musick* had then been advertised. I asked if this was not unlucky : would not they hurt one another ? —JOHNSON. " No, sir. They will do good to one another. Some will buy the one, some the other, and compare them ; and so a talk is made about a thing, and the books are sold."

He was angry at me for proposing to carry lemons with us to Sky, that he might be sure to have his lemonade. " Sir, (said he,) I do not wish to be thought that feeble man who cannot do without any thing. Sir, it is very bad manners to carry provisions to any man's house, as if he could not entertain you. To an inferior, it is oppressive ; to a superior, it is insolent."

Having taken the liberty, this evening, to remark to Dr. Johnson, that he very often sat quite silent for a long time, even when in company with only a single friend, which I myself had sometimes sadly experienced, he smiled and said, " It is true, sir. Tom Tyers, (for so he familiarly called our ingenious friend, who, since his death, has paid a biographical tribute to his memory,) Tom Tyers described me the best. He once said to me, ' Sir, you are like a ghost : you never speak till you are spoken to.' "

Saturday, 21st August

Neither the Rev. Mr. Nisbet, the established minister, nor the Rev. Mr. Spooner, the episcopal minister, were in town. Before breakfast, we went and saw the town-hall, where is a good dancing-room, and other rooms for tea-drinking. The appearance of the town from it is very well ; but many of the houses are built with their ends to the street, which looks awkward. When we came down from it, I met Mr. Gleg, a merchant here. He went with us to see the English chapel. It is situated on a pretty dry spot, and there is a fine walk to it. It is really an elegant building, both within and without. The organ is adorned with green and gold. Dr. Johnson gave a shilling extraordinary to the clerk, saying, " He belongs to an honest church." I put him in mind, that episcopals were but *dissenters* here ; they were only *tolerated*. " Sir, (said he,) we are here, as Christians in Turkey."—He afterwards went into an apothecary's shop, and ordered some medicine for himself, and wrote the prescription in technical characters. The boy took him for a physician.

I doubted much which road to take, whether to go by the coast, or by Laurence Kirk and Monboddo. I knew Lord Monboddo and Dr. Johnson did not love each other : yet I was unwilling not to visit his lordship ; and was also curious to see them together. I mentioned my doubts to Dr. Johnson, who said, he would go two miles out of his way to see Lord Monboddo. I therefore sent Joseph forward, with the following note :

" MONTROSE, 21 *August.*

" MY DEAR LORD,
" THUS far I am come with Mr. Samuel Johnson. We must be at Aberdeen to-night. I know you do not admire him so much as I do ; but I cannot be in this country without making you a bow at your old place, as I do not know if I may again have an opportunity of seeing Monboddo. Besides, Mr. Johnson says, he would go two miles out of his way to see Lord

Monboddo. I have sent forward my servant, that we may know if your lordship be at home. I am ever, my dear lord,

" Most sincerely yours,
" JAMES BOSWELL."

As we travelled onwards from Montrose, we had the Grampian hills in our view, and some good land around us, but void of trees and hedges. Dr. Johnson has said ludicrously, in his *Journey*, that the *hedges* were of *stone ;* for, instead of the verdant *thorn* to refresh the eye, we found the bare *wall* or *dike* intersecting the Prospect. He observed, that it was wonderful to see a country so divested, so denuded of trees.

We stopped at Laurence Kirk, where our great Grammarian, Ruddiman, was once schoolmaster. We respectfully remembered that excellent man and eminent scholar, by whose labours a knowledge of the Latin language will be preserved in Scotland, if it shall be preserved at all. Lord Gardenston, one of our judges, collected money to raise a monument to him at this place, which I hope will be well executed. I know my father gave five guineas towards it. Lord Gardenston is the proprietor of Laurence Kirk, and has encouraged the building of a manufacturing village, of which he is exceedingly fond, and has written a pamphlet upon it, as if he had founded Thebes ; in which, however, there are many useful precepts strongly expressed. The village seemed to be irregularly built, some of the houses being of clay, some of brick, and some of brick and stone. Dr. Johnson observed, they thatched well here.

I was a little acquainted with Mr. Forbes, the minister of the parish. I sent to inform him that a gentleman desired to see him. He returned for answer, " that he would not come to a stranger." I then gave my name, and he came. I remonstrated to him for not coming to a stranger ; and, by presenting him to Dr. Johnson,

3

proved to him what a stranger might sometimes be. His Bible inculcates " be not forgetful to entertain strangers," and mentions the same motive. He defended himself by saying, " He had once come to a stranger who sent for him ; and he found him ' *a little worth person* ' ! "

Dr. Johnson insisted on stopping at the inn, as I told him that Lord Gardenston had furnished it with a collection of books, that travellers might have entertainment for the mind, as well as the body. He praised the design, but wished there had been more books, and those better chosen.

About a mile from Monboddo, where you turn off the road, Joseph was waiting to tell us my lord expected us to dinner. We drove over a wild moor. It rained, and the scene was somewhat dreary. Dr. Johnson repeated, with solemn emphasis, Macbeth's speech on meeting the witches. As we travelled on, he told me, " Sir, you got into our club by doing what a man can do. Several of the members wished to keep you out. Burke told me, he doubted if you were fit for it : but, now you are in, none of them are sorry. Burke says, that you have so much good humour naturally, it is scarce a virtue."—BOSWELL. " They were afraid of you, sir, as it was you who proposed me."—JOHNSON. " Sir, they knew, that if they refused you, they'd probably never have got in another. I'd have kept them all out. Beauclerk was very earnest for you."—BOSWELL. " Beauclerk has a keenness of mind which is very uncommon."—JOHNSON. " Yes, sir ; and every thing comes from him so easily. It appears to me that I labour, when I say a good thing."—BOSWELL. " You are loud, sir ; but it is not an effort of mind."

Monboddo is a wretched place, wild and naked, with a poor old house ; though, if I recollect right, there are two turrets which mark an old baron's residence. Lord Monboddo received us at his gate most courteously; pointed to the Douglas arms upon his house, and told us that his great-grandmother was of that family. "In such houses (said he,) our ancestors lived, who were better men than we."—"No, no, my lord (said Dr. Johnson). We are as strong as they, and a great deal wiser."—This was an assault upon one of Lord Monboddo's capital dogmas, and I was afraid there would have been a violent altercation in the very close, before we got into the house. But his lordship is distinguished not only for "ancient metaphysicks," but for ancient *politesse,* "*la vieille cour,*" and he made no reply.

His lordship was drest in a rustick suit, and wore a little round hat; he told us, we now saw him as *Farmer Burnet,* and we should have his family dinner, a farmer's dinner. He said, "I should not have forgiven Mr. Boswell, had he not brought you here, Dr. Johnson." He produced a very long stalk of corn, as a specimen of his crop, and said, "You see here the *lætas segetes :*" he added, that Virgil seemed to be as enthusiastick a farmer as he, and was certainly a practical one.— JOHNSON. "It does not always follow, my lord, that a man who has written a good poem on an art, has practised it. Philip Miller told me, that in Philips's *Cyder,* a poem, all the precepts were just, and indeed better than in books written for the purpose of instructing; yet Philips had never made cyder."

I started the subject of emigration.—JOHNSON. "To a man of mere animal life, you can urge no argument against going to America, but that it will be some time before he will get the earth to produce. But a man of any intellectual enjoyment will not easily go and immerse himself and his posterity for ages in barbarism."

He and my lord spoke highly of Homer.—JOHNSON. "He had all the learning of his age. The shield of Achilles shews a nation in war, a nation in peace; harvest sport, nay stealing."—MONBODDO. "Ay, and what we (looking to me) would call a parliament-house scene; a cause pleaded."—JOHNSON. "That is part of the life of a nation in peace. And there are in Homer such characters of heroes, and combinations of qualities of heroes, that the united powers of mankind ever since have not produced any but what are to be found there." —MONBODDO. "Yet no character is described."— JOHNSON. "No; they all develope themselves. Agamemnon is always a gentleman-like character; he has always Βασιλικον τι. That the ancients held so, is plain from this; that Euripides, in his Hecuba, makes him the person to interpose."—MONBODDO. "The history of manners is the most valuable. I never set a high value on any other history."—JOHNSON. "Nor I; and therefore I esteem biography, as giving us what comes near to ourselves, what we can turn to use."—BOSWELL. "But in the course of general history, we find manners. In wars, we see the dispositions of people, their degrees of humanity, and other particulars." —JOHNSON. "Yes; but then you must take all the facts to get this; and it is but a little you get."— MONBODDO. "And it is that little which makes history valuable."—Bravo! thought I; they agree like two brothers.—MONBODDO. "I am sorry, Dr. Johnson, you were not longer at Edinburgh, to receive the homage of our men of learning."—JOHNSON. "My lord, I received great respect and great kindness."—BOSWELL. "He goes back to Edinburgh after our tour."—We talked of the decrease of learning in Scotland, and of the *Muses' Welcome.*—JOHNSON. "Learning is much decreased in England, in my remembrance."—MONBODDO. "You, sir, have lived to see its decrease in England, I its extinction in Scotland." However, I brought him to confess that the High School of Edinburgh did well.—JOHNSON. "Learning has decreased in England, because learning will not do so much for a man as formerly. There are other ways of getting preferment. Few bishops are now made for their learning. To be a bishop, a man must be learned in a learned age,—factious in a factious age; but always of eminence. Warburton is an exception; though his learning alone did not raise him. He was first an antagonist to Pope, and helped Theobald to publish his *Shakspeare*; but, seeing Pope the rising man,—when Crousaz attacked his *Essay on Man*, for some faults which it has, and some which it has not, Warburton defended it in the Review of that time. This brought him acquainted with Pope, and he gained his friendship. Pope introduced him to Allen, Allen married him to his niece: so, by Allen's interest and his own, he was made a bishop. But then his learning was the *sine quà non*: He knew how to make the most of it; but I do not find by any dishonest means."—MONBODDO. "He is a great man."—JOHNSON. "Yes; he has great knowledge,—great power of mind. Hardly any man brings greater variety of learning to bear upon his point."—MONBODDO. "He is one of the greatest lights of your church."—JOHNSON. "Why, we are not so sure of his being very friendly to us. He blazes, if you will, but that is not always the steadiest light.— Lowth is another bishop who has risen by his learning."

Dr. Johnson examined young Arthur, Lord Monboddo's son, in Latin. He answered very well; upon which he said, with complacency, "Get you gone! When King James comes back, you shall be in the *Muses' Welcome*!"—My lord and Dr. Johnson disputed a little, whether the Savage or the London Shopkeeper had the best existence; his lordship, as usual, preferring the Savage.—My lord was extremely hospitable, and I saw both Dr. Johnson and him liking each other better every hour.

Dr. Johnson having retired for a short time, his lordship spoke of his conversation as I could have wished. Dr. Johnson had said, "I have done greater

feats with my knife than this ; " though he had eaten
a very hearty dinner.—My lord, who affects or believes
he follows an abstemious system, seemed struck with
Dr. Johnson's manner of living. I had a particular
satisfaction in being under the roof of Monboddo, my
lord being my father's old friend, and having been
always very good to me. We were cordial together.
He asked Dr. Johnson and me to stay all night. When
I said we *must* be at Aberdeen, he replied, " Well, I
am like the Romans : I shall say to you, ' Happy to
come ;—happy to depart ! ' " He thanked Dr. Johnson
for his visit.—JOHNSON. " I little thought, when I
had the honour to meet your lordship in London, that
I should see you at Monboddo." After dinner, as the
ladies were going away, Dr. Johnson would stand up.
He insisted that politeness was of great consequence
in society. " It is, (said he,) fictitious benevolence.
It supplies the place of it amongst those who see each
other only in publick, or but little. Depend upon it,
the want of it never fails to produce something disagreeable to one or other. I have always applied to
good breeding, what Addison in his *Cato* says of honour :

> " ' Honour's a sacred tie ; the law of Kings ;
> The noble mind's distinguishing perfection,
> That aids and strengthens Virtue where it meets her,
> And imitates her actions where she is not.' "

When he took up his large oak stick, he said, " My
lord, that's *Homerick* ; " thus pleasantly alluding to his
lordship's favourite writer.

Gory, my lord's black servant, was sent as our guide,
to conduct us to the high road. The circumstance
of each of them having a black servant was another
point of similarity between Johnson and Monboddo.
I observed how curious it was to see an African in the
north of Scotland, with little or no difference of manners
from those of the natives. Dr. Johnson laughed to see

Gory and Joseph riding together most cordially. "Those two fellows, (said he,) one from Africa, the other from Bohemia, seem quite at home."—He was much pleased with Lord Monboddo to-day. He said, he would have pardoned him for a few paradoxes, when he found he had so much that was good : but that, from his appearance in London, he thought him all paradox ; which would not do. He observed, that his lordship had talked no paradoxes to-day. "And as to the savage and the London shopkeeper, (said he,) I don't know but I might have taken the side of the savage equally, had any body else taken the side of the shopkeeper."— He had said to my lord, in opposition to the value of the savage's courage, that it was owing to his limited power of thinking, and repeated Pope's verses, in which " Macedonia's madman " is introduced, and the conclusion is,

" Yet ne'er looks forward farther than his nose."

I objected to the last phrase, as being low.—JOHNSON. "Sir, it is intended to be low : it is satire. The expression is debased, to debase the character."

When Gory was about to part from us, Dr. Johnson called to him, " Mr. Gory, give me leave to ask you a question : are you baptised ? " Gory told him he was, —and confirmed by the Bishop of Durham. He then gave him a shilling.

We had tedious driving this afternoon, and were somewhat drowsy. Last night I was afraid Dr. Johnson was beginning to faint in his resolution ; for he said, " If we must ride much, we shall not go ; and there's an end on't."—To-day, when he talked of Sky with spirit, I said, " Why, sir, you seemed to me to despond yesterday. You are a delicate Londoner ;—you are a maccaroni ; you can't ride."—JOHNSON. " Sir, I shall ride better than you. I was only afraid I should not find a horse able to carry me."—I hoped then there would be no fear of getting through our wild Tour.

We came to Aberdeen at half an hour past eleven. The New Inn, we were told, was full. This was comfortless. The waiter, however, asked if one of our names was Boswell, and brought me a letter left at the inn; it was from Mr. Thrale, enclosing one to Dr. Johnson. Finding who I was, we were told they would contrive to lodge us by putting us for a night into a room with two beds. The waiter said to me in the broad strong Aberdeenshire dialect, "I thought I knew you, by your likeness to your father."—My father puts up at the New Inn, when on his circuit. Little was said to-night. I was to sleep in a little press-bed in Dr. Johnson's room. I had it wheeled out into the dining-room, and there I lay very well.

Sunday, 22nd August

I sent a message to Professor Thomas Gordon, who came and breakfasted with us. He had secured seats for us at the English chapel. We found a respectable congregation, and an admirable organ, well played by Mr. Tait.

We walked down to the shore. Dr. Johnson laughed to hear that Cromwell's soldiers taught the Aberdeen people to make shoes and stockings, and to plant cabbages. He asked, if weaving the plaids was ever a domestick art in the Highlands, like spinning or knitting. They could not inform him here. But he conjectured probably, that where people lived so remote from each other, it was likely to be a domestick art as we see it was among the ancients, from Penelope. —I was sensible to-day, to an extraordinary degree, of Dr. Johnson's excellent English pronunciation. I

cannot account for its striking me more than any
other day : but it was as if new to me ; and I listened
to every sentence which he spoke, as to a musical composition.—Professor Gordon gave him an account of
the plan of education in his college. Dr. Johnson
said, it was similar to that at Oxford.—Waller the
poet's great grandson was studying here. Dr. Johnson
wondered that a man should send his son so far off,
when there were so many good schools in England.
He said, " At a great school there is all the splendour
and illumination of many minds ; the radiance of all is
concentrated in each, or at least reflected upon each.
But we must own that neither a dull boy, nor an idle
boy, will do so well at a great school as at a private
one. For at a great school there are always boys
enough to do well easily, who are sufficient to keep
up the credit of the school ; and after whipping being
tried to no purpose, the dull or idle boys are left at the
end of a class, having the appearance of going through
the course, but learning nothing at all. Such boys may
do good at a private school, where constant attention is
paid to them, and they are watched. So that the question of publick or private education is not properly a
general one ; but whether one or the other is best for
my son."

We were told the present Mr. Waller was a plain
country gentleman ; and his son would be such another.
I observed, a family could not expect a poet but in a
hundred generations.—" Nay, (said Dr. Johnson,) not
one family in a hundred can expect a poet in a hundred
generations." He then repeated Dryden's celebrated
lines,

Three poets in three distant ages born, etc.

and a part of a Latin translation of it done at Oxford :
he did not then say by whom.

He received a card from Sir Alexander Gordon,

who had been his acquaintance twenty years ago in London, and who, " if forgiven for not answering a line from him," would come in the afternoon. Dr. Johnson rejoiced to hear of him, and begged he would come and dine with us. I was much pleased to see the kindness with which Dr. Johnson received his old friend Sir Alexander ; a gentleman of good family, Lismore, but who had not the estate. The King's College here made him Professor of Medicine, which affords him a decent subsistence. He told us that the value of the stockings exported from Aberdeen was, in peace, a hundred thousand pounds ; and amounted, in time of war, to one hundred and seventy thousand pounds. Dr. Johnson asked, What made the difference ? Here we had a proof of the comparative sagacity of the two professors. Sir Alexander answered, " Because there is more occasion for them in war." Professor Thomas Gordon answered, " Because the Germans, who are our great rivals in the manufacture of stockings, are otherwise employed in time of war."— JOHNSON. " Sir, you have given a very good solution."

At dinner, Dr. Johnson ate several plate-fulls of Scotch broth, with barley and peas in it, and seemed very fond of the dish. I said, " You never ate it before."—JOHNSON. " No, sir ; but I don't care how soon I eat it again."—My cousin, Miss Dallas, formerly of Inverness, was married to Mr. Riddoch, one of the ministers of the English chapel here. He was ill, and confined to his room ; but she sent us a kind invitation to tea, which we all accepted. She was the same lively, sensible, cheerful woman, as ever. Dr. Johnson here threw out some jokes against Scotland. He said, " You go first to Aberdeen ; then to Enbru (the Scottish pronunciation of Edinburgh) ; then to Newcastle, to be polished by the colliers ; then to York ; then to London." And he laid hold of a little girl, Stuart Dallas, niece to Mrs. Riddoch, and, representing him-

self as a giant, said, he would take her with him! telling
her, in a hollow voice, that he lived in a cave, and had
a bed in the rock, and she should have a little bed cut
opposite to it!

He thus treated the point, as to prescription of murder in Scotland. " A jury in England would make
allowance for deficiencies of evidence, on account of
lapse of time : but a general rule that a crime should
not be punished, or tried for the purpose of punishment, after twenty years, is bad : It is cant to talk
of the King's advocate delaying a prosecution from
malice. How unlikely is it the King's advocate should
have malice against persons who commit murder, or
should even know them at all.—If the son of the murdered man should kill the murderer who got off merely
by prescription, I would help him to make his escape ;
though, were I upon his jury, I would not acquit him.
I would not advise him to commit such an act. On
the contrary, I would bid him submit to the determination of society, because a man is bound to submit
to the inconveniences of it, as he enjoys the good :
but the young man, though politically wrong, would
not be morally wrong. He would have to say, ' Here
I am amongst barbarians, who not only refuse to do
justice, but encourage the greatest of all crimes. I am
therefore in a state of nature : for, so far as there is
no law, it is a state of nature : and consequently, upon
the eternal and immutable law of justice, which requires that he who sheds man's blood should have his
blood shed, I will stab the murderer of my father.' "

We went to our inn, and sat quietly. Dr. Johnson
borrowed, at Mr. Riddoch's, a volume of Massillon's
Discourses on the Psalms : but I found he read little
in it. Ogden too he sometimes took up, and glanced
at ; but threw it down again. I then entered upon
religious conversation. Never did I see him in a better
frame : calm, gentle, wise, holy.—I said, " Would

not the same objection hold against the Trinity as against Transubstantiation ?"—"Yes, (said he,) if you take three and one in the same sense. If you do so, to be sure you cannot believe it : but the three persons in the Godhead are Three in one sense, and One in another. We cannot tell how ; and that is the mystery !"

I spoke of the satisfaction of Christ. He said his notion was, that it did not atone for the sins of the world ; but, by satisfying divine justice, by shewing that no less than the Son of God suffered for sin, it shewed to men and innumerable created beings, the heinousness of it, and therefore rendered it unnecessary for divine vengeance to be exercised against sinners, as it otherwise must have been ; that in this way it might operate even in favour of those who had never heard of it : as to those who did hear of it, the effect it should produce would be repentance and piety, by impressing upon the mind a just notion of sin : that original sin was the propensity to evil, which no doubt was occasioned by the fall. He presented this solemn subject in a new light to me, and rendered much more rational and clear the doctrine of what our Saviour has done for us ;—as it removed the notion of imputed righteousness in co-operating ; whereas by this view, Christ has done all already that he had to do, or is ever to do, for mankind, by making his great satisfaction ; the consequences of which will affect each individual according to the particular conduct of each. I would illustrate this by saying, that Christ's satisfaction resembles a sun placed to shew light to men, so that it depends upon themselves whether they will walk the right way or not, which they could not have done without that sun, "*the sun of righteousness*." There is, however, more in it than merely giving light—*a light to lighten the Gentiles :* for we are told, there is *healing under his wings.* Dr. Johnson said to me, "Richard Baxter commends a treatise by Grotius, *De Satisfactione Christi*. I have never read it : but I intend to read it ; and you may read it." I remarked, upon the principle now laid down, we might explain the difficult and seemingly hard text, " They that believe shall be saved ; and they that believe not shall be damned : " They that believe shall have such an impression made upon their minds, as will make them act so that they may be accepted by GOD.

We talked of one of our friends taking ill, for a length of time, a hasty expression of Dr. Johnson's to him, on his attempting to prosecute a subject that had a reference to religion, beyond the bounds within which the Doctor thought such topicks should be confined in a mixed company.—JOHNSON. " What is to become of society, if a friendship of twenty years is to be broken off for such a cause ? " As Bacon says,

> " Who then to frail mortality shall trust,
> But limns the water, or but writes in dust."

I said, he should write expressly in support of Christianity ; for that, although a reverence for it shines through his works in several places, that is not enough. " You know, (said I,) what Grotius has done, and what Addison has done.—You should do also."—He replied, " I hope I shall."

Monday, 23rd August

Principal Campbell, Sir Alexander Gordon, Professor Gordon, and Professor Ross, visited us in the morning, as did Dr. Gerard, who had come six miles from the country on purpose. We went and saw the Marischal College, and at one o'clock we waited on the magistrates in the town-hall, as they had invited us in order to present Dr. Johnson with the freedom of the town, which Provost Jopp did with a very good grace. Dr. Johnson was much pleased with this mark of attention, and received it very politely. There was a pretty numerous company assembled. It was striking to hear all of them drinking " Dr. Johnson ! Dr. Johnson ! " in the town-hall of Aberdeen, and then to see him with his burgess-ticket, or diploma, in his hat, which he wore as he walked along the street, according to the usual custom.—It gave me great satisfaction to observe the regard, and indeed fondness too, which every body here had for my father.

While Sir Alexander Gordon conducted Dr. Johnson to old Aberdeen, Professor Gordon and I called on Mr. Riddoch, whom I found to be a grave worthy clergyman. He observed, that, whatever might be said of Dr. Johnson while he was alive, he would, after he was dead, be looked upon by the world with regard and astonishment, on account of his Dictionary.

Professor Gordon and I walked over to the Old College, which Dr. Johnson had seen by this time. I stepped into the chapel, and looked at the tomb of the founder, Archbishop Elphinston, of whom I shall have occasion to write in my History of James IV. of Scotland, the patron of my family.

We dined at Sir Alexander Gordon's. The Provost, Professor Ross, Professor Dunbar, Professor Thomas Gordon, were there. After dinner came in Dr. Gerard, Professor Leslie, Professor Macleod. We had little or no conversation in the morning ; now we were but barren. The professors seemed afraid to speak.

Dr. Gerard told us that an eminent printer was very intimate with Warburton.—JOHNSON. " Why, sir, he has printed some of his works, and perhaps bought the property of some of them. The intimacy is such as one of the professors here may have with one of the carpenters who is repairing the college."—"But, (said Gerard,) I saw a letter from him to this printer, in which he says, that the one half of the clergy of the church of Scotland are fanaticks, and the other half infidels."—JOHNSON. "Warburton has accustomed himself to write letters just as he speaks, without thinking any more of what he throws out. When I read Warburton first, and observed his force, and his contempt of mankind, I thought he had driven the world before him; but I soon found that was not the case; for Warburton, by extending his abuse, rendered it ineffectual."

He told me, when we were by ourselves, that he thought it very wrong in the printer, to shew Warburton's letter, as it was raising a body of enemies against him. He thought it foolish in Warburton to write so to the printer; and added, "Sir, the worst way of being intimate, is by scribbling." He called Warburton's *Doctrine of Grace* a poor performance, and so he said was Wesley's Answer. "Warburton," he observed, "had laid himself very open. In particular, he was weak enough to say, that, in some disorders of the imagination, people had spoken with tongues, had spoken languages which they never knew before; a thing as absurd as to say, that, in some disorders of the imagination, people had been known to fly."

I talked of the difference of genius, to try if I could engage Gerard in a disquisition with Dr. Johnson; but I did not succeed. I mentioned, as a curious fact, that Locke had written verses.—JOHNSON. "I know of none, sir, but a kind of exercise prefixed to Dr. Sydenham's Works, in which he has some conceits about the dropsy, in which water and burning are united; and how Dr. Sydenham removed fire by drawing off water, contrary to the usual practice, which is to extinguish fire by bringing water upon it.—I am not sure that there is a word of all this; but it is such kind of talk."

We spoke of Fingal. Dr. Johnson said calmly, " If the poems were really translated, they were certainly first written down. Let Mr. Macpherson deposit the manuscript in one of the colleges at Aberdeen, where there are people who can judge ; and, if the professors certify the authenticity, then there will be an end of the controversy. If he does not take this obvious and easy method, he gives the best reason to doubt ; considering too, how much is against it *à priori*."

We sauntered after dinner in Sir Alexander's garden, and saw his little grotto, which is hung with pieces of poetry written in a fair hand. It was agreeable to observe the contentment and kindness of this quiet, benevolent man. Professor Macleod was brother to Macleod of Talisker, and brother-in-law to the Laird of Col. He gave me a letter to young Col. I was weary of this day, and began to think wishfully of being again in motion. I was uneasy to think myself too fastidious, whilst I fancied Dr. Johnson quite satisfied. But he owned to me that he was fatigued and teased by Sir Alexander's doing too much to entertain him. I said, it was all kindness.—JOHNSON. " True, sir : but sensation is sensation."—BOSWELL. " It is so : we feel pain equally from the surgeon's probe, as from the sword of the foe."

We visited two booksellers' shops, and could not find Arthur Johnston's Poems. We went and sat near an hour at Mr. Riddoch's. He could not tell distinctly how much education at the college here costs, which disgusted Dr. Johnson. I had pledged myself that we should go to the inn, and not stay supper. They pressed us, but he was resolute. I saw Mr. Riddoch did not please him. He said to me, afterwards, " Sir, he has no vigour in his talk." But my friend should have considered that he himself was not in good humour ; so that it was not easy to talk to his satisfaction.—We sat contentedly at our inn. He then became merry,

and observed how little we had either heard or said at
Aberdeen : That the Aberdonians had not started a
single *mawkin* (the Scottish word for hare) for us to
pursue.

Tuesday, 24th August

We set out about eight in the morning, and breakfasted at Ellon. The landlady said to me, " Is not
this the great Doctor that is going about through the
country ? "—I said, " Yes."—" Ay, (said she,) we
heard of him, I made an errand into the room on purpose to see him. There's something great in his appearance : it is a pleasure to have such a man in one's
house ; a man who does so much good. If I had
thought of it, I would have shewn him a child of mine,
who has had a lump on his throat for some time."—
" But, (said I,) he is not a doctor of physick."—" Is he
an oculist ? " said the landlord.—" No, (said I,) he is
only a very learned man."—LANDLORD. " They say he
is the greatest man in England, except Lord Mansfield."—Dr. Johnson was highly entertained with this,
and I do think he was pleased too. He said, " I like
the exception : to have called me the greatest man in
England, would have been an unmeaning compliment :
but the exception marked that the praise was in earnest ;
and, in Scotland, the exception must be Lord Mansfield,
or—Sir John Pringle."

He told me a good story of Dr. Goldsmith. Graham,
who wrote *Telemachus, a Masque*, was sitting one night
with him and Dr. Johnson, and was half drunk. He
rattled away to Dr. Johnson : " You are a clever
fellow, to be sure ; but you cannot write an essay like
Addison, or verses like the *Rape of the Lock.*" At
last he said, " Doctor, I should be happy to see you
at Eaton."—" I shall be glad to wait on you," answered

Goldsmith.—" No, (said Graham,) 'tis not you I mean,
Dr. Minor ; 'tis Dr. Major, there.''—Goldsmith was
excessively hurt by this. He afterwards spoke of it
himself. " Graham, (said he,) is a fellow to make one
commit suicide.''

We had received a polite invitation to Slains castle,
We arrived there just at three o'clock, as the bell for
dinner was ringing. Though, from its being just on
the North-east Ocean, no trees will grow here, Lord
Errol has done all that can be done. He has cultivated his fields so as to bear rich crops of every kind,
and he has made an excellent kitchen-garden, with a
hot-house. I had never seen any of the family : but
there had been a card of invitation written by the
honourable Charles Boyd, the earl's brother. We were
conducted into the house, and at the dining-room door
were met by that gentleman, whom both of us at first
took to be Lord Errol ; but he soon corrected our mis-
take. My lord was gone to dine in the neighbourhood,
at an entertainment given by Mr. Irvine of Drum. Lady
Errol received us politely, and was very attentive to us
during the time of dinner. There was nobody at table
but her ladyship, Mr. Boyd, and some of the children,
their governour and governess. Mr. Boyd put Dr.
Johnson in mind of having dined with him at Cumming
the Quaker's, along with a Mr. Hall and Miss Williams :
this was a bond of connection between them. For me,
Mr. Boyd's acquaintance with my father was enough.
After dinner, Lady Errol favoured us with a sight of
her young family, whom she made stand up in a row.
There were six daughters and two sons. It was a very
pleasing sight.

Dr. Johnson proposed our setting out. Mr. Boyd
said, he hoped we would stay all night ; his brother
would be at home in the evening, and would be very
sorry if he missed us. Mr. Boyd was called out of
the room. I was very desirous to stay in so comfort-

able a house, and I wished to see Lord Errol. Dr. Johnson, however, was right in resolving to go, if we were not asked again, as it is best to err on the safe side in such cases, and to be sure that one is quite welcome. To my great joy, when Mr. Boyd returned, he told Dr. Johnson that it was Lady Errol who had called him out, and said that she would never let Dr. Johnson into the house again, if he went away that night ; and that she had ordered the coach, to carry us to view a great curiosity on the coast, after which we should see the house. We cheerfully agreed.

Mr. Boyd was engaged, in 1745-6, on the same side with many unfortunate mistaken noblemen and gentlemen. He escaped, and lay concealed for a year in the island of Arran, the ancient territory of the Boyds. He then went to France, and was about twenty years on the continent. He married a French Lady, and now lived very comfortably at Aberdeen, and was much at Slains castle. He entertained us with great civility. He had a pompousness or formal plenitude in his conversation, which I did not dislike. Dr. Johnson said, " there was too much elaboration in his talk." It gave me pleasure to see him, a steady branch of the family, setting forth all its advantages with much zeal. He told us that Lady Errol was one of the most pious and sensible women in the island ; had a good head, and as good a heart. He said, she did not use force or fear in educating her children.—JOHNSON. " Sir, she is wrong ; I would rather have the rod to be the general terror to all, to make them learn, than tell a child, if you do thus or thus, you will be more esteemed than your brothers or sisters. The rod produces an effect which terminates in itself. A child is afraid of being whipped, and gets his task, and there's an end on't ; whereas, by exciting emulation, and comparisons of superiority, you lay the foundation of lasting mischief; you make brothers and sisters hate each other."

During Mr. Boyd's stay in Arran, he had found a chest of medical books, left by a surgeon there, and had read them till he acquired some skill in physick, in consequence of which he is often consulted by the poor. There were several here waiting for him as patients. We walked round the house till stopped by a cut made by the influx of the sea. The house is built quite upon the shore; the windows look upon the main ocean, and the King of Denmark is Lord Errol's nearest neighbour on the north-east.

We got immediately into the coach, and drove to Dunbui, a rock near the shore, quite covered with sea-fowls; then to a circular basin of large extent, surrounded with tremendous rocks. On the quarter next the sea, there is a high arch in the rock, which the force of the tempest has driven out. This place is called Buchan's Buller, or the Buller of Buchan, and the country people call it the Pot. Mr. Boyd said it was so called from the French *Bouloir*. It may be more simply traced from *Boiler* in our own language. We walked round this monstrous cauldron. In some places, the rock is very narrow; and on each side there is a sea deep enough for a man of war to ride in; so that it is somewhat horrid to move along. However, there is earth and grass upon the rock, and a kind of road marked out by the print of feet; so that one makes it out pretty safely: yet it alarmed me to see Dr. Johnson striding irregularly along. He insisted on taking a boat, and sailing into the Pot. We did so. He was stout, and wonderfully alert. The Buchanmen all shewing their teeth, and speaking with that strange sharp accent which distinguishes them, was to me a matter of curiosity. He was not sensible of the difference of pronunciation in the South, and North of Scotland, which I wondered at.

As the entry into the Buller is so narrow that oars cannot be used as you go in, the method taken is, to row very hard when you come near it, and give the boat such a rapidity of motion that it glides in. Dr. Johnson observed what an effect this scene would have had, were we entering into an unknown place. There are caves of considerable depth ; I think, one on each side. The boatmen had never entered either of them far enough to know the size. Mr. Boyd told us that it is customary for the company at Peterhead well, to make parties, and come and dine in one of the caves here.

He told us, that, as Slains is at a considerable distance from Aberdeen, Lord Errol, who has a very large family, resolved to have a surgeon of his own. With this view he educated one of his tenants' sons, who is now settled in a very neat house and farm just by, which we saw from the road. By the salary which the earl allows him, and the practice which he has had, he is in very easy circumstances. He had kept an exact account of all that had been laid out on his education, and he came to his lordship one day, and told him that he had arrived at a much higher situation than ever he expected ; that he was now able to repay what his lordship had advanced, and begged he would accept of it. The earl was pleased with the generous gratitude and genteel offer of the man ; but refused it. —Mr. Boyd also told us, Cumming the Quaker first began to distinguish himself, by writing against Dr. Leechman on Prayer, to prove it unnecessary, as GOD knows best what should be, and will order it without our asking :—the old hackneyed objection.

When we returned to the house we found coffee and tea in the drawing-room. Lady Errol was not there, being, as I supposed, engaged with her young family. There is a bow-window fronting the sea. Dr. Johnson repeated the ode, *Jam satis terris*, while Mr. Boyd was with his patients. He spoke well in favour of entails, to preserve lines of men whom mankind are accustomed to reverence. His opinion was that so much land should be entailed as that families should never fall into contempt, and as much left free as to give them all the advantages of property in case of any emergency. "If (said he,) the nobility are suffered to sink into indigence, they of course become corrupt ; they are ready to do whatever the king chooses ; therefore it is fit they should be kept from becoming poor, unless it is fixed that when they fall below a certain standard of wealth they shall lose their peerages. We know the House of Peers have made noble stands, when the House of Commons durst not. The two last years of parliament they dare not contradict the populace."

This room is ornamented with a number of fine prints, and with a whole length picture of Lord Errol, by Sir Joshua Reynolds. This led Dr. Johnson and me to talk of our amiable and elegant friend, whose panegyrick he concluded by saying, "Sir Joshua Reynolds, sir, is the most invulnerable man I know ; the man with whom if you should quarrel, you would find the most difficulty how to abuse."

Dr. Johnson observed, the situation here was the noblest he had ever seen,—better than Mount Edgecumbe, reckoned the first in England ; because, at Mount Edgecumbe, the sea is bounded by land on the other side, and, though there is there the grandeur of a fleet, there is also the impression of there being a dockyard, the circumstances of which are not agreeable. At Slains is an excellent old house. The noble owner has built of brick, along the square in the inside, a gallery, both on the first and second story, the house being no higher ; so that he has always a dry walk, and the rooms, to which formerly there was no approach but through each other, have now all separate entries from the gallery, which is hung with Hogarth's works, and other prints. We went and sat a while in the library. There is a valuable numerous collection. It was chiefly made by Mr. Falconer, husband to the late Countess of Errol in her own right. This earl has added a good many modern books.

About nine the earl came home. Captain Gordon of Park was with him. His lordship put Dr. Johnson in mind of their having dined together in London, along with Mr. Beauclerk. I was exceedingly pleased with Lord Errol. His dignified person and agreeable countenance, with the most unaffected affability, gave me high satisfaction. From perhaps a weakness, or, as I rather hope, more fancy and warmth of feeling than is quite reasonable, my mind is ever impressed with admiration for persons of high birth, and I could, with the most perfect honesty, expatiate on Lord Errol's good qualities ; but he stands in no need of my praise. His agreeable manners and softness of address prevented that constraint which the idea of his being Lord High Constable of Scotland might otherwise have occasioned. He talked very easily and sensibly with his learned guest. I observed that Dr. Johnson, though he shewed that respect to his lordship, which, from principle, he always does to high rank, yet, when they came to argument, maintained that manliness which becomes the force and vigour of his understanding. To shew external deference to our superiors, is proper : to seem to yield to them in opinion, is meanness. The earl said grace, both before and after supper, with much decency. He told us a story of a man who was executed at Perth, some years ago, for murdering a woman who was with child by him, and a former child he had by her. His hand was cut off : he was then pulled up ; but the rope broke, and he was forced to lie an hour on the ground, till another rope was brought from Perth, the execution being in a wood at some distance,

—at the place where the murders were committed.
"*There*, (said my lord,) *I see the hand of Providence.*"
—I was really happy here. I saw in this nobleman
the best dispositions and best principles ; and I saw
him, *in my mind's eye*, to be the representative of the
ancient Boyds of Kilmarnock. I was afraid he might
have urged drinking, as, I believe, he used formerly to
do, but he drank port and water out of a large glass
himself, and let us do as we pleased. He went with
us to our ro ms at night ; said, he took the visit very
kindly ; and told me, my father and he were very old
acquaintance ;—that I now knew the way to Slains,
and he hoped to see me there again.

I had a most elegant room ; but there was a fire in
it which blazed ; and the sea, to which my windows
looked, roared ; and the pillows were made of the
feathers of some sea-fowl, which had to me a disagreeable smell : so that, by all these causes, I was kept
awake a good while. I saw, in imagination, Lord
Errol's father, Lord Kilmarnock, (who was beheaded
on Tower-hill in 1746,) and I was somewhat dreary.
But the thought did not last long, and I fell asleep.

Wednesday, 25th August

We got up between seven and eight, and found Mr.
Boyd in the dining-room, with tea and coffee before
him, to give us breakfast. We were in an admirable
humour. Lady Errol had given each of us a copy of
an ode by Beattie, on the birth of her son, Lord Hay.
Mr. Boyd asked Dr. Johnson, how he liked it. Dr.
Johnson, who did not admire it, got off very well, by
taking it out, and reading the second and third stanzas
of it with much melody. This, without his saying a
word, pleased Mr. Boyd. He observed, however, to

Dr. Johnson, that the expression as to the family of Errol,

"*A thousand years* have seen it shine,"

compared with what went before, was an anti-climax, and that it would have been better

Ages have seen, etc.

Dr. Johnson said, " So great a number as a thousand is better. *Dolus latet in universalibus.* Ages might be only two ages."—He talked of the advantage of keeping up the connections of relationship, which produce much kindness. " Every man (said he,) who comes into the world, has need of friends. If he has to get them for himself, half his life is spent, before his merit is known. Relations are a man's ready friends who support him. When a man is in real distress, he flies into the arms of his relations. An old lawyer, who had much experience in making wills, told me, that after people had deli-berated long, and thought of many for their executors, they settled at last by fixing on their relations. This shews the universality of the principle."

I regretted the decay of respect for men of family, and that a Nabob now would carry an election from them.—JOHNSON. " Why, sir, the Nabob will carry it by means of his wealth, in a country where money is highly valued, as it must be where nothing can be had without money ; but, if it comes to personal preference, the man of family will always carry it. There is generally a *scoundrelism* about a low man."—Mr. Boyd said, that was a good *ism*.

I said, I believed mankind were happier in the ancient feudal state of subordination, than they are in the modern state of independency.—JOHNSON. " To be sure, the *Chief* was : but we must think of the number of individuals. That *they* were less happy, seems plain; for that state from which all escape as soon as they can, and to which none return after they have left it, must be less happy; and this is the case with the state of dependance on a chief or great man."

I mentioned the happiness of the French in their subordination, by the reciprocal benevolence and attachment between the great and those in lower rank.—Mr. Boyd gave us an instance of their gentlemanly spirit. An old Chevalier de Malthe, of ancient *noblesse*, but in low circumstances, was in a coffee-house at Paris, where was Julien, the great Manufacturer at the Gobelins, of the fine tapestry, so much distinguished both for the figures and the *colours*. The chevalier's carriage was very old. Says Julien, with a plebeian insolence, " I think, sir, you had better have your carriage new painted." The chevalier looked at him with indignant contempt, and answered, " Well, sir, you may take it home and *dye* it ! "—All the coffee-house rejoiced at Julien's confusion.

We set out about nine. Dr. Johnson was curious to see one of those structures which northern antiquarians call a Druid's temple. I had a recollection of one at Strichen; which I had seen fifteen years ago; so we went four miles out of our road, after passing Old Deer, and went thither. Mr. Fraser, the proprietor, was at home, and shewed it to us. But I had augmented it in my mind; for all that remains is two stones set up on end, with a long one laid upon them, as was usual, and one stone at a little distance from them. That stone was the capital one of the circle which surrounded what now remains. Mr. Fraser was very hospitable. There was a fair at Strichen; and he had several of his neighbours from it at dinner. One of them, Dr. Fraser, who had been in the army, remembered to have seen Dr. Johnson at a lecture on experimental philosophy, at Lichfield. The doctor

recollected being at the lecture ; and he was surprised
to find here somebody who knew him.

Mr. Fraser sent a servant to conduct us by a short
passage into the high road. I observed to Dr. Johnson, that I had a most disagreeable notion of the life of
country gentlemen ; that I left Mr. Fraser just now,
as one leaves a prisoner in a jail.—Dr. Johnson said,
that I was right in thinking them unhappy ; for that
they had not enough to keep their minds in motion.

I started a thought this afternoon which amused
us a great part of the way. " If, (said I,) our club
should come and set up in St. Andrews, as a college,
to teach all that each of us can, in the several depart-
ments of learning and taste, we should rebuild the city :
we should draw a wonderful concourse of students."—
Dr. Johnson entered fully into the spirit of this project.
We immediately fell to distributing the offices. I was
to teach Civil and Scotch law ; Burke, politicks and
eloquence ; Garrick, the art of publick speaking ; Langton was to be our Grecian, Colman our Latin professor ;
Nugent to teach physick ; Lord Charlemont, modern
history ; Beauclerk, natural philosophy ; Vesey, Irish
antiquities, or Celtick learning ; Jones, Oriental learning ; Goldsmith, poetry and ancient history ; Chamier,
commercial politicks ; Reynolds, painting, and the arts
which have beauty for their object ; Chambers, the law
of England. Dr. Johnson at first said, " I'll trust
theology to nobody but myself." But, upon due consideration, that Percy is a clergyman, it was agreed
that Percy should teach practical divinity and British
antiquities ; Dr. Johnson himself, logick, metaphysicks,
and scholastick divinity. In this manner did we amuse
ourselves ;—each suggesting, and each varying or adding,
till the whole was adjusted. Dr. Johnson said, we
only wanted a mathematician since Dyer died, who was
a very good one ; but as to every thing else, we should
have a very capital university.

We got at night to Banff. I sent Joseph on to Duff-house : but Earl Fife was not at home, which I regretted much, as we should have had a very elegant reception from his lordship. We found here but an indifferent inn. Dr. Johnson wrote a long letter to Mrs. Thrale. I wondered to see him write so much so easily. He verified his own doctrine that " a man may always write when he will set himself *doggedly* to it."

Thursday, 26th August

We got a fresh chaise here, a very good one, and very good horses. We breakfasted at Cullen. They set down dried haddocks broiled, along with our tea. I ate one ; but Dr. Johnson was disgusted by the sight of them, so they were removed. Cullen has a com-fortable appearance, though but a very small town, and the houses mostly poor buildings.

I called on Mr. Robertson, who has the charge of Lord Findlater's affairs, and was formerly Lord Mon-boddo's clerk, was three times in France with him, and translated Condamine's *Account of the Savage Girl*, to which his lordship wrote a preface, containing several remarks of his own. Robertson said, he did not believe so much as his lordship did ; that it was plain to him, the girl confounded what she imagined with what she remembered : that, besides, she perceived Condamine and Lord Monboddo forming theories, and she adapted her story to them.

Dr. Johnson said, " It is a pity to see Lord Mon-boddo publish such notions as he has done ; a man of sense, and of so much elegant learning. There would be little in a fool doing it ; we should only laugh ; but when a wise man does it, we are sorry. Other people have strange notions ; but they conceal them. If they

have tails, they hide them ; but Monboddo is as jealous
of his tail as a squirrel."—I shall here put down some
more remarks of Dr. Johnson's on Lord Monboddo,
which were not made exactly at this time, but come in
well from connection. He said, he did not approve of
a judge's calling himself *Farmer* Burnett, and going
about with a little round hat. He laughed heartily at
his lordship's saying he was an *enthusiastical* farmer ;
" for, (said he,) what can he do in farming by his *enthusiasm ?* " Here, however, I think Dr. Johnson mistaken.
He who wishes to be successful, or happy, ought to be
enthusiastical, that is to say, very keen in all the occupations or diversions of life. An ordinary gentleman-
farmer will be satisfied with looking at his fields once
or twice a day : an enthusiastical farmer will be constantly employed on them ;—will have his mind earnestly
engaged ; will talk perpetually of them. But Dr. Johnson has much of the *nil admirari* in smaller concerns.
That survey of life which gave birth to his *Vanity
of Human Wishes* early sobered his mind. Besides,
so great a mind as his cannot be moved by inferior
objects : an elephant does not run and skip like lesser
animals.

Mr. Robertson sent a servant with us, to shew us
through Lord Findlater's wood, by which our way was
shortened, and we saw some part of his domain, which
is indeed admirably laid out. Dr. Johnson did not
choose to walk through it. He always said, that he
was not come to Scotland to see fine places, of which
there were enough in England ; but wild objects,——
mountains, —— waterfalls,—— peculiar manners ; in
short, things which he had not seen before. I have a
notion that he at no time has had much taste for rural
beauties. I have myself very little.

Dr. Johnson said, there was nothing more con
temptible than a country gentleman living beyond his
income, and every year growing poorer and poorer.

He spoke strongly of the influence which a man has by being rich. "A man, (said he,) who keeps his money, has in reality more use from it, than he can have by spending it." I observed that this looked very like a paradox; but he explained it thus: "If it were certain that a man would keep his money locked up for ever, to be sure he would have no influence; but, as so many want money, and he has the power of giving it, and they know not but by gaining his favour they may obtain it, the rich man will always have the greatest influence. He again who lavishes his money, is laughed at as foolish, and in a great degree with justice, considering how much is spent from vanity. Even those who partake of a man's hospitality, have but a transient kindness for him. If he has not the command of money, people know he cannot help them, if he would; whereas the rich man always can, if he will, and for the chance of that, will have much weight."—BOSWELL. "But philosophers and satirists have all treated a miser as contemptible."—JOHNSON. "He is so philosophically; but not in the practice of life."—BOSWELL. "Let me see now:—I do not know the instances of misers in England, so as to examine into their influence."—JOHNSON. "We have had few misers in England."—BOSWELL. "There was Lowther."—JOHNSON. "Why, sir, Lowther, by keeping his money, had the command of the county, which the family has now lost, by spending it. I take it, he lent a great deal; and that is the way to have influence, and yet preserve one's wealth. A man may lend his money upon very good security, and yet have his debtor much under his power."—BOSWELL. "No doubt, sir. He can always distress him for the money; as no man borrows, who is able to pay on demand quite conveniently."

We dined at Elgin, and saw the noble ruins of the cathedral. Though it rained much, Dr. Johnson examined them with a most patient attention. He could not here feel any abhorrence at the Scottish reformers, for he had been told by Lord Hailes, that it was destroyed before the Reformation, by the Lord of Badenoch, who had a quarrel with the bishop. The bishop's house, and those of the other clergy, which are still pretty entire, do not seem to have been proportioned to the magnificence of the cathedral, which has been of great extent, and had very fine carved work. The ground within the walls of the cathedral is employed as a burying-place. The family of Gordon have their vault here ; but it has nothing grand.

We passed Gordon Castle this forenoon, which has a princely appearance. Fochabers, the neighbouring village, is a poor place, many of the houses being ruinous ; but it is remarkable, they have in general orchards well stored with apple-trees. Elgin has what in England are called piazzas, that run in many places on each side of the street. It must have been a much better place formerly. Probably it had piazzas all along the town, as I have seen at Bologna. I approved much of such structures in a town, on account of their conveniency in wet weather. Dr. Johnson disapproved of them, " because (said he) it makes the under story of a house very dark, which greatly over-balances the conveniency, when it is considered how small a part of the year it rains ; how few are usually in the street at such times ; that many who are might as well be at home ; and the little that people suffer, supposing them to be as much wet as they commonly are in walking a street."

We fared but ill at our inn here ; and Dr. Johnson said, this was the first time he had seen a dinner in Scotland that he could not eat.

In the afternoon, we drove over the very heath where Macbeth met the witches, according to tradition. Dr. Johnson again solemnly repeated—

How far is't called to Fores ?   What are these,
So wither'd, and so wild in their attire ?
That look not like the inhabitants o' the earth,
And yet are on't ?

He repeated a good deal more of *Macbeth*. His re-
citation was grand and affecting, and, as Sir Joshua
Reynolds has observed to me, had no more tone than
it should have : it was the better for it. He then
parodied the *All-hail* of the witches to Macbeth, addressing himself to me. I had purchased some land
called Dalblair ; and, as in Scotland it is customary
to distinguish landed men by the name of their estates,
I had thus two titles, Dalblair and Young Auchinleck,
So my friend, in imitation of

All hail Macbeth ! hail to thee, Thane of Cawdor !

condescended to amuse himself with uttering—

All hail Dalblair ! hail to thee, Laird of Auchinleck !

We got to Fores at night, and found an admirable
inn, in which Dr. Johnson was pleased to meet with
a landlord, who styled himself "Wine-Cooper, from
LONDON."

Friday, 27th August

It was dark when we came to Fores last night ; so
we did not see what is called King Duncan's monument.—I shall now mark some gleanings of Dr. Johnson's conversation. I spoke of *Leonidas*, and said
there were some good passages in it.—JOHNSON. " Why,
you must *seek* for them."—He said, Paul Whitehead's
Manners was a poor performance.—Speaking of Derrick, he told me " he had a kindness for him, and had
often said, that if his letters had been written by one

of a more established name, they would have been thought very pretty letters."

This morning I introduced the subject of the origin of evil.—JOHNSON. "Moral evil is occasioned by free will, which implies choice between good and evil. With all the evil that there is, there is no man but would rather be a free agent, than a mere machine without the evil; and what is best for each individual, must be best for the whole. If a man would rather be the machine, I cannot argue with him. He is a different being from me."—BOSWELL. "A man, as a machine, may have agreeable sensations; for instance, he may have pleasure in musick."—JOHNSON. "No, sir, he cannot have pleasure in musick; at least no power of producing musick; for he who can produce musick may let it alone: he who can play upon a fiddle may break it: such a man is not a machine." This reasoning satisfied me. It is certain, there cannot be a free agent, unless there is the power of being evil as well as good. We must take the inherent possibilities of things into consideration, in our reasonings or conjectures concerning the works of GOD.

We came to Nairn to breakfast. Though a county town and a royal burgh, it is a miserable place. Over the room where we sat, a girl was spinning wool with a great wheel, and singing an Erse song: "I'll warrant you, (said Dr. Johnson,) one of the songs of Ossian." He then repeated these lines:

> "Verse sweetens toil, however rude the sound.
>   All at her work the village maiden sings;
>   Nor, while she turns the giddy wheel around,
>   Revolves the sad vicissitude of things."

I thought I had heard these lines before.—JOHNSON. "I fancy not, sir; for they are in a detached poem, the name of which I do not remember, written by one Giffard, a parson."

I expected Mr. Kenneth M'Aulay, the minister of Calder, who published the history of St. Kilda, a book which Dr. Johnson liked, would have met us here, as I had written to him from Aberdeen. But I received a letter from him, telling me that he could not leave home, as he was to administer the sacrament the following Sunday, and earnestly requesting to see us at his manse. "We'll go," said Dr. Johnson; which we accordingly did. Mrs. M'Aulay received us, and told us her husband was in the church distributing tokens. We arrived between twelve and one o'clock, and it was near three before he came to us.

Dr. Johnson thanked him for his book, and said "it was a very pretty piece of topography." M'Aulay did not seem much to mind the compliment. From his conversation, Dr. Johnson was persuaded that he had not written the book which goes under his name. I myself always suspected so; and I have been told it was written by the learned Dr. John M'Pherson of Sky, from the materials collected by M'Aulay. Dr. Johnson said privately to me, "There is a combination in it of which M'Aulay is not capable." However, he was exceedingly hospitable; and, as he obligingly promised us a route for our Tour through the Western Isles, we agreed to stay with him all night.

After dinner, we walked to the old castle of Calder, (pronounced Cawder) the Thane of Cawdor's seat. I was sorry that my friend, this "prosperous gentleman," was not there. The old tower must be of great antiquity. There is a draw-bridge,—what has been a moat,—and an ancient court. There is a hawthorn-tree, which rises like a wooden pillar through the rooms of the castle; for, by a strange conceit, the walls have been built round it. The thickness of the walls, the small slaunting windows, and a great iron door at the entrance on the second story as you ascend the stairs, all indicate the rude times in which this castle was erected. There were here some large venerable trees.

I was afraid of a quarrel between Dr. Johnson and Mr. M'Aulay, who talked slightingly of the lower English clergy. The Doctor gave him a frowning look, and said, " This is a day of novelties : I have seen old trees in Scotland, and I have heard the English clergy treated with disrespect."

I dreaded that a whole evening at Calder-manse would be heavy ; however, Mr. Grant, an intelligent and well bred minister in the neighbourhood, was there, and assisted us by his conversation. Dr. Johnson, talking of hereditary occupations in the Highlands, said, " There is no harm in such a custom as this ; but it is wrong to enforce it, and oblige a man to be a taylor or a smith, because his father has been one." This custom, however, is not peculiar to our Highlands ; it is well known that in India a similar practice prevails.

Mr. M'Aulay began a rhapsody against creeds and confessions. Dr. Johnson shewed, that " what he called *imposition*, was only a voluntary declaration of agreement in certain articles of faith, which a church has a right to require, just as any other society can insist on certain rules being observed by its members. Nobody is compelled to be of the church, as nobody is compelled to enter into a society."—This was a very clear and just view of the subject : but, M'Aulay could not be driven out of his track. Dr. Johnson said, " Sir, you are a *bigot to laxness*."

Mr. M'Aulay and I laid the map of Scotland before us ; and he pointed out a route for us from Inverness, by Fort Augustus, to Glenelg, Sky, Mull, Icolmkill, Lorn, and Inverary, which I wrote down. As my father was to begin the northern circuit about the 18th of September, it was necessary for us either to make our tour with great expedition, so as to get to Auchinleck before he set out, or to protract it, so as not to be there till his return, which would be about the 10th of October. By M'Aulay's calculation, we were not to land in Lorn till the 20th of September. I thought that the interruptions by bad days, or by occasional excursions, might make it ten days later; and I thought too, that we might perhaps go to Benbecula, and visit Clanranald, which would take a week of itself.

Dr. Johnson went up with Mr. Grant to the library, which consisted of a tolerable collection; but the Doctor thought it rather a lady's library, with some Latin books in it by chance, than the library of a clergyman. It had only two of the Latin fathers, and one of the Greek fathers in Latin. I doubted whether Dr. Johnson would be present at a Presbyterian prayer. I told Mr. M'Aulay so, and said that the Doctor might sit in the library while we were at family worship. Mr. M'Aulay said, he would omit it, rather than give Dr. Johnson offence: but I would by no means agree that an excess of politeness, even to so great a man, should prevent what I esteem as one of the best pious regulations. I know nothing more beneficial, more comfortable, more agreeable, than that the little societies of each family should regularly assemble, and unite in praise and prayer to our heavenly Father, from whom we daily receive so much good, and may hope for more in a higher state of existence. I mentioned to Dr. Johnson the over-delicate scrupulosity of our host. He said, he had no objection to hear the prayer. This was a pleasing surprise to me; for he refused to go and hear Principal Robertson preach. "I will hear him, (said he,) if he will get up into a tree and preach; but I will not give a sanction, by my presence, to a Presbyterian assembly."

Mr. Grant having prayed, Dr. Johnson said, his prayer was a very good one; but objected to his not having introduced the Lord's Prayer. He told us, that an Italian of some note in London said once to him, " We have in our service a prayer called the *Pater Noster,* which is a very fine composition. I wonder who is the author of it."—A singular instance of ignorance in a man of some literature and general inquiry !

Saturday, 28th August

Dr. Johnson had brought a Sallust with him in his pocket from Edinburgh. He gave it last night to Mr. M'Aulay's son, a smart young lad about eleven years old. Dr. Johnson had given an account of the education at Oxford, in all its gradations. The advantage of being a servitor to a youth of little fortune struck Mrs. M'Aulay much. I observed it aloud. Dr. Johnson very handsomely and kindly said, that, if they would send their boy to him, when he was ready for the university, he would get him made a servitor, and perhaps would do more for him. He could not promise to do more ; but would undertake for the servitorship.

I should have mentioned that Mr. White, a Welchman, who has been many years factor (*i.e.* steward) on the estate of Calder, drank tea with us last night, and upon getting a note from Mr. M'Aulay, asked us to his house. We had not time to accept of his invitation. He gave us a letter of introduction to Mr. Ferne, master of stores at Fort George. He shewed it to me. It recommended " two celebrated gentlemen ; no less than Dr. Johnson, *author of his Dictionary,*— and Mr. Boswell, known at Edinburgh by the name of Paoli."—He said, he hoped I had no objection to what he had written ; if I had, he would alter it. I thought it was a pity to check his effusions, and acqui-

esced ; taking care, however, to seal the letter, that it
might not appear that I had read it.

A conversation took place, about saying grace at
breakfast (as we do in Scotland) as well as at dinner
and supper ; in which Dr. Johnson said, " It is enough
if we have stated seasons of prayer ; no matter when.
A man may as well pray when he mounts his horse, or
a woman when she milks her cow, (which Mr. Grant
told us is done in the Highlands,) as at meals ; and
custom is to be followed."

We proceeded to Fort George. When we came
into the square, I sent a soldier with the letter to Mr.
Ferne. He came to us immediately, and along with
him came Major Brewse of the Engineers, pronounced
Bruce. He said he believed it was originally the
same Norman name with Bruce. That he had dined
at a house in London, where were three Bruces, one
of the Irish line, one of the Scottish line, and himself
of the English line. He said he was shewn it in the
Herald's office spelt fourteen different ways. I told
him the different spellings of my name. Dr. Johnson
observed, that there had been great disputes about the
spelling of Shakspear's name ; at last it was thought it
would be settled by looking at the original copy of his
will ; but, upon examining it, he was found to have
written it himself no less than three different ways.

Mr. Ferne and Major Brewse first carried us to wait
on Sir Eyre Coote, whose regiment, the 37th, was lying
here, and who then commanded the fort. He asked
us to dine with him, which we agreed to do.

Before dinner we examined the fort. The Major
explained the fortification to us, and Mr. Ferne gave
us an account of the stores. Dr. Johnson talked of
the proportions of charcoal and salt-petre in making
gunpowder, of granulating it, and of giving it a gloss.
He made a very good figure upon these topics. He
said to me afterwards, that " he had talked *ostenta-*

tiously."—We reposed ourselves a little in Mr. Ferne's house. He had every thing in neat order as in England ; and a tolerable collection of books. I looked into Pennant's *Tour in Scotland*. He says little of this fort ; but that " the barracks, &c. form several streets." This is aggrandising. Mr. Ferne observed, if he had said they form a square, with a row of buildings before it, he would have given a juster description. Dr. Johnson remarked, " how seldom descriptions correspond with realities ; and the reason is, that people do not write them till some time after, and then their imagination has added circumstances."

We talked of Sir Adolphus Oughton. The Major said, he knew a great deal for a military man.—JOHNSON. " Sir, you will find few men, of any profession, who know more. Sir Adolphus is a very extraordinary man ; a man of boundless curiosity and unwearied diligence."

I know not how the Major contrived to introduce the contest between Warburton and Lowth.—JOHNSON. " Warburton kept his temper all along, while Lowth was in a passion. Lowth published some of Warburton's letters. Warburton drew *him* on to write some very abusive letters, and then asked his leave to publish them ; which he knew Lowth could not refuse, after what *he* had done. So that Warburton contrived that he should publish, apparently with Lowth's consent, what could not but shew Lowth in a disadvantageous light."

At three the drum beat for dinner. I, for a little while, fancied myself a military man, and it pleased me. We went to Sir Eyre Coote's, at the governour's house, and found him a most gentleman-like man. His lady is a very agreeable woman, with an uncommonly mild and sweet tone of voice. There was a pretty large company : Mr. Ferne, Major Brewse, and several officers. Sir Eyre had come from the East-Indies by land, through the Desarts of Arabia. He told us, the Arabs could live five days without victuals, and subsist for three weeks on nothing else but the blood of their camels, who could lose so much of it as would suffice for that time, without being exhausted. He highly praised the virtue of the Arabs; their fidelity, if they undertook to conduct any person; and said, they would sacrifice their lives rather than let him be robbed. Dr. Johnson, who is always for maintaining the superiority of civilized over uncivilized men, said, " Why, sir, I can see no superiour virtue in this. A serjeant and twelve men, who are my guard, will die, rather than that I shall be robbed."—Colonel Pennington, of the 37th regiment, took up the argument with a good deal of spirit and ingenuity.—PENNINGTON. " But the soldiers are compelled to this, by fear of punishment."—JOHNSON. " Well, sir, the Arabs are compelled by the fear of infamy."—PENNINGTON. " The soldiers have the same fear of infamy, and the fear of punishment besides; so have less virtue; because they act less voluntarily." —Lady Coote observed very well, that it ought to be known if there was not, among the Arabs, some punishment for not being faithful on such occasions.

We talked of the stage. I observed, that we had not now such a company of actors as in the last age; Wilks, Booth, &c. &c.—JOHNSON. " You think so, because there is one who excels all the rest so much : you compare them with Garrick, and see the deficiency. Garrick's great distinction is his universality. He can represent all modes of life, but that of an easy fine bred gentleman."—PENNINGTON. " He should give over playing young parts."—JOHNSON. " He does not take them now; but he does not leave off those which he has been used to play, because he does them better than any one else can do them. If you had generations of actors, if they swarmed like bees, the young ones might drive off the old. Mrs. Cibber, I think, got more

reputation than she deserved, as she had a great same-
ness ; though her expression was undoubtedly very
fine. Mrs. Clive was the best player I ever saw. Mrs.
Pritchard was a very good one ; but she had something affected in her manner : I imagine she had some
player of the former age in her eye, which occasioned it."

Colonel Pennington said, Garrick sometimes failed
in emphasis ; as for instance, in *Hamlet,*

> I will speak *daggers* to her ; but use *none,*

instead of

> I will *speak* daggers to her ; but *use* none.

We had a dinner of two complete courses, variety of
wines, and the regimental band of musick playing in the
square, before the windows, after it. I enjoyed this
day much. We were quite easy and cheerful. Dr.
Johnson said, " I shall always remember this fort with
gratitude." I could not help being struck with some
admiration, at finding upon this barren sandy point,
such buildings,—such a dinner,—such company : it
was like enchantment. Dr. Johnson, on the other
hand, said to me more rationally, that " it did not strike
him as any thing extraordinary ; because he knew, here
was a large sum of money expended in building a fort ;
here was a regiment. If there had been less than what
we found, it would have surprized him." *He* looked
coolly and deliberately through all the gradations : my
warm imagination jumped from the barren sands to the
splendid dinner and brilliant company, to borrow the
expression of an absurd poet,

> " Without ands or ifs,
> I leapt from off the sands upon the cliffs."

The whole scene gave me a strong impression of the
power and excellence of human art.

We left the fort between six and seven o'clock : Sir Eyre Coote, Colonel Pennington, and several more, accompanied us down stairs, and saw us into our chaise. There could not be greater attention paid to any visitors. Sir Eyre spoke of the hardships which Dr. Johnson had before him.—BOSWELL. " Considering what he has said of us, we must make him feel something rough in Scotland."—Sir Eyre said to him, " You must change your name, sir."—BOSWELL. " Ay, to Dr. M'Gregor."

We got safely to Inverness, and put up at Mackenzie's inn. Mr. Keith, the collector of Excise here, my old acquaintance at Ayr, who had seen us at the Fort, visited us in the evening, and engaged us to dine with him next day, promising to breakfast with us, and take us to the English chapel ; so that we were at once commodiously arranged.

Not finding a letter here that I expected, I felt a momentary impatience to be at home. Transient clouds darkened my imagination, and in those clouds I saw events from which I shrunk ; but a sentence or two of the Rambler's conversation gave me firmness, and I considered that I was upon an expedition for which I had wished for years, and the recollection of which would be a treasure to me for life.

Sunday, 29th August

Mr. Keith breakfasted with us. Dr. Johnson expatiated rather too strongly upon the benefits derived to Scotland from the Union, and the bad state of our people before it. I am entertained with his copious exaggeration upon that subject ; but I am uneasy when people are by, who do not know him as well as I do, and may be apt to think him narrow-minded. I therefore diverted the subject.

The English chapel, to which we went this morning, was but mean. The altar was a bare fir table, with a coarse stool for kneeling on, covered with a piece of thick sailcloth doubled, by way of cushion. The congregation was small. Mr. Tait, the clergyman, read prayers very well, though with much of the Scotch accent. He preached on " Love your Enemies." It was remarkable that, when talking of the connections amongst men, he said, that some connected themselves with men of distinguished talents, and since they could not equal them, tried to deck themselves with their merit, by being their companions. The sentence was to this purpose. It had an odd coincidence with what might be said of my connecting myself with Dr. Johnson.

After church, we walked down to the Quay. We then went to Macbeth's castle. I had a romantick satisfaction in seeing Dr. Johnson actually in it. It perfectly corresponds with Shakspeare's description, which Sir Joshua Reynolds has so happily illustrated, in one of his notes on our immortal poet :

> "This castle hath a pleasant seat : the air
> Nimbly and sweetly recommends itself
> Unto our gentle sense," &c.

Just as we came out of it, a raven perched on one of the chimney-tops, and croaked. Then I repeated

> " —— The raven himself is hoarse,
> That croaks the fatal enterance of Duncan
> Under my battlements."

We dined at Mr. Keith's. Mrs. Keith was rather too attentive to Dr. Johnson, asking him many questions about his drinking only water. He repressed that observation, by saying to me, " You may remember that Lady Errol took no notice of this."

Dr. Johnson has the happy art (for which I have

heard my father praise the old Earl of Aberdeen) of
instructing himself, by making every man he meets tell
him something of what he knows best. He led Keith
to talk to him of the Excise in Scotland, and, in the
course of conversation, mentioned that his friend Mr.
Thrale, the great brewer, paid twenty thousand pounds
a year to the revenue ; and that he had four casks,
each of which holds sixteen hundred barrels,—above a
thousand hogsheads.

After this there was little conversation that deserves
to be remembered. I shall therefore here again glean
what I have omitted on former days. Dr. Gerard,
at Aberdeen, told us, that when he was in Wales, he
was shewn a valley inhabited by Danes, who still retain
their own language, and are quite a distinct people.
Dr. Johnson thought it could not be true, or all the
kingdom must have heard of it. He said to me, as
we travelled, " these people, sir, that Gerard talks
of, may have somewhat of a *peregrinity* in their dialect,
which relation has augmented to a different language."
I asked him if *peregrinity* was an English word : he
laughed, and said, " No." I told him this was the
second time that I had heard him coin a word. When
Foote broke his leg, I observed that it would make
him fitter for taking off George Faulkner as Peter
Paragraph, poor George having a wooden leg. Dr.
Johnson at that time said, " George will rejoice at the
depeditation of Foote ; " and when I challenged that
word, laughed, and owned he had made it, and added that
he had not made above three or four in his dictionary.

Having conducted Dr. Johnson to our inn, I begged
permission to leave him for a little, that I might run
about and pay some short visits to several good people
of Inverness. He said to me, " You have all the old-
fashioned principles, good and bad." I acknowledge
I have. That of attention to relations in the remotest
degree, or to worthy persons, in every state whom I

have once known, I inherit from my father. It gave me much satisfaction to hear every body at Inverness speak of him with uncommon regard.—Mr. Keith and Mr. Grant, whom we had seen at Mr. M'Aulay's, supped with us at the inn. We had roasted kid, which Dr. Johnson had never tasted before. He relished it much.

Monday, 30th August

This day we were to begin our *equitation*, as I said ; for *I* would needs make a word too. It is remarkable, that my noble, and to me most constant friend, the Earl of Pembroke, (who, if there is too much ease on my part, will please to pardon what his benevolent, gay, social intercourse, and lively correspondence, have insensibly produced,) has since hit upon the very same word. The title of the first edition of his lordship's very useful book was, in simple terms, *A Method of breaking Horses and teaching Soldiers to ride.* The title of the second edition is, *Military Equitation.*

We might have taken a chaise to Fort Augustus, but, had we not hired horses at Inverness, we should not have found them afterwards : so we resolved to begin here to ride. We had three horses, for Dr. Johnson, myself, and Joseph, and one which carried our portmanteaus, and two Highlanders who walked along with us, John Hay and Lauchland Vass, whom Dr. Johnson has remembered with credit in his *Journey*, though he has omitted their names. Dr. Johnson rode very well.

About three miles beyond Inverness, we saw, just by the road, a very complete specimen of what is called a Druid's temple. There was a double circle, one of very large, the other of smaller stones. Dr. Johnson justly observed, that, " to go and see one druidical temple is only to see that it is nothing, for there is neither art nor power in it; and seeing one is quite enough."

It was a delightful day. Lochness, and the road upon the side of it, shaded with birch trees, and the hills above it, pleased us much. The scene was as sequestered and agreeably wild as could be desired, and for a time engrossed all our attention.

To see Dr. Johnson in any new situation is always an interesting object to me; and, as I saw him now for the first time on horseback, jaunting about at his ease in quest of pleasure and novelty, the very different occupations of his former laborious life, his admirable productions, his *London*, his *Rambler*, &c. &c. immediately presented themselves to my mind, and the contrast made a strong impression on my imagination.

When we had advanced a good way by the side of Lochness, I perceived a little hut, with an old looking woman at the door of it. I thought here might be a scene that would amuse Dr. Johnson; so I mentioned it to him. "Let's go in," said he. We dismounted, and we and our guides entered the hut. It was a wretched little hovel of earth only, I think, and for a window had only a small hole, which was stopped with a piece of turf, that was taken out occasionally to let in light. In the middle of the room or space which we entered, was a fire of peat, the smoke going out at a hole in the roof. She had a pot upon it, with goat's flesh, boiling. There was at one end under the same roof, but divided by a kind of partition made of wattles, a pen or fold in which we saw a good many kids.

Dr. Johnson was curious to know where she slept. I asked one of the guides, who questioned her in Erse. She answered with a tone of emotion, saying, (as he told us,) she was afraid we wanted to go to bed to her. This coquetry, or whatever it may be called, of so wretched a being, was truly ludicrous. Dr. Johnson and I afterwards were merry upon it. I said, it was he who alarmed the poor woman's virtue.—" No, sir, (said he,) she'll say, " There came a wicked young fellow, a wild dog, who I believe would have ravished me, had there not been with him a grave old gentleman, who repressed him : but when he gets out of the sight of his tutor, I'll warrant you he'll spare no woman he meets, young or old.' "—" No, sir, (I replied,) she'll say, ' There was a terrible ruffian who would have forced me, had it not been for a civil decent young man who, I take it, was an angel sent from heaven to protect me.' "

Dr. Johnson would not hurt her delicacy, by insisting on " seeing her bed-chamber," like Archer in the *Beaux Stratagem*. But my curiosity was more ardent ; I lighted a piece of paper, and went into the place where the bed was. There was a little partition of wicker, rather more neatly done than that for the fold, and close by the wall was a kind of bedstead of wood with heath upon it by way of bed ; at the foot of which I saw some sort of blankets or covering rolled up in a heap. The woman's name was Fraser ; so was her husband's. He was a man of eighty. Mr. Fraser of Balnain allows him to live in this hut, and keep sixty goats, for taking care of his woods, where he then was. They had five children, the eldest only thirteen. Two were gone to Inverness to buy meal ; the rest were looking after the goats. This contented family had four stacks of barley, twenty-four sheaves in each. They had a few fowls. We were informed that they lived all the spring without meal, upon milk and curds and whey alone. What they get for their goats, kids, and fowls, maintains them during the rest of the year.

She asked us to sit down and take a dram. I saw one chair. She said she was as happy as any woman in Scotland. She could hardly speak any English except a few detached words. Dr. Johnson was pleased at seeing, for the first time, such a state of human life. She asked for snuff. It is her luxury, and she uses a great deal. We had none; but gave her six pence a-piece. She then brought out her whisky bottle. I tasted it; as did Joseph and our guides: so I gave her sixpence more. She sent us away with many prayers in Erse.

We dined at a publick house called the General's Hut, from General Wade, who was lodged there when he commanded in the North. Near it is the meanest parish Kirk I ever saw. It is a shame it should be on a high road. After dinner, we passed through a good deal of mountainous country. I had known Mr. Trapaud, the deputy governour of Fort Augustus, twelve years ago, at a circuit at Inverness, where my father was judge. I sent forward one of our guides, and Joseph, with a card to him, that he might know Dr. Johnson and I were coming up, leaving it to him to invite us or not. It was dark when we arrived. The inn was wretched. Government ought to build one, or give the resident governour an additional salary; as in the present state of things, he must necessarily be put to a great expence in entertaining travellers. Joseph announced to us, when we alighted, that the governour waited for us at the gate of the fort. We walked to it. He met us, and with much civility conducted us to his house. It was comfortable to find ourselves in a well built little square, and a neatly furnished house, in good company, and with a good supper before us; in short, with all the conveniencies of civilized life in the midst of rude mountains. Mrs. Trapaud, and the governour's daughter, and her husband, Captain Newmarsh, were all most obliging and polite. The governour had excellent animal spirits, the conversation of a soldier, and somewhat of a Frenchman, to which his extraction entitles him. He is brother to General Cyrus Trapaud. We passed a very agreeable evening.

Tuesday, 31st August

The governour has a very good garden. We looked at it, and at the rest of the fort, which is but small, and may be commanded from a variety of hills around. We also looked at the galley or sloop belonging to the fort, which sails upon the Loch, and brings what is wanted for the garrison. Captains Urie and Darippe, of the 15th regiment of foot, breakfasted with us. They had served in America, and entertained Dr. Johnson much with an account of the Indians. He said, he could make a very pretty book out of them, were he to stay there. Governour Trapaud was much struck with Dr. Johnson. "I like to hear him, (said he,) it is so majestick. I should be glad to hear him speak in your court."—He pressed us to stay dinner; but I considered that we had a rude road before us, which we could more easily encounter in the morning, and that it was hard to say when we might get up, were we to sit down to good entertainment, in good company: I therefore begged the governour would excuse us.—Here too, I had another very pleasing proof how much my father is regarded. The governour expressed the highest respect for him, and bade me tell him, that, if he would come that way on the Northern circuit, he would do him all the honours of the garrison.

Between twelve and one we set out, and travelled eleven miles, through a wild country, till we came to a house in Glenmorison, called Anoch, kept by a M'Queen. Our landlord was a sensible fellow: he had learnt his grammar, and Dr. Johnson justly observed, that "a man is the better for that as long as he lives." There were some books here: a *Treatise against Drunkenness*, translated from the French; a volume of the *Spectator;* a volume of Prideaux's

Connection, and Cyrus's *Travels*. M'Queen said he
had more volumes ; and his pride seemed to be much
piqued that we were surprised at his having books.

Near to this place we had passed a party of soldiers,
under a serjeant's command, at work upon the road.
We gave them two shillings to drink. They came to
our inn, and made merry in the barn. We went and
paid them a visit, Dr. Johnson saying, " Come, let's
go and give 'em another shilling a-piece." We did
so ; and he was saluted " MY LORD " by all of them.
He is really generous, loves influence, and has the way
of gaining it. He said, " I am quite feudal, sir,"
Here I agree with him. I said, I regretted I was not
the head of a clan ; however, though not possessed of
such an hereditary advantage, I would always endeavour
to make my tenants follow me. I could not be a *patriarchal* chief, but I would be a *feudal* chief.

The poor soldiers got too much liquor. Some of
them fought, and left blood upon the spot, and cursed
whisky next morning. The house here was built of
thick turfs, and thatched with thinner turfs and heath.
It had three rooms in length, and a little room which
projected. Where we sat, the side-walls were wains-
cotted, as Dr. Johnson said, with wicker, very neatly
plaited. Our landlord had made the whole with his
own hands.

After dinner, M'Queen sat by us a while, and talked
with us. He said, all the Laird of Glenmorison's
people would bleed for him, if they were well used ; but
that seventy men had gone out of the Glen to America.
That he himself intended to go next year ; for that
the rent of his farm, which twenty years ago was only
five pounds, was now raised to twenty pounds. That
he could pay ten pounds, and live ; but no more.—Dr.
Johnson said, he wished M'Queen laird of Glenmorison,
and the laird to go to America. M'Queen very gener-
ously answered, he should be sorry for it ; for the

laird could not shift for himself in America as he could do.

I talked of the officers whom we had left to-day; how much service they had seen, and how little they got for it, even of fame.—JOHNSON. "Sir, a soldier gets as little as any man can get."—BOSWELL. "Goldsmith has acquired more fame than all the officers last war, who were not Generals."—JOHNSON. "Why, sir, you will find ten thousand fit to do what they did, before you find one who does what Goldsmith has done. You must consider, that a thing is valued according to its rarity. A pebble that paves the street is in itself more useful than the diamond upon a lady's finger."—I wish our friend Goldsmith had heard this.

I yesterday expressed my wonder that John Hay, one of our guides, who had been pressed aboard a man of war, did not choose to continue in it longer than nine months, after which time he got off.—JOHNSON. "Why, sir, no man will be a sailor, who has contrivance enough to get himself into a jail; for, being in a ship is being in a jail, with the chance of being drowned."

We had tea in the afternoon, and our landlord's daughter, a modest civil girl, very neatly drest, made it for us. She told us, she had been a year at Inverness, and learnt reading and writing, sewing, knotting, working lace, and pastry. Dr. Johnson made her a present of a book which he had bought at Inverness.

The room had some deals laid across the joists, as a kind of ceiling. There were two beds in the room, and a woman's gown was hung on a rope to make a curtain of separation between them. Joseph had sheets, which my wife had sent with us, laid on them. We had much hesitation, whether to undress, or lie down with our clothes on. I said at last, " I'll plunge in ! There will be less harbour for vermin about me, when I am stripped ! "—Dr. Johnson said, he was like one hesitating whether to go into the cold bath. At last he

resolved too. I observed, he might serve a campaign.
—JOHNSON. " I could do all that can be done by
patience : whether I should have strength enough, I
know not."—He was in excellent humour. To see
the Rambler as I saw him to-night, was really an
amusement. I yesterday told him, I was thinking of
writing a poetical letter to him, *on his return from
Scotland*, in the stile of Swift's humorous epistle in the
character of Mary Gulliver to her husband, Captain
Lemuel Gulliver, on his return to England from the
country of the Houyhnhnms :

> " At early morn I to the market haste,
> Studious in ev'ry thing to please thy taste.
> A curious *fowl* and *sparagrass* I chose ;
> (For I remember you were fond of those :)
> Three shillings cost the first, the last sev'n groats ;
> Sullen you turn from both, and call for OATS."

He laughed, and asked in whose name I would write
it. I said, in Mrs. Thrale's. He was angry. " Sir,
if you have any sense of decency or delicacy, you won't
do that ! "—BOSWELL. " Then let it be in Cole's, the
landlord of the Mitre tavern ; where we have so often
sat together."—JOHNSON. " Ay, that may do."

After we had offered up our private devotions, and
had chatted a little from our beds, Dr. Johnson said,
" GOD bless us both, for Jesus Christ's sake ! Good
night ! "—I pronounced " Amen."—He fell asleep
immediately. I was not so fortunate for a long time.
I fancied myself bit by innumerable vermin under the
clothes ; and that a spider was travelling from the wains-
cot towards my mouth. At last I fell into insensibility.

Wednesday, 1st September

I awaked very early. I began to imagine that the
landlord, being about to emigrate, might murder us

to get our money, and lay it upon the soldiers in the barn. Such groundless fears will arise in the mind, before it has resumed its vigour after sleep! Dr. Johnson had had the same kind of ideas; for he told me afterwards, that he considered so many soldiers, having seen us, would be witnesses, should any harm be done, and that circumstance, I suppose, he considered as a security. When I got up, I found him sound asleep in his miserable *stye*, as I may call it, with a coloured handkerchief tied round his head. With difficulty could I awaken him. It reminded me of Henry the Fourth's fine soliloquy on sleep; for there was here as *uneasy a pallet* as the poet's imagination could possibly conceive.

A *red coat* of the 15th regiment, whether officer, or only serjeant, I could not be sure, came to the house, in his way to the mountains to shoot deer, which it seems the Laird of Glenmorison does not hinder any body to do. Few, indeed, can do them harm. We had him to breakfast with us. We got away about eight. M'Queen walked some miles to give us a convoy. He had, in 1745, joined the Highland army at Fort Augustus, and continued in it till after the battle of Culloden. As he narrated the particulars of that ill-advised, but brave attempt, I could not refrain from tears. There is a certain association of ideas in my mind upon that subject, by which I am strongly affected. The very Highland names, or the sound of a bagpipe, will stir my blood, and fill me with a mixture of melancholy and respect for courage; with pity for an unfortunate and superstitious regard for antiquity, and thoughtless inclination for war; in short, with a crowd of sensations with which sober rationality has nothing to do.

We passed through Glensheal, with prodigious mountains on each side. We saw where the battle was fought in the year 1719. Dr. Johnson owned he was

now in a scene of as wild nature as he could see; but
he corrected me sometimes in my inaccurate observations.—" There, (said I,) is a mountain like a cone."
—JOHNSON. " No, sir. It would be called so in a
book; and when a man comes to look at it, he sees it
is not so. It is indeed pointed at the top; but one
side of it is larger than the other."—Another mountain
I called immense.—JOHNSON. " No; it is no more
than a considerable protuberance."

We came to a rich green valley, comparatively speaking, and stopped a while to let our horses rest and eat
grass. We soon afterwards came to Auchnasheal, a
kind of rural village, a number of cottages being built
together, as we saw all along in the Highlands. We
passed many miles this day without seeing a house, but
only little summer-huts, called *shielings*. Even Campbell, servant to Mr. Murchison, factor to the Laird of
Macleod in Glenelg, ran along with us to-day. He
was a very obliging fellow. At Auchnasheal, we sat
down on a green turf-seat at the end of a house; they
brought us out two wooden dishes of milk, which we
tasted. One of them was frothed like a syllabub. I
saw a woman preparing it with such a stick as is used
for chocolate, and in the same manner. We had a
considerable circle about us, men, women, and children,
all M'Craas, Lord Seaforth's people. Not one of them
could speak English. I observed to Dr. Johnson, it
was much the same as being with a tribe of Indians.
—JOHNSON. " Yes, sir; but not so terrifying." I gave
all who chose it, snuff and tobacco. Governour Trapaud had made us buy a quantity at Fort Augustus, and
put them up in small parcels. I also gave each person
a bit of wheat bread, which they had never tasted
before. I then gave a penny apiece to each child.
I told Dr. Johnson of this; upon which he called to
Joseph and our guides, for change for a shilling, and
declared that he would distribute among the children.

Upon this being announced in Erse, there was a great stir ; not only did some children come running down from neighbouring huts, but I observed one black-haired man, who had been with us all along, had gone off, and returned, bringing a very young child. My fellow traveller then ordered the children to be drawn up in a row ; and he dealt about his copper, and made them and their parents all happy. The poor M'Craas, whatever may be their present state, were of considerable estimation in the year 1715, when there was a line in a song,

And aw the brave M'Craas are coming.

There was great diversity in the faces of the circle around us : Some were as black and wild in their appearance as any American savages whatever. One woman was as comely almost as the figure of Sappho, as we see it painted. We asked the old woman, the mistress of the house where we had the milk, (which by the bye, Dr. Johnson told me, for I did not observe it myself, was built not of turf, but of stone,) what we should pay. She said, what we pleased. One of our guides asked her, in Erse, if a shilling was enough. She said, " Yes." But some of the men bade her ask more. This vexed me ; because it showed a desire to impose upon strangers, as they knew that even a shilling was high payment. The woman, however, honestly persisted in her first price ; so I gave her half a crown. —Thus we had one good scene of life uncommon to us. The people were very much pleased, gave us many blessings, and said they had not had such a day since the old Laird of Macleod's time.

Dr. Johnson was much refreshed by this repast. He was pleased when I told him he would make a good Chief. He said, " Were I a chief, I would dress my servants better than myself, and knock a fellow down if he looked saucy to a Macdonald in rags : but I would not treat men as brutes. I would let them know why all my clan were to have attention paid to them. I would tell my upper servants why, and make them tell the others."

We rode on well, till we came to the high mountain called the Rattakin, by which time both Dr. Johnson and the horses were a good deal fatigued. It is a terrible steep to climb, notwithstanding the road is formed slanting along it ; however, we made it out. On the top of it we met Captain M'Leod of Balmenoch (a Dutch officer who had come from Sky) riding with his sword slung across him. He asked, " Is this Mr. Boswell ? " which was a proof that we were expected. Going down the hill on the other side was no easy task. As Dr. Johnson was a great weight, the two guides agreed that he should ride the horses alternately. Hay's were the two best, and the Doctor would not ride but upon one or other of them, a black or a brown. But, as Hay complained much after ascending the Rattakin, the Doctor was prevailed with to mount one of Vass's greys. As he rode upon it down hill, it did not go well ; and he grumbled. I walked on a little before, but was excessively entertained with the method taken to keep him in good humour. Hay led the horse's head, talking to Dr. Johnson as much as he could ; and (having heard him, in the forenoon, express a pastoral pleasure on seeing the goats browzing) just when the Doctor was uttering his displeasure, the fellow cried, with a very Highland accent, " See such pretty goats ! " Then he whistled, *whu !* and made them jump.—Little did he conceive what Doctor Johnson was. Here now was a common ignorant Highland clown imagining that he could divert, as one does a child,—Dr. Samuel Johnson !—The ludicrousness, absurdity, and extraordinary contrast between what the fellow fancied, and the reality, was truly comick.

It grew dusky ; and we had a very tedious ride for

what was called five miles; but I am sure would measure ten. We had no conversation. I was riding forward to the inn at Glenelg, on the shore opposite to Sky, that I might take proper measures, before Dr. Johnson, who was now advancing in dreary silence, Hay leading his horse, should arrive. Vass also walked by the side of his horse, and Joseph followed behind: as therefore he was thus attended, and seemed to be in deep meditation, I thought there could be no harm in leaving him for a little while. He called me back with a tremendous shout, and was really in a passion with me for leaving him. I told him my intentions, but he was not satisfied, and said, " Do you know, I should as soon have thought of picking a pocket, as doing so."—BOSWELL. " I am diverted with you, sir." —JOHNSON. " Sir, I could never be diverted with incivility. Doing such a thing, makes one lose confidence in him who has done it, as one cannot tell what he may do next."—His extraordinary warmth confounded me so much, that I justified myself but lamely to him; yet my intentions were not improper. I wished to get on, to see how we were to be lodged, and how we were to get a boat; all which I thought I could best settle myself, without his having any trouble. To apply his great mind to minute particulars, is wrong: it is like taking an immense balance, such as is kept on quays for weighing cargoes of ships,—to weigh a guinea. I knew I had neat little scales, which would do better; and that his attention to every thing which falls in his way, and his uncommon desire to be always in the right, would make him weigh, if he knew of the particulars: it was right therefore for me to weigh them, and let him have them only in effect. I however continued to ride by him, finding he wished I should do so.

As we passed the barracks at Bernéra, I looked at them wishfully, as soldiers have always every thing in the best order: but there was only a serjeant and a

few men there.   We came on to the inn at Glenelg.
There was no provender for our horses ; so they were
sent to grass, with a man to watch them.   A maid
shewed us up stairs into a room damp and dirty, with
bare walls, a variety of bad smells, a coarse black greasy
fir table, and forms of the same kind ; and out of a
wretched bed started a fellow from his sleep, like Edgar
in *King Lear,* " *Poor Tom's a cold.*"

This inn was furnished with not a single article that
we could either eat or drink ; but Mr. Murchison,
factor to the Laird of Macleod in Glenelg, sent us a
bottle of rum and some sugar, with a polite message, to
acquaint us, that he was very sorry that he did not hear
of us till we had passed his house, otherwise he should
have insisted on our sleeping there that night ; and
that, if he were not obliged to set out for Inverness
early next morning, he would have waited upon us.
—Such extraordinary attention from this gentleman,
to entire strangers, deserves the most honourable commemoration.

Our bad accommodation here made me uneasy, and
almost fretful.   Dr. Johnson was calm.   I said, he
was so from vanity.—JOHNSON.   " No, sir, it is from
philosophy."—It pleased me to see that the Rambler
could practise so well his own lessons.

I resumed the subject of my leaving him on the
road, and endeavoured to defend it better.   He was
still violent upon that head, and said, " Sir, had you
gone on, I was thinking that I should have returned
with you to Edinburgh, and then have parted from
you, and never spoken to you more."

I sent for fresh hay, with which we made beds for
ourselves, each in a room equally miserable.   Like
Wolfe, we had a " choice of difficulties."   Dr. Johnson
made things easier by comparison.   At M'Queen's,
last night, he observed, that few were so well lodged
in a ship.   To-night he said, we were better than if

we had been upon the hill. He lay down buttoned up in his great coat. I had my sheets spread on the hay, and my clothes and great coat laid over me, by way of blankets.

Thursday, 2nd September

I had slept ill. Dr. Johnson's anger had affected me much. I considered that, without any bad intention, I might suddenly forfeit his friendship; and was impatient to see him this morning. I told him how uneasy he had made me, by what he had said, and reminded him of his own remark at Aberdeen, upon old friendships being hastily broken off. He owned, he had spoken to me in passion; that he would not have done what he threatened; and that, if he had, he should have been ten times worse than I; that forming intimacies, would indeed be " limning the water," were they liable to such sudden dissolution; and he added, " Let's think no more on't."—BOSWELL. " Well then, sir, I shall be easy. Remember, I am to have fair warning in case of any quarrel. You are never to spring a mine upon me. It was absurd in me to believe you."—JOHNSON. " You deserved about as much, as to believe me from night to morning."

After breakfast, we got into a boat for Sky. It rained much when we set off, but cleared up as we advanced. One of the boatmen, who spoke English, said, that a mile at land was two miles at sea. I then observed, that from Glenelg to Armidale in Sky, which was our present course, and is called twelve, was only six miles: but this he could not understand. " Well, (said Dr. Johnson,) never talk to me of the native good sense of the Highlanders. Here is a fellow who calls one mile two, and yet cannot comprehend that twelve such imaginary miles make in truth but six."

We reached the shore of Armidale before one o'clock. Sir Alexander M'Donald came down to receive us. He and his lady, (formerly Miss Bosville of Yorkshire,) were then in a house built by a tenant at this place, which is in the district of Slate, the family mansion here having been burned in Sir Donald Macdonald's time.

The most ancient seat of the chief of the Macdonalds in the isle of Sky was at Duntulm, where there are the remains of a stately castle. The principal residence of the family is now at Mugstot. at which there is a considerable building. Sir Alexander and Lady Macdonald had come to Armidale in their way to Edinburgh, where it was necessary for them to be soon after this time.

Armidale is situated on a pretty bay of the narrow sea, which flows between the main land of Scotland and the Isle of Sky. In front there is a grand prospect of the rude mountains of Moidart and Knoidart. Behind are hills gently rising and covered with a finer verdure than I expected to see in this climate, and the scene is enlivened by a number of little clear brooks.

Sir Alexander Macdonald having been an Eton scholar, and being a gentleman of talents, Dr. Johnson had been very well pleased with him in London. But my fellow-traveller and I were now full of the old Highland spirit, and were dissatisfied at hearing of racked rents and emigration ; and finding a chief not surrounded by his clan. Dr. Johnson said, " Sir, the Highland chiefs should not be allowed to go farther south than Aberdeen. A strong-minded man, like Sir James Macdonald, may be improved by an English education ; but in general, they will be tamed into insignificance."

We found here Mr. Janes of Aberdeenshire, a naturalist. Janes said he had been at Dr. Johnson's in London, with Ferguson the astronomer.—JOHNSON. " It is strange that, in such distant places, I should meet with any one

who knows me.   I should have thought I might hide
myself in Sky."

Friday, 3rd September

This day proving wet, we should have passed our
time very uncomfortably, had we not found in the house
two chests of books, which we eagerly ransacked.
After dinner, when I alone was left at table with the
few Highland gentlemen who were of the company,
having talked with very high respect of Sir James
Macdonald, they were all so much affected as to shed
tears.   One of them was Mr. Donald Macdonald,
who had been lieutenant of grenadiers in the Highland regiment, raised by Colonel Montgomery, now
Earl of Eglintoune, in the war before last ; one of
those regiments which the late Lord Chatham prided
himself in having brought from " the mountains of the
North : " by doing which he contributed to extinguish
in the Highlands the remains of disaffection to the
present Royal Family.   From this gentleman's conversation, I first learnt how very popular his Colonel
was among the Highlanders ; of which I had such
continued proofs, during the whole course of my Tour,
that on my return I could not help telling the noble
Earl himself, that I did not before know how great a
man he was.

We were advised by some persons here to visit Rasay,
in our way to Dunvegan, the seat of the Laird of Macleod.   Being informed that the Rev. Mr. Donald
M'Queen was the most intelligent man in Sky, and
having been favoured with a letter of introduction
to him, by the learned Sir James Foulis, I sent it to
him by an express, and requested he would meet us at
Rasay ; and at the same time enclosed a letter to the
Laird of Macleod, informing him that we intended in

a few days to have the honour of waiting on him at Dunvegan.

Dr. Johnson this day endeavoured to obtain some knowledge of the state of the country; but complained that he could get no distinct information about any thing, from those with whom he conversed.

Saturday, 4th September

My endeavours to rouse the English-bred Chieftain, in whose house we were, to the feudal and patriarchal feelings, proving ineffectual, Dr. Johnson this morning tried to bring him to our way of thinking.—JOHNSON. "Were I in your place, sir, in seven years I would make this an independant island. I would roast oxen whole, and hang out a flag as a signal to the Macdonalds to come and get beef and whisky."—Sir Alexander was still starting difficulties.—JOHNSON. "Nay, sir; if you are born to object, I have done with you. Sir, I would have a magazine of arms."—SIR ALEXANDER. "They would rust."—JOHNSON. "Let there be men to keep them clean. Your ancestors did not use to let their arms rust."

We attempted in vain to communicate to him a portion of our enthusiasm. He bore with so polite a good-nature our warm, and what some might call Gothick, expostulations, on this subject, that I should not forgive myself, were I to record all that Dr. Johnson's ardour led him to say.—This day was little better than a blank.

Sunday, 5th September

I walked to the parish church of Slate, which is a very poor one. There are no church bells in the island.

I was told there were once some ; what has become of them, I could not learn. The minister not being at home, there was no service. I went into the church, and saw the monument of Sir James Macdonald, which was elegantly executed at Rome, and has the following inscription, written by his friend, George Lord Lyttelton :

To the memory

Of Sir JAMES MACDONALD, Bart.

Who in the flower of youth,
Had attained to so eminent a degree of knowledge
In Mathematics, Philosophy, Languages,
And in every other branch of useful and polite learning,
As few have acquired in a long life
Wholly devoted to study :
Yet to this erudition he joined
What can rarely be found with it
Great talents for business,
Great propriety of behaviour,
Great politeness of manners !
His eloquence was sweet, correct, and flowing ;
His memory vast and exact ;
His judgement strong and acute ;
All which endowments, united
With the most amiable temper
And every private virtue,
Procured him, not only in his own country,
But also from foreign nations,
The highest marks of esteem.
In the year of our Lord
1766,
The 25th of his life,
After a long and extremely painful illness,
Which he supported with admirable patience and fortitude,
He died at Rome,
Where, notwithstanding the difference of religion,
Such extraordinary honours were paid to his memory,
As had never graced that of any other British subject,
Since the death of Sir Philip Sydney.

The fame he left behind him is the best consolation
To his afflicted family,
And to his countrymen in this isle,
For whose benefit he had planned
Many useful improvements,
Which his fruitful genius suggested,
And his active spirit promoted,
Under the sober direction
Of a clear and enlightened understanding.
Reader, bewail our loss,
And that of all Britain.
In testimony of her love,
And as the best return she can make
To her departed son,
For the constant tenderness and affection
Which, even to his last moments,
He shewed for her,
His much afflicted mother,
The LADY MARGARET MACDONALD,
Daughter to the EARL of EGLINTOUNE,
Erected this Monument,
A.D. 1768.

Dr. Johnson said, the inscription should have been in Latin, as every thing intended to be universal and permanent, should be.

This being a beautiful day, my spirits were cheered by the mere effect of climate. I had felt a return of spleen during my stay at Armidale, and had it not been that I had Dr. Johnson to contemplate, I should have sunk into dejection ; but his firmness supported me. I looked at him, as a man whose head is turning giddy at sea looks at a rock, or any fixed object. I wondered at his tranquillity. He said, " Sir, when a man retires into an island, he is to turn his thoughts intirely to another world. He has done with this."— BOSWELL. " It appears to me, sir, to be very difficult to unite a due attention to this world, and that which is to come ; for, if we engage eagerly in the affairs of life, we are apt to be totally forgetful of a future state ; and, on the other hand, a steady contemplation of the awful concerns of eternity renders all objects here so insignificant, as to make us indifferent and negligent about them."—JOHNSON. " Sir, Dr. Cheyne has laid down a rule to himself on this subject, which should be imprinted on every mind : *'To neglect nothing to secure my eternal peace, more than if I had been certified I should die within the day : nor to mind any thing that my secular obligations and duties demanded of me, less than if I had been ensured to live fifty years more.'* "

I must here observe, that though Dr. Johnson appeared now to be philosophically calm, yet his genius did not shine forth as in companies, where I have listened to him with admiration. The vigour of his mind was, however, sufficiently manifested, by his discovering no symptoms of feeble relaxation in the dull, " weary, flat and unprofitable " state in which we now were placed.

I am inclined to think that it was on this day he composed the following Ode upon the Isle of Sky, which a few days afterwards he shewed me at Rasay :

ODA

Ponti profundis clausa recessibus,
Strepens procellis, rupibus obsita,
Quam grata defesso virentem
Skia sinum nebulosa pandis.

His cura, credo, sedibus exulat ;
His blanda certe pax habitat locis :
Non ira, non mœror quietis
Insidias meditatur horis.

At non cavata rupe latescere,
Menti nec ægræ montibus aviis
Prodest vagari, nec frementes
E scopulo numerare fluctus.

Humana virtus non sibi sufficit,
Datur nec æquum cuique animum sibi
Parare posse, ut Stoicorum
Secta crepet nimis alta fallax.

Excæstuantis pectoris impetum,
Rex summe, solus tu regis arbiter,
Mentisque, te tollente, surgunt,
Te recidunt moderante fluctus.

After supper, Dr. Johnson told us, that Isaac Hawkins Browne drank freely for thirty years, and that he wrote his poem, *De Animi Immortalitate*, in some of the last of these years.—I listened to this with the eagerness of one, who, conscious of being himself fond of wine, is glad to hear that a man of so much genius and good thinking as Browne had the same propensity.

Monday, 6th September

We set out, accompanied by Mr. Donald M'Leod (late of Canna) as our guide. We rode for some time along the district of Slate, near the shore. The houses in general are made of turf, covered with grass. The country seemed well peopled. We came into the district of Strath, and passed along a wild moorish tract of land till we arrived at the shore. There we found good verdure, and some curious whin-rocks, or collections of stones like the ruins of the foundations of old buildings. We saw also three Cairns of considerable size.

About a mile beyond Broadfoot, is Corrichatachin, a farm of Sir Alexander Macdonald's, possessed by Mr. M'Kinnon, who received us with a hearty welcome, as did his wife, who was what we call in Scotland a *lady-like* woman. Mr. Pennant, in the course of his tour to the Hebrides, passed two nights at this gentleman's house. On its being mentioned, that a present had here been made to him of a curious specimen of Highland antiquity, Dr. Johnson said, " Sir, it was more than he deserved : the dog is a whig."

We here enjoyed the comfort of a table plentifully furnished, the satisfaction of which was heightened by a numerous and cheerful company ; and we for the first time had a specimen of the joyous social manners of the inhabitants of the Highlands. They talked in their own ancient language, with fluent vivacity, and sung many Erse songs with such spirit, that, though Dr. Johnson was treated with the greatest respect and attention, there were moments in which he seemed to be forgotten. For myself, though but a *Lowlander*, having picked up a few words of the language, I presumed to mingle in their mirth, and joined in the chorusses with as much glee as any of the company. Dr. Johnson being fatigued with his journey, retired early to his chamber, where he composed the following Ode, addressed to Mrs. Thrale :

O D A

Permeo terras, ubi nuda rupes
Saxeas miscet nebulis ruinas,
Torva ubi rident steriles coloni
                         Rura labores.

Pervagor gentes, hominum ferorum
Vita ubi nullo decorata cultu
Squallet informis, tugurique fumis
                         Fœda latescit.

Inter erroris salebrosa longi,
Inter ignotæ strepitus loquelæ,
Quot modis mecum, quid agat, requiro,
                         Thralia dulcis?

Seu viri curas pia nupta mulcet,
Seu fovet mater sobolem benigna,
Sive cum libris novitate pascet
                         Sedula mentem ;

Sit memor nostri, fideique merces,
Stet fides constans, meritoque blandum
Thraliæ discant resonare nomen
                         Littora Skiæ.

Scriptum in Skiá, *Sept. 6, 1773.*

Tuesday, 7th September

Dr. Johnson was much pleased with his entertainment here. There were many good books in the house : Hector Boethius in Latin ; Cave's *Lives of the Fathers ;* Baker's *Chronicle ;* Jeremy Collier's *Church History ;* Dr. Johnson's small Dictionary ; Craufurd's *Officers of State,* and several more :—a mezzotinto of Mrs. Brooks the actress (by some strange chance in Sky) ; and also a print of Macdonald of Clanranald, with a Latin inscription about the cruelties after the battle of Culloden, which will never be forgotten.

It was a very wet stormy day ; we were therefore obliged to remain here, it being impossible to cross the sea to Rasay.

I employed a part of the forenoon in writing this Journal. The rest of it was somewhat dreary, from the gloominess of the weather, and the uncertain state which we were in, as we could not tell but it might clear up every hour. Nothing is more painful to the mind than a state of suspence, especially when it depends upon the weather, concerning which there can be so little calculation. As Dr. Johnson said of our weariness on the Monday at Aberdeen, " Sensation is sensation : " Corrichatachin, which was last night a hospitable house, was, in my mind, changed to-day into a prison.—After dinner I read some of Dr. Macpherson's *Dissertations on the Ancient Caledonians.* I was disgusted by the unsatisfactory conjectures as to antiquity, before the days of record. I was happy when tea came. Such, I take it, is the state of those who live in the country. Meals are wished for from the cravings of vacuity of mind, as well as from the desire of eating. I was hurt to find even such a temporary feebleness, and that I was so far from being that robust wise man who is sufficient for his own happiness. I felt a kind of lethargy of indolence. I did not exert myself to get Dr. Johnson to talk, that I might not have the labour of writing down his conversation.—He enquired here, if there were any remains of the second sight. Mr. M'Pherson, Minister of Slate, said, he was *resolved* not to believe it, because it was founded on no principle.—JOHNSON. " There are many things then, which we are sure are true, that you will not believe. What principle is there, why a loadstone attracts iron ? why an egg produces a chicken by heat ? why a tree grows upwards, when the natural tendency of all things is downwards ? Sir, it depends upon the degree of evidence that you have."——Young Mr. M'Kinnon mentioned one M'Kenzie, who is still alive, who had often fainted in his presence, and when he recovered, mentioned visions which had been presented to him. He told Mr. M'Kinnon, that at such a place he should meet a funeral, and that such and such people would be the bearers, naming four ; and three weeks afterwards he saw what M'Kenzie had predicted. The naming the very spot in a country where a funeral comes a long way, and the very people as bearers, when there are so many out of whom a choice may be made, seems extraordinary. We should have sent for M'Kenzie, had we not been informed that he could speak no English. Besides, the facts were not related with sufficient accuracy.

Mrs. M'Kinnon, who is a daughter of old Kingsburgh, told us that her father was one day riding in Sky, and some women, who were at work in a field on the side of the road, said to him, they had heard two *taiscks*, (that is, two voices of persons about to die,) and what was remarkable, one of them was an *English taisck*, which they never heard before. When he returned, he at that very place met two funerals, and one of them was that of a woman who had come from the main land, and could speak only English. This, she remarked, made a great impression upon her father.

How all the people here were lodged, I know not. It was partly done by separating man and wife, and putting a number of men in one room, and of women in another.

Wednesday, 8th September

When I waked, the rain was much heavier than yesterday; but the wind had abated. By breakfast, the day was better, and in a little while it was calm and clear. I felt my spirits much elated. The propriety of the expression, "the sunshine of the breast," now struck me with peculiar force; for the brilliant rays penetrated into my very soul. We were all in better humour than before. Mrs. M'Kinnon, with unaffected hospitality and politeness, expressed her happiness in having such company in her house, and appeared to understand and relish Dr. Johnson's conversation, as indeed all the company seemed to do. When I knew she was old Kingsburgh's daughter, I did not wonder at the good appearance which she made.

She talked as if her husband and family would emigrate, rather than be oppressed by their landlord; and said, "how agreeable would it be, if these gentlemen should come in upon us when we are in America."—Somebody observed that Sir Alexander Macdonald was always frightened at sea.—JOHNSON. "*He* is frightened at sea; and his tenants are frightened when he comes to land."

We resolved to set out directly after breakfast. We had about two miles to ride to the sea-side, and there we expected to get one of the boats belonging to the fleet of bounty herring-busses then on the coast, or at least a good country fishing-boat. But while we were preparing to set out, there arrived a man with the following card from the Reverend Mr. Donald M'Queen :

" Mr. M'Queen's compliments to Mr. Boswell, and begs leave to acquaint him that, fearing the want of a proper boat, as much as the rain of yesterday, might have caused a stop, he is now at Skianwden with Macgillichallum's carriage, to convey him and Dr. Johnson to Rasay, where they will meet with a most hearty welcome, and where Macleod, being on a visit, now attends their motions.

" *Wednesday afternoon.*"

This card was most agreeable ; it was a prologue to that hospitable and truly polite reception which we found at Rasay. In a little while arrived Mr. Donald M'Queen himself ; a decent minister, an elderly man with his own black hair, courteous, and rather slow of speech, but candid, sensible and well informed, nay learned. Along with him came, as our pilot, a gentleman whom I had a great desire to see, Mr. Malcolm Macleod, one of the Rasay family, celebrated in the year 1745-6. He was now sixty-two years of age, hale, and well proportioned,—with a manly countenance, tanned by the weather, yet having a ruddiness in his cheeks, over a great part of which his rough beard extended.—His eye was quick and lively, yet his look was not fierce, but he appeared at once firm and good-humoured. He wore a pair of brogues,—Tartan hose which came up only near to his knees, and left them bare,—a purple camblet kilt,—a black waistcoat,—a short green cloth coat bound with gold cord,—a yellowish bushy wig,—a large blue bonnet with a gold thread button. I never saw a figure that gave a more perfect representation of a Highland gentleman. I wished much to have a picture of him just as he was.

I found him frank and *polite*, in the true sense of the word.

The good family at Corrichatachin said, they hoped to see us on our return. We rode down to the shore ; but Malcolm walked with graceful agility.

We got into Rasay's *carriage*, which was a good strong open boat made in Norway. The wind had now risen pretty high, and was against us ; but we had four stout rowers, particularly a Macleod, a robust, black-haired fellow, half naked, and bare-headed, something between a wild Indian and an English tar. Dr. Johnson sat high on the stern, like a magnificent Triton. Malcolm sung an Erse song, the chorus of which was " *Hatyin foam foam eri*," with words of his own. The tune resembled " Owr the muir amang the heather." The boatmen and Mr. M'Queen chorused, and all went well. At length Malcolm himself took an oar, and rowed vigorously. We sailed along the coast of Scalpa, a rugged island, about four miles in length. Dr. Johnson proposed that he and I should buy it, and found a good school, and an episcopal church, (Malcolm said, he would come to it,) and have a printing-press, where he would print all the Erse that could be found.

Here I was strongly struck with our long projected scheme of visiting the Hebrides being realized. I called to him, " We are contending with seas ; " which I think were the words of one of his letters to me. " Not much," said he ; and though the wind made the sea lash considerably upon us, he was not discomposed. After we were out of the shelter of Scalpa, and in the sound between it and Rasay, which extended about a league, the wind made the sea very rough. I did not like it.—JOHNSON. " This now is the Atlantick. If I should tell at a tea table in London, that I have crossed the Atlantick in an open boat, how they'd shudder, and what a fool they'd think me to expose myself to such danger!" He then repeated Horace's ode,

> *Otium Divos rogat in patenti*
> *Prensus Ægæo——*

In the confusion and hurry of this boisterous sail, Dr. Johnson's spurs, of which Joseph had charge, were carried over-board into the sea, and lost. This was the first misfortune that had befallen us. Dr. Johnson was a little angry at first, observing that "there was something wild in letting a pair of spurs be carried into the sea out of a boat;" but then he remarked, "that, as Janes the naturalist had said upon losing his pocket-book, it was rather an inconvenience than a loss." He told us, he now recollected that he dreamt the night before, that he put his staff into a river, and chanced to let it go, and it was carried down the stream and lost. "So now you see, (said he,) that I have lost my spurs; and this story is better than many of those which we have concerning second sight and dreams." Mr. M'Queen said he did not believe the second sight; that he never met with any well attested instances; and if he should, he should impute them to chance; because all who pretend to that quality often fail in their predictions, though they take a great scope, and sometimes interpret literally, sometimes figuratively, so as to suit the events. He told us, that, since he came to be minister of the parish where he now is, the belief of witchcraft, or charms, was very common, insomuch that he had many prosecutions before his session (the parochial ecclesiastical court) against women, for having by these means carried off the milk from people's cows. He disregarded them; and there is not now the least vestige of that superstition. He preached against it; and in order to give a strong proof to the people that there was nothing in it, he said from the pulpit, that every woman in the parish was welcome to take the milk from his cows, provided she did not touch them.

Dr. Johnson asked him as to Fingal. He said he could repeat some passages in the original, that he heard his grandfather had a copy of it; but that he could not affirm that Ossian composed all that poem as it is now published. This came pretty much to what Dr. Johnson had maintained; though he goes farther, and contends that it is no better than such an epick poem as he could make from the song of Robin Hood; that is to say, that, except a few passages, there is nothing truly ancient but the names and some vague traditions. Mr. M'Queen alleged that Homer was made up of detached fragments. Dr. Johnson denied this; observing, that it had been one work originally, and that you could not put a book of the *Iliad* out of its place; and he believed the same might be said of the *Odyssey*.

The approach to Rasay was very pleasing. We saw before us a beautiful bay, well defended by a rocky coast; a good family mansion; a fine verdure about it, —with a considerable number of trees;—and beyond it hills and mountains in gradation of wildness. Our boatmen sung with great spirit. Dr. Johnson observed, that naval musick was very ancient. As we came near the shore, the singing of our rowers was succeeded by that of reapers, who were busy at work, and who seemed to shout as much as to sing, while they worked with a bounding activity. Just as we landed, I observed a cross, or rather the ruins of one, upon a rock, which had to me a pleasing vestige of religion. I perceived a large company coming out from the house. We met them as we walked up. There were Rasay himself; his brother Dr. Macleod; his nephew the Laird of M'Kinnon; the Laird of Macleod; Colonel Macleod of Talisker, an officer in the Dutch service, a very genteel man, and a faithful branch of the family; Mr. Macleod of Muiravenside, best known by the name of Sandie

Macleod, who was long in exile on account of the part which he took in 1745; and several other persons. We were welcomed upon the green, and conducted into the house, where we were introduced to Lady Rasay, who was surrounded by a numerous family, consisting of three sons and ten daughters. The Laird of Rasay is a sensible, polite, and most hospitable gentleman. I was told that his island of Rasay, and that of Rona, (from which the eldest son of the family has his title,) and a considerable extent of land which he has in Sky, do not altogether yield him a very large revenue : and yet he lives in great splendour ; and so far is he from distressing his people, that, in the present rage for emigration, not a man has left his estate.

It was past six o'clock when we arrived. Some excellent brandy was served round immediately, according to the custom of the Highlands, where a dram is generally taken every day. They call it a *scalch*. On a side-board was placed for us, who had come off the sea, a substantial dinner, and a variety of wines. Then we had coffee and tea. I observed in the room several elegantly bound books and other marks of improved life. Soon afterwards a fidler appeared, and a little ball began. Rasay himself danced with as much spirit as any man, and Malcolm bounded like a roe. Sandie Macleod, who has at times an excessive flow of spirits, and had it now, was, in his days of absconding, known by the name of *M'Cruslick*, which it seems was the designation of a kind of wild man in the Highlands, something between Proteus and Don Quixotte ; and so he was called here. He made much jovial noise. Dr. Johnson was so delighted with this scene, that he said, " I know not how we shall get away." It entertained me to observe him sitting by, while we danced, sometimes in deep meditation,—sometimes smiling complacently,—sometimes looking upon Hooke's *Roman History*,—and sometimes talking a little, amidst the noise of the ball, to Mr. Donald M'Queen, who anxiously gathered knowledge from him. He was pleased with M'Queen, and said to me, " This is a critical man, sir. There must be great vigour of mind to make him cultivate learning so much in the isle of Sky, where he might do without it. It is wonderful how many of the new publications he has. There must be a snatch of every opportunity." Mr. M'Queen told me that his brother (who is the fourth generation of the family following each other as ministers of the parish of Snizort,) and he joined together, and bought from time to time such books as had reputation. Soon after we came in, a black cock and grey hen, which had been shot, were shewn, with their feathers on, to Dr. Johnson, who had never seen that species of bird before. We had a company of thirty at supper ; and all was good humour and gaiety, without intemperance.

Thursday, 9th September

At breakfast this morning, among a profusion of other things, there were oat-cakes, made of what is called *graddaned* meal, that is, meal made of grain separated from the husks, and toasted by fire, instead of being threshed and kiln dried.—This seems to be bad management, as so much fodder is consumed by it. Mr. M'Queen however defended it, by saying, that it is doing the thing much quicker, as one operation effects what is otherwise done by two. His chief reason however was, that the servants in Sky are, according to him, a faithless pack, and steal what they can ; so that much is saved by the corn passing but once through their hands, as at each time they pilfer some. It appears to me, that the gradaning is a strong proof of the laziness of the Highlanders, who will rather make fire act for them, at the expence of fodder, than labour themselves. There was also, what I cannot help disliking at breakfast, cheese : it is the custom over all the Highlands to have it ; and it often smells very strong, and poisons to a certain degree the elegance of an Indian repast. The day was showery ; however, Rasay and I took a walk, and had some cordial conversation. I conceived a more than ordinary regard for this worthy gentleman. His family has possessed this island above four hundred years. It is the remains of the estate of Macleod of Lewis, whom he represents.—When we returned, Dr. Johnson walked with us to see the old chapel. He was in fine spirits. He said, " This is truly the patriarchal life : this is what we came to find."

After dinner, M'Cruslick, Malcolm, and I, went out with guns, to try if we could find any black-cock ; but we had no sport, owing to a heavy rain. I saw here what is called a Danish fort. Our evening was passed as last night was. One of our company, I was told, had hurt himself by too much study, particularly of infidel metaphysicians, of which he gave a proof, on second sight being mentioned. He immediately retailed some of the fallacious arguments of Voltaire and Hume against miracles in general. Infidelity in a Highland gentleman appeared to me peculiarly offensive. I was sorry for him, as he had otherwise a good character. I told Dr. Johnson that he had studied himself into infidelity.—JOHNSON. " Then he must study himself out of it again. That is the way. Drinking largely will sober him again."

Friday, 10th September

Having resolved to explore the island of Rasay, which could be done only on foot, I last night obtained my fellow-traveller's permission to leave him for a day, he being unable to take so hardy a walk. Old Mr. Malcolm M'Cleod, who had obligingly promised to accompany me, was at my bedside between five and six. I sprang up immediately, and he and I, attended by two other gentlemen, traversed the country during the whole of this day. Though we had passed over not less than four-and-twenty miles of very rugged ground, and had a Highland dance on the top of Dun Can, the highest mountain in the island, we returned in the evening not at all fatigued, and piqued ourselves at not being outdone at the nightly ball by our less active friends, who had remained at home.

My survey of Rasay did not furnish much which can interest my readers; I shall therefore put into as short a compass as I can, the observations upon it, which I find registered in my Journal. It is about fifteen English miles long, and four broad. On the south side is the laird's family seat, situated on a pleasing low spot. The old tower of three stories, mentioned by Martin, was taken down soon after 1746, and a modern house supplies its place. There are very good grass-fields and corn-lands about it, well-dressed. I observed, however, hardly any inclosures, except a good garden plentifully stocked with vegetables, and strawberries, raspberries, currants, &c.

On one of the rocks just where we landed, which are not high, there is rudely carved a square, with a crucifix in the middle. Here, it is said, the Lairds of Rasay, in old times, used to offer up their devotions. I could not approach the spot, without a grateful recollection of the event commemorated by this symbol.

A little from the shore, westward, is a kind of subterraneous house. There has been a natural fissure, or separation of the rock, running towards the sea, which has been roofed over with long stones, and above them turf has been laid. In that place the inhabitants used to keep their oars. There are a number of trees near the house, which grow well ; some of them of a pretty good size. They are mostly plane and ash. A little to the west of the house is an old ruinous chapel, unroofed, which never has been very curious. We here saw some human bones of an uncommon size. There was a heel-bone, in particular, which Dr. Macleod said was such, that if the foot was in proportion, it must have been twenty-seven inches long. Dr. Johnson would not look at the bones. He started back from them with a striking appearance of horrour. Mr. M'Queen told us, it was formerly much the custom, in these isles, to have human bones lying above ground, especially in the windows of churches. On the south of the chapel is the family burying-place. Above the door, on the east end of it, is a small bust or image of the Virgin Mary, carved upon a stone which makes part of the wall. There is no church upon the island. It is annexed to one of the parishes of Sky ; and the minister comes and preaches either in Rasay's house, or some other house, on certain Sundays. I could not but value the family seat more, for having even the ruins of a chapel close to it. There was something comfortable in the thought of being so near a piece of consecrated ground. Dr. Johnson said, " I look with reverence upon every place that has been set apart for religion ; " and he kept off his hat while he was within the walls of the chapel.

The eight crosses, which Martin mentions as pyramids for deceased ladies, stood in a semicircular line, which contained within it the chapel. They marked out the boundaries of the sacred territory within which an asylum was to be had. One of them, which we observed upon our landing, made the first point of the semicircle. There are few of them now remaining. A good way farther north, there is a row of buildings about four feet high : they run from the shore on the east along the top of a pretty high eminence, and so down to the shore on the west, in much the same direction with the crosses. Rasay took them to be the marks for the asylum; but Malcolm thought them to be false sentinels, a common deception, of which instances occur in Martin, to make invaders imagine an island better guarded. Mr. Donald M'Queen, justly in my opinion, supposed the crosses which form the inner circle to be the church's land-marks.

The south end of the island is much covered with large stones or rocky strata. The laird has enclosed and planted part of it with firs, and he shewed me a considerable space marked out for additional plantations.

Dun Can is a mountain three computed miles from the laird's house. The ascent to it is by consecutive risings, if that expression may be used when vallies intervene, so that there is but a short rise at once; but it is certainly very high above the sea. The palm of altitude is disputed for by the people of Rasay and those of Sky; the former contending for Dun Can, the latter for the mountains in Sky, over against it. We went up the east side of Dun Can pretty easily. It is mostly rocks all around, the points of which hem the summit of it. Sailors, to whom it was a good object as they pass along, call it Rasay's cap. Before we reached this mountain, we passed by two lakes. Of the first, Malcolm told me a strange fabulous tradition. He said, there was a wild beast in it, a seahorse, which came and devoured a man's daughter; upon which the man lighted a great fire, and had a sow roasted at it, the smell of which attracted the monster. In the fire was put a spit. The man lay concealed behind a low wall of loose stones, and he had an avenue formed for the monster, with two rows of large flat stones, which extended from the fire over the summit of the hill, till it reached the side of the loch. The monster came, and the man with the red-hot spit destroyed it.   Malcolm showed me the little hiding-place, and the rows of stones.   He did not laugh when he told this story.   I recollect having seen in the *Scots Magazine*, several years ago, a poem upon a similar tale, perhaps the same, translated from the Erse, or Irish, called *Albin and the Daughter of Mey*.

There is a large tract of land, possessed as a common, in Rasay.   They have no regulations as to the number of cattle.   Every man puts upon it as many as he chooses.   From Dun Can northward, till you reach the other end of the island, there is much good natural pasture unincumbered by stones.   We passed over a spot, which is appropriated for the exercising ground. In 1745, a hundred fighting men were reviewed here, as Malcolm told me, who was one of the officers that led them to the field.   They returned home all but about fourteen.   What a princely thing is it to be able to furnish such a band !   Rasay has the true spirit of a chief.   He is, without exaggeration, a father to his people.

There is plenty of lime-stone in the island, a great quarry of free-stone, and some natural woods, but none of any age, as they cut the trees for common country uses.   The lakes, of which there are many, are well stocked with trout.   Malcolm catched one of four-and-twenty pounds weight in the loch next to Dun Can, which, by the way, is certainly a Danish name, as most names of places in these islands are.

The old castle, in which the family of Rasay formerly resided, is situated upon a rock very near the sea. The rock is not one mass of stone, but a concretion of pebbles and earth, so firm that it does not appear to have mouldered.   In this remnant of antiquity I found nothing worthy of being noticed, except a certain accommodation rarely to be found at the modern houses of Scotland, and which Dr. Johnson and I sought for in vain at the Laird of Rasay's new-built mansion, where nothing else was wanting. I took the liberty to tell the Laird it was a shame there should be such a deficiency in civilized times. He acknowledged the justice of the remark. But perhaps some generations may pass before the want is supplied. Dr. Johnson observed to me, how quietly people will endure an evil, which they might at any time very easily remedy; and mentioned as an instance, that the present family of Rasay had possessed the island for more than four hundred years, and never made a commodious landing place, though a few men with pickaxes might have cut an ascent of stairs out of any part of the rock in a week's time.

The north end of Rasay is as rocky as the south end. From it I saw the little isle of Fladda, belonging to Rasay, all fine green ground;—and Rona, which is of so rocky a soil that it appears to be a pavement. I was told however that it has a great deal of grass, in the interstices. The Laird has it all in his own hands. At this end of the island of Rasay is a cave in a striking situation. It is in a Recess of a great cleft, a good way up from the sea. Before it the ocean roars, being dashed against monstrous broken rocks; grand and aweful *propugnacula*. On the right hand of it is a longitudinal cave, very low at the entrance, but higher as you advance. The sea having scooped it out, it seems strange and unaccountable that the interior part, where the water must have operated with less force, should be loftier than that which is more immediately exposed to its violence. The roof of it is all covered with a kind of petrifications formed by drops, which perpetually distil from it. The first cave has been a place of much safety. I find a great difficulty in describing visible objects. I must own too that the old castle and cave, like many other things, of which one hears much, did not answer my expectations. People are every where apt to magnify the curiosities of their country.

This island has abundance of black cattle, sheep, and goats ;—a good many horses, which are used for ploughing, carrying out dung, and other works of husbandry. I believe the people never ride. There are indeed no roads through the island, unless a few detached beaten tracks deserve that name. Most of the houses are upon the shore ; so that all the people have little boats, and catch fish. There is great plenty of potatoes here. There are black-cock in extraordinary abundance, moor-fowl, plover and wild pigeons, which seemed to me to be the same as we have in pigeon-houses, in their state of nature. Rasay has no pigeon-house. There are no hares nor rabbits in the island, nor was there ever known to be a fox, till last year, when one was landed on it by some malicious person, without whose aid he could not have got thither, as that animal is known to be a very bad swimmer. He has done much mischief. There is a great deal of fish caught in the sea round Rasay ; it is a place where one may live in plenty, and even in luxury. There are no deer ; but Rasay told us he would get some.

They reckon it rains nine months in the year in this island, owing to its being directly opposite to the western coast of Sky, where the watery clouds are broken by high mountains. The hills here, and indeed all the heathy grounds in general, abound with the sweet-smelling plant which the Highlanders call *gaul*, and (I think) with dwarf juniper in many places. There is enough of turf, which is their fuel, and it is thought there is a mine of coal,—Such are the observations which I made upon the island of Rasay, upon comparing it with the description given by Martin, whose book we had with us.

There has been an ancient league between the families of Macdonald and Rasay. Whenever the head of either family dies, his sword is given to the head of the other. The present Rasay has the late Sir James

Macdonald's sword. Old Rasay joined the Highland army in 1745, but prudently guarded against a forfeiture, by previously conveying his estate to the present gentleman, his eldest son. On that occasion, Sir Alexander, father of the late Sir James Macdonald, was very friendly to his neighbour. " Don't be afraid, Rasay," said he ; " I'll use all my interest to keep you safe ; and if your estate should be taken, I'll buy it for the family."—And he would have done it.

Let me now gather some gold dust,—some more fragments of Dr. Johnson's conversation, without regard to order of time. He said, " he thought very highly of Bentley ; that no man now went so far in the kinds of learning that he cultivated ; that the many attacks on him were owing to envy, and to a desire of being known, by being in competition with such a man ; that it was safe to attack him, because he never answered his opponents, but let them die away. It was attacking a man who would not beat them, because his beating them would make them live the longer. And he was right not to answer ; for, in his hazardous method of writing, he could not but be often enough wrong ; so it was better to leave things to their general appearance, than own himself to have erred in particulars."—He said, " Mallet was the prettiest drest puppet about town, and always kept good company. That, from his way of talking, he saw, and always said, that he had not written any part of the *Life of the Duke of Marlborough*, though perhaps he intended to do it at some time, in which case he was not culpable in taking the pension. That he imagined the Duchess furnished the materials for her *Apology*, which Hooke wrote, and Hooke furnished the words and the order, and all that in which the art of writing consists. That the duchess had not superior parts, but was a bold frontless woman, who knew how to make the most of her opportunities in life. That Hooke got a *large* sum of money for writing her *Apology*. That he wondered Hooke should have been weak enough to insert so profligate a maxim, as that to tell another's secret to one's friend, is no breach of confidence ; though perhaps Hooke, who was a virtuous man, as his *History* shews, and did not wish her well, though he wrote her *Apology*, might see its ill tendency, and yet insert it at her desire. He was acting only ministerially."—I apprehend, however, that Hooke was bound to give his best advice. I speak as a lawyer. Though I have had clients whose causes I could not, as a private man, approve ; yet, if I undertook them, I would not do any thing that might be prejudicial to them, even at their desire, without warning them of their danger.

Saturday, 11th September

It was a storm of wind and rain ; so we could not set out. I wrote some of this Journal, and talked awhile with Dr. Johnson in his room, and passed the day, I cannot well say how, but very pleasantly. I was here amused to find Mr. Cumberland's comedy of the *Fashionable Lover*, in which he has very well drawn a Highland character, Colin M'Cleod, of the same name with the family under whose roof we now were. Dr. Johnson was much pleased with the Laird of Macleod, who is indeed a most promising youth, and with a noble spirit struggles with difficulties, and endeavours to preserve his people. He has been left with an incumbrance of forty thousand pounds debt, and annuities to the amount of thirteen hundred pounds a year. Dr. Johnson said, " If he gets the better of all this, he'll be a hero ; and I hope he will. I have not met with a young man who had more desire to learn, or who has learnt more. I have seen nobody

that I wish more to do a kindness to than Macleod."
—Such was the honourable eulogium, on this young
chieftain, pronounced by an accurate observer, whose
praise was never lightly bestowed.

There is neither justice of peace, nor constable in
Rasay. Sky has Mr. M'Cleod of Ulinish, who is the
sheriff substitute, and no other justice of peace. The
want of the execution of justice is much felt among
the islanders. Macleod very sensibly observed, that
taking away the heritable jurisdictions had not been of
such service in the islands, as was imagined. They
had not authority enough in lieu of them. What could
formerly have been settled at once, must now either
take much time and trouble, or be neglected. Dr.
Johnson said, " A country is in a bad state, which is
governed only by laws ; because a thousand things
occur for which laws cannot provide, and where authority ought to interpose. Now destroying the authority
of the chiefs set the people loose. It did not pretend
to bring any positive good, but only to cure some evil ;
and I am not well enough acquainted with the country
to know what degree of evil the heritable jurisdictions
occasioned."—I maintained hardly any ; because the
chiefs generally acted right, for their own sakes.

Dr. Johnson was now wishing to move. There was
not enough of intellectual entertainment for him, after
he had satisfied his curiosity, which he did, by asking
questions, till he had exhausted the island ; and where
there was so numerous a company, mostly young people,
there was such a flow of familiar talk, so much noise, and
so much singing and dancing, that little opportunity was
left for his energetick conversation. He seemed sensible of this ; for when I told him how happy they were
at having him there, he said, " Yet we have not been
able to entertain them much."—I was fretted, from
irritability of nerves, by M'Cruslick's too obstreperous
mirth. I complained of it to my friend, observing we

should be better if he was gone.—" No, sir (said he). He puts something into our society, and takes nothing out of it."—Dr. Johnson, however, had several opportunities of instructing the company ; but I am sorry to say, that I did not pay sufficient attention to what passed, as his discourse now turned chiefly on mechanicks, agriculture and such subjects, rather than on science and wit.—Last night Lady Rasay showed him the operation of *wawking* cloth, that is, thickening it in the same manner as is done by a mill. Here it is performed by women, who kneel upon the ground, and rub it with both their hands, singing an Erse song all the time. He was asking questions while they were performing this operation, and, amidst their loud and wild howl, his voice was heard even in the room above.

They dance here every night. The queen of our ball was the eldest Miss Macleod, of Rasay, an elegant well-bred woman, and celebrated for her beauty over all those regions, by the name of Miss Flora Rasay. There seemed to be no jealousy, no discontent among them ; and the gaiety of the scene was such, that I for a moment doubted whether unhappiness had any place in Rasay. But my delusion was soon dispelled, by recollecting the following lines of my fellow-traveller :

" Yet hope not life from pain or danger free,
    Or think the doom of man revers'd for thee ! "

Sunday, 12th September

It was a beautiful day, and although we did not approve of travelling on Sunday, we resolved to set out, as we were in an island from whence one must take occasion as it serves. Macleod and Talisker sailed in a boat of Rasay's for Sconser, to take the shortest way to Dunvegan. M'Cruslick went with them to

Sconser, from whence he was to go to Slate, and so to the main land. We were resolved to pay a visit at Kingsburgh, and see the celebrated Miss Flora Macdonald, who is married to the present Mr. Macdonald of Kingsburgh; so took that road, though not so near. All the family, but Lady Rasay, walked down to the shore to see us depart. Rasay himself went with us in a large boat, with eight oars, built in his island; as did Mr. Malcolm M'Cleod, Mr. Donald M'Queen, Dr. Macleod, and some others. We had a most pleasant sail between Rasay and Sky; and passed by a cave, where Martin says fowls were caught by lighting fire in the mouth of it. Malcolm remembers this. But it is not now practised, as few fowls come into it.

We spoke of Death. Dr. Johnson on this subject observed, that the boastings of some men, as to dying easily, were idle talk, proceeding from partial views. I mentioned Hawthornden's Cypress-grove, where it is said that the world is a mere show; and that it is unreasonable for a man to wish to continue in the show-room, after he has seen it. Let him go cheerfully out, and give place to other spectators.—JOHNSON. " Yes, sir, if he is sure he is to be well, after he goes out of it. But if he is to grow blind after he goes out of the show-room, and never to see any thing again; or if he does not know whither he is to go next, a man will not go cheerfully out of a show-room. No wise man will be contented to die, if he thinks he is to go into a state of punishment. Nay, no wise man will be contented to die, if he thinks he is to fall into annihilation: for however unhappy any man's existence may be, he yet would rather have it, than not exist at all. No; there is no rational principle by which a man can die contented, but a trust in the mercy of GOD, through the merits of Jesus Christ."—This short sermon, delivered with an earnest tone, in a boat upon the sea, which was perfectly calm, on a day appropriated to religious worship, while every one listened with an air of satisfaction, had a most pleasing effect upon my mind.

Pursuing the same train of serious reflection, he added, that it seemed certain that happiness could not be found in this life, because so many had tried to find it, in such a variety of ways, and had not found it.

We reached the harbour of Portree, in Sky, which is a large and good one. There was lying in it a vessel to carry off the emigrants, called the *Nestor*. It made a short settlement of the differences between a chief and his clan :

> ――*Nestor* componere lites
> Inter Peleiden festinat & inter Atriden.

We approached her, and she hoisted her colours. Dr. Johnson and Mr. M'Queen remained in the boat : Rasay and I, and the rest went on board of her. She was a very pretty vessel, and, as we were told, the largest in Clyde. Mr. Harrison, the captain shewed her to us. The cabin was commodious, and even elegant. There was a little library, finely bound. Portree has its name from King James the Fifth having landed there in his tour through the Western Isles, *Ree* in Erse being King, as *Re* is in Italian ; so it is *Port-Royal*. There was here a tolerable inn. On our landing, I had the pleasure of finding a letter from home ; and there were also letters to Dr. Johnson and me, from Lord Elibank, which had been sent after us from Edinburgh.—His lordship's letter to me was as follows :

" DEAR BOSWELL,

" I FLEW to Edinburgh the moment I heard of Mr. Johnson's arrival ; but so defective was my intelligence, that I came too late.

" It is but justice to believe, that I could never forgive myself, nor deserve to be forgiven by others, if I was to fail in any mark of respect to that very great

genius.—I hold him in the highest veneration ; for that
very reason I was resolved to take no share in the
merit, perhaps guilt, of enticing him to honour this
country with a visit.—I could not persuade myself
there was anything in Scotland worthy to have a
Summer of Samuel Johnson bestowed on it ; but since
he has done us that compliment, for heaven's sake
inform me of your motions. I will attend them most
religiously ; and though I should regret to let Mr.
Johnson go a mile out of his way on my account, old
as I am, I shall be glad to go five hundred miles to
enjoy a day of his company. Have the charity to send
a council-post with intelligence ; the post does not
suit us in the country.—At any rate write to me. I
will attend you in the north, when I shall know where
to find you.

> " I am,
> > " My dear Boswell,
> > > " Your sincerely
> > > > " Obedient humble servant,
> > > > > " ELIBANK."

" *August* 21*st*, 1773."

The letter to Dr. Johnson was in these words :

" DEAR SIR,
    " I WAS to have kissed your hands at Edinburgh,
the moment I heard of you ; but you was gone.
    " I hope my friend Boswell will inform me of your
motions. It will be cruel to deprive me an instant of
the honour of attending you. As I value you more
than any King in Christendom, I will perform that
duty with infinitely greater alacrity than any courtier. I
can contribute but little to your entertainment ; but, my
sincere esteem for you gives me some title to the opportunity of expressing it.
    " I dare say you are by this time sensible that things

are pretty much the same, as when Buchanan complained of being born *solo et seculo inerudito*. Let me hear of you, and be persuaded that none of your admirers is more sincerely devoted to you, than,

> " Dear Sir,
> > " Your most obedient
> > > " And most humble servant,
> > > > " ELIBANK."

Dr. Johnson, on the following Tuesday, answered for both of us, thus :

" MY LORD,

  " ON the rugged shore of Skie, I had the honour of your Lordship's letter, and can with great truth declare, that no place is so gloomy but that it would be cheered by such a testimony of regard, from a mind so well qualified to estimate characters, and to deal out approbation in its due proportions. If I have more than my share, it is your Lordship's fault ; for I have always reverenced your judgment too much, to exalt myself in your presence by any false pretensions.

  " Mr. Boswell and I are at present at the disposal of the winds, and therefore cannot fix the time at which we shall have the honour of seeing your lordship. But we should either of us think ourselves injured by the supposition that we would miss your lordship's conversation, when we could enjoy it ; for I have often declared that I never met you without going away a wiser man.

> " I am, my Lord,
> > " Your lordship's most obedient
> > > " And most humble servant,
> > > > " SAM. JOHNSON.'

" SKIE, *Sept.* 14*th*, 1773."

At Portree, Mr. Donald M'Queen went to church and officiated in Erse, and then came to dinner. Dr. Johnson and I resolved that we should treat the company, so I played the landlord, or master of the feast, having previously ordered Joseph to pay the bill.

Sir James Macdonald intended to have built a village here, which would have done great good. A village is like a heart to a country. It produces a perpetual circulation, and gives the people an opportunity to make profit of many little articles, which would otherwise be in a good measure lost. We had here a dinner, *et præterea nihil.* Dr. Johnson did not talk. When we were about to depart, we found that Rasay had been before-hand with us, and that all was paid : I would fain have contested this matter with him, but seeing him resolved, I declined it. We parted with cordial embraces from him and worthy Malcolm. In the evening Dr. Johnson and I remounted our horses, accompanied by Mr. M'Queen and Dr. Macleod. It rained very hard. We rode what they call six miles, upon Rasay's lands in Sky, to Dr. Macleod's house. On the road Dr. Johnson appeared to be somewhat out of spirits. When I talked of our meeting Lord Elibank, he said, " I cannot be with him much. I long to be again in civilized life ; but can stay but a short while ; " (he meant at Edinburgh). He said, " let us go to Dunvegan to-morrow."—" Yes, (said I,) if it is not a deluge."—" At any rate," he replied.—This shewed a kind of fretful impatience ; nor was it to be wondered at, considering our disagreeable ride. I feared he would give up Mull and Icolmkill, for he said something of his apprehensions of being detained by bad weather in going to Mull and Iona. However I hoped well. We had a dish of tea at Dr. Macleod's, who had a pretty good house, where was his brother, a half-pay officer. His lady was a polite, agreeable woman. Dr. Johnson said, he was glad to see that he was so well married, for he had an esteem for physicians. The doctor accompanied us to Kingsburgh, which is called a mile farther ; but the computation of Sky has no connection whatever with real distance.

I was highly pleased to see Dr. Johnson safely arrived at Kingsburgh, and received by the hospitable Mr. Macdonald, who, with a most respectful attention, supported him into the house. Kingsburgh was completely the figure of a gallant Highlander,—exhibiting " the graceful mien and manly looks," which our popular Scotch song has justly attributed to that character. He had his Tartan plaid thrown about him, a large blue bonnet with a knot of black ribband like a cockade, a brown short coat of a kind of duffil, a Tartan waistcoat with gold buttons and gold button-holes, a bluish philibeg, and Tartan hose. He had jet black hair tied behind, and was a large stately man, with a steady sensible countenance.

There was a comfortable parlour with a good fire, and a dram went round. By and by supper was served, at which there appeared the lady of the house, the celebrated Miss Flora Macdonald. She is a little woman, of a genteel appearance, and uncommonly mild and well bred. To see Dr. Samuel Johnson, the great champion of the English Tories, salute Miss Flora Macdonald in the isle of Sky, was a striking sight ; for though somewhat congenial in their notions, it was very improbable they should meet here.

Miss Flora Macdonald (for so I shall call her) told me, she heard upon the main land, as she was returning home about a fortnight before, that Mr. Boswell was coming to Sky, and one Mr. Johnson, a young English buck, with him. He was highly entertained with this fancy. Giving an account of the afternoon which we passed at Anock, he said, " I, being a *buck*, had miss in to make tea."—He was rather quiescent to-night, and went early to bed. I was in a cordial humour, and promoted a cheerful glass. The punch was excellent. Honest Mr. M'Queen observed that I was in high glee, "my *governour* being gone to bed." Yet in reality my heart was grieved, when I recollected that Kingsburgh was embarrassed in his affairs, and intended to go to America. However, nothing but what was good was present, and I pleased myself in thinking that so spirited a man would be well every where. I slept in the same room with Dr. Johnson. Each had a neat bed, with Tartan curtains, in an upper chamber.

Monday, 13th September

The room where we lay was a celebrated one. Dr. Johnson's bed was the very bed in which the grandson of the unfortunate King James the Second lay, on one of the nights after the failure of his rash attempt in 1745-6, while he was eluding the pursuit of the emissaries of government, which had offered thirty thousand pounds as a reward for apprehending him. To see Dr. Samuel Johnson lying in that bed, in the isle of Sky, in the house of Miss Flora Macdonald, struck me with such a group of ideas as it is not easy for words to describe, as they passed through the mind. He smiled, and said, " I have had no ambitious thoughts in it.— The room was decorated with a great variety of maps and prints. Among others, was Hogarth's print of Wilkes grinning, with the cap of liberty on a pole by him. That too was a curious circumstance in the scene this morning ; such a contrast was Wilkes to the above group. It reminded me of Sir William Chambers's Account of Oriental Gardening, in which we are told all odd, strange, ugly, and even terrible objects, are introduced, for the sake of variety ; a wild extravagance of taste which is so well ridiculed in the celebrated Epistle to him. The following lines of that poem immediately occurred to me :

> " Here too, O king of vengeance ! in thy fane,
>   Tremendous Wilkes shall rattle his gold chain."

Upon the table in our room I found in the morning a slip of paper, on which Dr. Johnson had written with his pencil these words :

> " Quantum cedat virtutibus aurum."

What he meant by writing them I could not tell. He had caught cold a day or two ago, and the rain yester day having made it worse, he was become very deaf. At breakfast he said, he would have given a good deal rather than not have lain in that bed. I owned he was the lucky man ; and observed, that without doubt it had been contrived between Mrs. Macdonald and him. She seemed to acquiesce ; adding, " You know young *bucks* are always favourites of the ladies." He spoke of Prince Charles being here, and asked Mrs. Macdonald, " *Who* was with him ? We were told, madam, in England, there was one Miss Flora Macdonald with him."—She said, " they were very right ; " and perceiving Dr. Johnson's curiosity, though he had delicacy enough not to question her, very obligingly entertained him with a recital of the particulars which she herself knew of that escape, which does so much honour to the humanity, fidelity, and generosity, of the Highlanders. Dr. Johnson listened to her with placid attention, and said, " All this should be written down."

From what she told us, and from what I was told by others personally concerned, and from a paper of information which Rasay was so good as to send me, at my desire, I have compiled the following abstract, which, as it contains some curious anecdotes, will, I imagine, not be uninteresting to my readers, and even, perhaps, be of some use to future historians.

Prince Charles Edward, after the battle of Culloden, was conveyed to what is called the Long Island, where he lay for some time concealed. But intelligence having been obtained where he was, and a number of troops having come in quest of him, it became absolutely necessary for him to quit that country without delay. Miss Flora Macdonald, then a young lady, animated by what she thought the sacred principle of loyalty, offered, with the magnanimity of a Heroine, to accompany him in an open boat to Sky, though the coast they were to quit was guarded by ships. He dressed himself in women's clothes, and passed as her supposed maid, by the name of Betty Bourke, an Irish girl. They got off undiscovered, though several shots were fired to bring them to, and landed at Mugstot, the seat of Sir Alexander Macdonald. Sir Alexander was then at Fort Augustus, with the Duke of Cumberland ; but his lady was at home. Prince Charles took his post upon a hill near the house. Flora Macdonald waited on Lady Margaret, and acquainted her of the enterprise in which she was engaged. Her ladyship, whose active benevolence was ever seconded by superior talents, shewed a perfect presence of mind, and readiness of invention, and at once settled that Prince Charles should be conducted to old Rasay, who was himself concealed with some select friends. The plan was instantly communicated to Kingsburgh, who was dispatched to the hill to inform the Wanderer, and carry him refreshments. When Kingsburgh approached, he started up, and advanced, holding a large knotted stick, and in appearance ready to knock him down, till he said, " I am Macdonald of Kingsburgh, come to serve your highness." The Wanderer answered, " It is well," and was satisfied with the plan.

Flora Macdonald dined with Lady Margaret, at whose table there sat an officer of the army, stationed here with a party of soldiers, to watch for Prince Charles in case of his flying to the isle of Sky. She afterwards often laughed in good humour with this gentleman, on her having so well deceived him.

After dinner, Flora Macdonald on horseback, and her supposed maid, and Kingsburgh, with a servant carrying some linen, all on foot, proceeded towards that gentleman's house. Upon the road was a small rivulet which they were obliged to cross. The Wanderer, forgetting his assumed sex, that his clothes might not be wet, held them up a great deal too high. Kingsburgh mentioned this to him, observing, it might make a discovery. He said he would be more careful for the future. He was as good as his word ; for the next brook they crossed, he did not hold up his clothes at all, but let them float upon the water. He was very awkward in his female dress. His size was so large, and his strides so great, that some women whom they met reported that they had seen a very big woman, who looked like a man in women's clothes, and that perhaps it was (as they expressed themselves) the Prince, after whom so much search was making.

At Kingsburgh he met with a most cordial reception ; seemed gay at supper, and after it indulged himself in a cheerful glass with his worthy host. As he had not had his clothes off for a long time, the comfort of a good bed was highly relished by him, and he slept soundly till next day at one o'clock.

The mistress of Corrichatachin told me, that in the forenoon she went into her father's room, who was also in bed, and suggested to him her apprehensions that a party of the military might come up, and that his guest and he had better not remain here too long. Her father said, " Let the poor man repose himself after his fatigues ; and as for me, I care not, though they

6

take off this old grey head ten or eleven years sooner than I should die in the course of nature." He then wrapped himself in the bed-clothes, and again fell fast asleep.

On the afternoon of that day, the Wanderer, still in the same dress, set out for Portree, with Flora Macdonald and a man servant. His shoes being very bad, Kingsburgh provided him with a new pair, and taking up the old ones, said, " I will faithfully keep them till you are safely settled at St. James's. I will then introduce myself by shaking them at you, to put you in mind of your night's entertainment and protection under my roof."—He smiled, and said, " Be as good as your word ! "—Kingsburgh kept the shoes as long as he lived. After his death, a zealous Jacobite gentleman gave twenty guineas for them.

Old Mrs. Macdonald, after her guest had left the house, took the sheets in which he had lain, folded them carefully, and charged her daughter that they should be kept unwashed, and that, when she died, her body should be wrapped in them as a winding sheet. Her will was religiously observed.

Upon the road to Portree, Prince Charles changed his dress, and put on man's clothes again ; a tartan short coat and waistcoat, with philibeg and short hose, a plaid, and a wig and bonnet.

Mr. Donald M'Donald, called Donald Roy, had been sent express to the present Rasay, then the young laird, who was at that time at his sister's house, about three miles from Portree, attending his brother, Dr. Macleod, who was recovering of a wound he had received at the battle of Culloden. Mr. M'Donald communicated to young Rasay the plan of conveying the Wanderer to where old Rasay was ; but was told that old Rasay had fled to Knoidart, a part of Glengary's estate. There was then a dilemma what should be done. Donald Roy proposed that he should conduct

the Wanderer to the main land; but young Rasay
thought it too dangerous at that time, and said it would
be better to conceal him in the island of Rasay, till old
Rasay could be informed where he was, and give his
advice what was best.   But the difficulty was, how to get
him to Rasay.   They could not trust a Portree crew,
and all the Rasay boats had been destroyed, or carried
off by the military, except two belonging to Malcolm
M'Leod, which he had concealed somewhere.

Dr. Macleod being informed of this difficulty, said
he would risk his life once more for Prince Charles;
and it having occurred, that there was a little boat
upon a fresh-water lake in the neighbourhood, young
Rasay and Dr. Macleod, with the help of some women,
brought it to the sea, by extraordinary exertion, across
a Highland mile of land, one half of which was bog,
and the other a steep precipice.

These gallant brothers, with the assistance of one
little boy, rowed the small boat to Rasay, where they
were to endeavour to find Captain M'Leod, as Malcolm
was then called, and get one of his good boats, with
which they might return to Portree, and receive the
Wanderer; or, in case of not finding him, they were
to make the small boat serve, though the danger was
considerable.

Fortunately, on their first landing, they found their
cousin Malcolm, who, with the utmost alacrity, got
ready one of his boats, with two strong men, John
M'Kenzie, and Donald M'Friar.   Malcolm, being the
oldest man, and most cautious, said, that as young
Rasay had not hitherto appeared in the unfortunate
business, he ought not to run any risk; but that Dr.
Macleod and himself, who were already publickly engaged, should go on this expedition.   Young Rasay
answered, with an oath, that he would go, at the risk
of his life and fortune.—" In GOD's name then (said
Malcolm) let us proceed."   The two boatmen, how-

ever, now stopped short, till they should be informed
of their destination ; and M'Kenzie declared he would
not move an oar till he knew where they were going.
Upon which they were both sworn to secrecy ; and the
business being imparted to them, they were eager to
put off to sea without loss of time. The boat soon
landed about half a mile from the inn at Portree.

All this was negotiated before the Wanderer got
forward to Portree. Malcolm M'Leod, and M'Friar,
were dispatched to look for him. In a short time he
appeared, and went into the publick house. Here
Donald Roy, whom he had seen at Mugstot, received
him, and informed him of what had been concerted.
He wanted silver for a guinea, but the landlord had
only thirteen shillings. He was going to accept of
this for his guinea ; but Donald Roy very judiciously
observed, that it would discover him to be some great
man ; so he desisted. He slipped out of the house,
leaving his fair protectress, whom he never again saw ;
and Malcolm Macleod was presented to him by Donald
Roy, as a captain in his army. Young Rasay and
Dr. Macleod had waited, in impatient anxiety, in the
boat. When he came, their names were announced to
him. He would not permit the usual ceremonies of
respect, but saluted them as his equals.

Donald Roy staid in Sky, to be in readiness to get
intelligence, and give an alarm in case the troops should
discover the retreat to Rasay ; and Prince Charles was
then conveyed in a boat to that island in the night. He
slept a little upon the passage, and they landed about
day-break. There was some difficulty in accommodating him with a lodging, as almost all the houses in the
island had been burnt by the soldiery. They repaired to
a little hut, which some shepherds had lately built, and
having prepared it as well as they could, and made a bed
of heath for the stranger, they kindled a fire, and partook
of some provisions which had been sent with him from

Kingsburgh. It was observed, that he would not taste wheat-bread, or brandy, while oat-bread and whisky lasted ; " for these," said he, " are my own country bread and drink."—This was very engaging to the Highlanders.

Young Rasay being the only person of the company that durst appear with safety, he went in quest of something fresh for them to eat ; but though he was amidst his own cows, sheep, and goats, he could not venture to take any of them for fear of a discovery, but was obliged to supply himself by stealth. He therefore caught a kid, and brought it to the hut in his plaid, and it was killed and drest, and furnished them a meal which they relished much. The distressed Wanderer, whose health was now a good deal impaired by hunger, fatigue, and watching, slept a long time, but seemed to be frequently disturbed. Malcolm told me he would start from broken slumbers, and speak to himself in different languages, French, Italian, and English. I must however acknowledge, that it is highly probable that my worthy friend Malcolm did not know precisely the difference between French and Italian. One of his expressions in English was, " O GOD ! poor Scotland ! "

While they were in the hut, M'Kenzie and M'Friar, the two boatmen, were placed as sentinels upon different eminences ; and one day an incident happened, which must not be omitted. There was a man wandering about the island, selling tobacco. Nobody knew him, and he was suspected to be a spy. M'Kenzie came running to the hut, and told that this suspected person was approaching. Upon which the three gentlemen, young Rasay, Dr. Macleod, and Malcolm, held a council of war upon him, and were unanimously of opinion that he should instantly be put to death. Prince Charles, at once assuming a grave and even severe countenance, said, " GOD forbid that we should take away a man's life, who may be innocent, while we can

preserve our own." The gentlemen however persisted
in their resolution, while he as strenuously continued
to take the merciful side. John M'Kenzie, who sat
watching at the door of the hut, and overheard the
debate, said in Erse, "Well, well; he must be shot.
You are the king, but we are the parliament, and will
do what we choose."—Prince Charles, seeing the gentlemen smile, asked what the man had said, and being
told it in English, he observed that he was a clever
fellow, and, notwithstanding the perilous situation in
which he was, laughed loud and heartily. Luckily
the unknown person did not perceive that there were
people in the hut, at least did not come to it, but walked
on past it, unknowing of his risk. It was afterwards
found out that he was one of the Highland army, who
was himself in danger. Had he come to them, they
were resolved to dispatch him; for, as Malcolm said
to me, "We could not keep him with us, and we durst
not let him go. In such a situation, I would have shot
my brother, if I had not been sure of him."—John
M'Kenzie was at Rasay's house, when we were there.
About eighteen years before, he hurt one of his legs
when dancing, and being obliged to have it cut off, he
now was going about with a wooden leg. The story
of his being a *member of parliament* is not yet forgotten.
I took him out a little way from the house, gave him a
shilling to drink Rasay's health, and led him into a
detail of the particulars which I have just related.—
With less foundation, some writers have traced the
idea of a parliament, and of the British constitution,
in rude and early times. I was curious to know if he
had really heard, or understood, any thing of that
subject, which, had he been a greater man, would probably have been eagerly maintained. "Why, John,
(said I,) did you think the king should be controuled
by a parliament?"—He answered, "I thought, sir,
there were many voices against one."

The conversation then turning on the times, the Wanderer said, that, to be sure, the life he had led of late was a very hard one ; but he would rather live in the way he now did, for ten years, than fall into the hands of his enemies. The gentlemen asked him, what he thought his enemies would do with him, should he have the misfortune to fall into their hands. He said, he did not believe they would dare to take his life publickly, but he dreaded being privately destroyed by poison or assassination.—He was very particular in his inquiries about the wound which Dr. Macleod had received at the battle of Culloden, from a ball which entered at one shoulder, and went cross to the other. The doctor happened still to have on the coat which he wore on that occasion. He mentioned, that he himself had his horse shot under him at Culloden ; that the ball hit the horse about two inches from his knee, and made him so unruly that he was obliged to change him for another. He threw out some reflections on the conduct of the disastrous affair at Culloden, saying, however, that perhaps it was rash in him to do so.—I am now convinced that his suspicions were groundless ; for I have had a good deal of conversation upon the subject with my very worthy and ingenious friend, Mr. Andrew Lumisden, who was under secretary to Prince Charles, and afterwards principal secretary to his father at Rome, who, he assured me, was perfectly satisfied both of the abilities and honour of the generals who commanded the Highland army on that occasion. Mr. Lumisden has written an account of the three battles in 1745–6, at once accurate and classical.—Talking of the different Highland corps, the gentlemen who were present wished to have his opinion which were the best soldiers. He said, he did not like comparisons among those corps : they were all best.

He told his conductors, he did not think it advisable

to remain long in any one place ; and that he expected a French ship to come for him to Lochbroom, among the Mackenzies. It then was proposed to carry him in one of Malcolm's boats to Lochbroom, though the distance was fifteen leagues coastwise. But he thought this would be too dangerous, and desired that at any rate, they might first endeavour to obtain intelligence. Upon which young Rasay wrote to his friend, Mr. M'Kenzie of Applecross, but received an answer, that there was no appearance of any French ship.

It was therefore resolved that they should return to Sky, which they did, and landed in Strath, where they reposed in a cow-house belonging to Mr. Niccolson of Scorbreck. The sea was very rough, and the boat took in a good deal of water. The Wanderer asked if there was danger, as he was not used to such a vessel. Upon being told there was not, he sung an Erse song with much vivacity. He had by this time acquired a good deal of the Erse language.

Young Rasay was now dispatched to where Donald Roy was, that they might get all the intelligence they could ; and the Wanderer, with much earnestness, charged Dr. Macleod to have a boat ready, at a certain place about seven miles off, as he said he intended it should carry him upon a matter of great consequence ; and gave the doctor a case, containing a silver spoon, knife, and fork, saying, " keep you that till I see you," which the doctor understood to be two days from that time. But all these orders were only blinds ; for he had another plan in his head, but wisely thought it safest to trust his secrets to no more persons than was absolutely necessary. Having then desired Malcolm to walk with him a little way from the house, he soon opened his mind, saying, " I deliver myself to you. Conduct me to the Laird of M'Kinnon's country."— Malcolm objected that it was very dangerous, as so many parties of soldiers were in motion. He answered,

" There is nothing now to be done without danger."
—He then said, that Malcolm must be the master,
and he the servant ; so he took the bag, in which his
linen was put up, and carried it on his shoulder ; and
observing that his waistcoat, which was of scarlet
tartan, with a gold twist button, was finer than Malcolm's, which was of a plain ordinary tartan, he put on
Malcolm's waistcoat, and gave him his ; remarking at
the same time, that it did not look well that the servant should be better dressed than the master.

Malcolm, though an excellent walker, found himself
excelled by Prince Charles, who told him, he should
not much mind the parties that were looking for him,
were he once but a musquet shot from them ; but that
he was somewhat afraid of the Highlanders who were
against him. He was well used to walking in Italy,
in pursuit of game ; and he was even now so keen a
sportsman, that, having observed some partridges, he
was going to take a shot ; but Malcolm cautioned him
against it, observing that the firing might be heard by
the tenders who were hovering upon the coast.

As they proceeded through the mountains, taking
many a circuit to avoid any houses, Malcolm, to try
his resolution, asked him what they should do, should
they fall in with a party of soldiers : he answered,
" Fight, to be sure ! "—Having asked Malcolm if he
should be known in his present dress, and Malcolm
having replied he would, he said, " Then I'll blacken my
face with powder."—" That," said Malcolm, " would
discover you at once."—" Then," said he, " I must be
put in the greatest dishabille possible." So he pulled off
his wig, tied a handkerchief round his head, and put
his nightcap over it, tore the ruffles from his shirt, took
the buckles out of his shoes, and made Malcolm fasten
them with strings ; but still Malcolm thought he would
be known. " I have so odd a face, (said he) that no
man ever saw me but he would know me again."

He seemed unwilling to give credit to the horrid narrative of men being massacred in cold blood, after victory had declared for the army commanded by the Duke of Cumberland. He could not allow himself to think that a general could be so barbarous.

When they came within two miles of M'Kinnon's house, Malcolm asked if he chose to see the laird. " No, (said he) by no means. I know M'Kinnon to be as good and as honest a man as any in the world, but he is not fit for my purpose at present. You must conduct me to some other house ; but let it be a gentleman's house."—Malcolm then determined that they should go to the house of his brother-in-law, Mr. John M'Kinnon, and from thence be conveyed to the main land of Scotland, and claim the assistance of Macdonald of Scothouse. The Wanderer at first objected to this, because Scothouse was cousin to a person of whom he had suspicions. But he acquiesced in Malcolm's opinion.

When they were near Mr. John M'Kinnon's house, they met a man of the name of Ross, who had been a private soldier in the Highland army. He fixed his eyes steadily on the Wanderer in his disguise, and having at once recognized him, he clapped his hands, and exclaimed, " Alas ! is this the case ? " Finding that there was now a discovery, Malcolm asked " What's to be done ? "—" Swear him to secrecy," answered Prince Charles. Upon which Malcolm drew his dirk, and on the naked blade, made him take a solemn oath, that he would say nothing of his having seen the Wanderer, till his escape should be made publick.

Malcolm's sister, whose house they reached pretty early in the morning, asked him who the person was that was along with him. He said it was one Lewis Caw, from Crieff, who being a fugitive like himself, for the same reason, he had engaged him as his servant, but that he had fallen sick. " Poor man ! (said she) I pity him. At the same time my heart warms to a man of his appearance."—Her husband was gone a little way from home ; but was expected every minute to return. She set down to her brother a plentiful Highland breakfast. Prince Charles acted the servant very well, sitting at a respectful distance, with his bonnet off. Malcolm then said to him, " Mr. Caw, you have as much need of this as I have ; there is enough for us both : you had better draw nearer and share with me."—Upon which he rose, made a profound bow, sat down at table with his supposed master, and eat very heartily. After this there came in an old woman, who, after the mode of ancient hospitality, brought warm water, and washed Malcolm's feet. He desired her to wash the feet of the poor man who attended him. She at first seemed averse to this, from pride, as thinking him beneath her, and in the periphrastick language of the Highlanders and the Irish, said warmly, " Though I wash your father's son's feet, why should I wash his father's son's feet ? " —She was however persuaded to do it.

They then went to bed, and slept for some time ; and when Malcolm awaked, he was told that Mr. John M'Kinnon, his brother-in-law, was in sight. He sprang out to talk to him before he should see Prince Charles. After saluting him, Malcolm, pointing to the sea, said, " What, John, if the prince should be prisoner on board one of those tenders ? "—" GOD forbid ! " replied John. —" What if we had him here ? " said Malcolm.— " I wish we had," answered John ; " we should take care of him."—" Well, John," said Malcolm, " he is in your house."—John, in a transport of joy, wanted to run directly in, and pay his obeisance ; but Malcolm stopped him, saying, " Now is your time to behave well, and do nothing that can discover him."—John composed himself, and having sent away all his servants upon different errands, he was introduced into the presence of his guest, and was then desired to go and get ready a boat lying near his house, which, though but a small leaky one, they resolved to take, rather than go to the Laird of M'Kinnon. John M'Kinnon, however, thought otherwise; and upon his return told them, that his Chief and lady M'Kinnon were coming in the laird's boat. Prince Charles said to his trusty Malcolm, "I am sorry for this, but must make the best of it."—M'Kinnon then walked up from the shore, and did homage to the Wanderer. His lady waited in a cave, to which they all repaired, and were entertained with cold meat and wine.—Mr. Malcolm M'Leod being now superseded by the Laird of M'Kinnon, desired leave to return, which was granted him, and Prince Charles wrote a short note, which he subscribed James Thompson, informing his friends that he had got away from Sky, and thanking them for their kindness; and he desired this might be speedily conveyed to young Rasay and Dr. Macleod, that they might not wait longer in expectation of seeing him again. He bade a cordial adieu to Malcolm, and insisted on his accepting of a silver stock-buckle, and ten guineas from his purse, though, as Malcolm told me, it did not appear to contain above forty. Malcolm at first begged to be excused, saying, that he had a few guineas at his service; but Prince Charles answered, "You will have need of money. I shall get enough when I come upon the main land."

The Laird of M'Kinnon then conveyed him to the opposite coast of Knoidart. Old Rasay, to whom intelligence had been sent, was crossing at the same time to Sky; but as they did not know of each other, and each had apprehensions, the two boats kept aloof.

These are the particulars which I have collected concerning the extraordinary concealment and escapes of Prince Charles, in the Hebrides. He was often in imminent danger. The troops traced him from the Long Island, across Sky, to Portree, but there lost him.

Here I stop,—having received no farther authentic

information of his fatigues and perils before he escaped to France.—Kings and subjects may both take a lesson of moderation from the melancholy fate of the House of Stuart ; that Kings may not suffer degradation and exile, and subjects may not be harassed by the evils of a disputed succession.

Let me close the scene on that unfortunate House with the elegant and pathetick reflections of Voltaire, in his *Histoire Generale.*—" Que les hommes privés (says that brilliant writer, speaking of Prince Charles) qui se croyent malheureux, jettent les yeux sur ce prince et ses ancêtres."

In another place he thus sums up the sad story of the family in general :—" Il n'y a aucun exemple dans l'histoire d'une maison si longtems infortunée. Le premier des Rois d'Ecosse, qui eut le nom de Jacques, apres avoir êté dix-huit ans prisonnier en Angleterre, mourut assassiné, avec sa femme, par la main de ses sujets. Jacques II. son fils, fut tué à vingt-neuf ans en combattant contre les Anglois. Jacques III. mis en prison par son peuple, fut tué ensuite par les revoltés, dans une bataille. Jacques IV. perit dans un combat qu'il perdit. Marie Stuart, sa petite fille, chassèe de son trone, fugitivê en Angleterre, ayant langui dix-huit ans en prison, se vit condamnée à mort par des juges Anglais, et eut la téte tranchée. Charles I. petit fils de Marie, Roi d'Ecosse et d'Angleterre, vendu par les Ecossois, et jugé à mort par les Anglais, mourut sur un échaffaut dans la place publique. Jacques, son fils, septiéme du nom, et deuxieme en Angleterre, fut chassé de ses trois royaumes ; et pour comble de malheur on contesta à son fils sa naissance ; le fils ne tenta de remonter sur le trone de ces peres, que pour faire périr ses amis par des bourreaux ; et nous avons vu le Prince Charles Édouard, reunuissant en vain les vertus de ses peres, et le courage do Roy Jean Sobieski, son ayeul maternel, executer les exploits et essuyer les malheurs les plus incroyables. Si quelque chose justifie ceux qui croyent une fatalité à laquelle rien ne peut se soustraire, c'est cette suite continuelle de malheurs qui a persecuté la maison de Stuart, pendant plus de trois-cent années.''

The gallant Malcolm was apprehended in about ten days after they separated, put aboard a ship and carried prisoner to London. He said, the prisoners in general were very ill treated in their passage ; but there were soldiers on board who lived well, and sometimes invited him to share with them : that he had the good fortune not to be thrown into jail, but was confined in the house of a messenger, of the name of Dick. To his astonishment, only one witness could be found against him, though he had been so openly engaged ; and therefore, for want of sufficient evidence, he was set at liberty. He added, that he thought himself in such danger, that he would gladly have compounded for banishment. Yet, he said, '' he should never be so ready for death as he then was.''—There is philosophical truth in this. A man will meet death much more firmly at one time than another. The enthusiasm even of a mistaken principle warms the mind, and sets it above the fear of death ; which in our cooler moments, if we really think of it, cannot but be terrible, or at least very awful.

Miss Flora Macdonald being then also in London, under the protection of Lady Primrose, that lady provided a post-chaise to convey her to Scotland, and desired she might choose any friend she pleased to accompany her. She chose Malcolm. '' So (said he, with a triumphant air) I went to London to be hanged, and returned in a post-chaise with Miss Flora Macdonald.''

Mr. Macleod of Muiravenside, whom we saw at Rasay, assured us that Prince Charles was in London in 1759, and that there was then a plan in agitation for restoring his family. Dr. Johnson could scarcely credit this story, and said, '' there could be no probable plan at that time. Such an attempt could not have succeeded, unless the King of Prussia had stopped the army in Germany ; for both the army and the fleet would, even without orders, have fought for the King, to whom they had engaged themselves.''

Having related so many particulars concerning the grandson of the unfortunate King James the Second ; having given due praise to fidelity and generous attachment, which, however erroneous the judgement may be, are honourable for the heart ; I must do the Highlanders the justice to attest, that I found every where amongst them a high opinion of the virtues of the King now upon the throne, and an honest disposition to be faithful subjects to his majesty, whose family has possessed the sovereignty of this country so long, that a change, even for the abdicated family, would now hurt the best feelings of all his subjects.

The *abstract* point of *right* would involve us in a discussion of remote and perplexed questions ; and after all, we should have no clear principle of decision. That establishment, which, from political necessity, took place in 1688, by a breach in the succession of our kings, and which, whatever benefits may have accrued from it, certainly gave a shock to our monarchy, —the able and constitutional Blackstone, wisely rests on the solid footing of authority.—'' Our ancestors having most indisputably a competent jurisdiction to decide this great and important question, and having, in fact, decided it, it is now become our duty, at this distance of time, to acquiesce in their determination.''

Mr. Paley, the present Archdeacon of Carlisle, in his *Principles of Moral and Political Philosophy*, having, with much clearness of argument, shown the duty of submission to civil government to be founded neither on an indefeasible *jus divinum*, nor on *compact*, but on *expediency*, lays down this rational position :—'' Irregularity in the first foundation of a state, or subsequent violence, fraud, or injustice, in getting possession of the supreme power, are not sufficient reasons for resistance, after the government is once peaceably settled. No subject of the British empire conceives himself engaged to vindicate the justice of the Norman claim or conquest, or apprehends that his duty in any manner depends upon that controversy. So likewise, if the house of Lancaster, or even the posterity of Cromwell, had been at this day seated upon the throne of England, we should have been as little concerned to enquire how the founder of the family came there."

In conformity with this doctrine, I myself, though fully persuaded that the House of Stuart had originally no right to the crown of Scotland; for that Baliol, and not Bruce, was the lawful heir; should yet have thought it very culpable to have rebelled, on that account, against Charles the First, or even a prince of that house much nearer the time, in order to assert the claim of the posterity of Baliol.

However convinced I am of the justice of that principle, which holds allegiance and protection to be reciprocal, I do however acknowledge, that I am not satisfied with the cold sentiment which would confine the exertions of the subject within the strict line of duty. I would have every breast animated with the *fervour* of loyalty; with that generous attachment which delights in doing somewhat more than is required, and makes " service perfect freedom." And, therefore, as our most gracious Sovereign, on his accession to the throne, gloried in being *born a Briton;* so, in my more private sphere, *Ego me nunc* denique natum, *gratulor.* I am happy that a disputed succession no longer distracts our minds; and that a monarchy, established by law, is now so sanctioned by time, that we can fully indulge those feelings of loyalty which I am ambitious to excite. They are feelings which have ever actuated the inhabitants of the Highlands and the

Hebrides. The plant of loyalty is there in full vigour, and the Brunswick graft now flourishes like a native shoot. To that spirited race of people I may with propriety apply the elegant lines of a modern poet, on the " facile temper of the beauteous sex : "

> " Like birds new-caught, who flutter for a time,
>   And struggle with captivity in vain ;
>   But by-and-by they rest, they smooth their plumes,
>   And to *new masters* sing their former notes."

Surely such notes are much better than the querulous growlings of suspicious Whigs and discontented Republicans.

Kingsburgh conducted us in his boat, across one of the lochs, as they call them, or arms of the sea, which flow in upon all the coasts of Sky,—to a mile beyond a place called Grishinish. Our horses had been sent round by land to meet us. By this sail we saved eight miles of bad riding. Dr. Johnson said, " When we take into the computation what we have saved, and what we have gained, by this agreeable sail, it is a great deal." He observed, " it is very disagreeable riding in Sky. The way is so narrow, one only at a time can travel, so it is quite unsocial ; and you cannot indulge in meditation by yourself, because you must be always attending to the steps which your horse takes."—This was a just and clear description of its inconveniencies.

The topick of emigration being again introduced, Dr. Johnson said, that " a rapacious chief would make a wilderness of his estate." Mr. Donald M'Queen told us, that the oppression, which then made so much noise, was owing to landlords listening to bad advice in the letting of their lands ; that interested and designing people flattered them with golden dreams of much higher rents than could reasonably be paid ; and that some of the gentlemen *tacksmen*, or upper tenants, were themselves in part the occasion of the mischief, by over-rating the farms of others. That many of the *tacksmen*, rather than comply with exorbitant demands, had gone off to America, and impoverished the country, by draining it of its wealth ; and that their places were filled by a number of poor people, who had lived under them, properly speaking, as servants, paid by a certain proportion of the produce of the lands, though called sub-tenants. I observed, that if the men of substance were once banished from a Highland estate, it might probably be greatly reduced in its value ; for one bad year might ruin a set of poor tenants, and men of any property would not settle in such a country, unless from the temptation of getting land extremely cheap ; for an inhabitant of any good county in Britain, had better go to America than to the Highlands or the Hebrides. Here, therefore, was a consideration that ought to induce a Chief to act a more liberal part, from a mere motive of interest, independent of the lofty and honourable principle of keeping a clan together, to be in readiness to serve his king. I added, that I could not help thinking a little arbitrary power in the sovereign, to control the bad policy and greediness of the Chiefs, might sometimes be of service. In France a Chief would not be permitted to force a number of the king's subjects out of the country.—Dr. Johnson concurred with me, observing, that " were an oppressive chieftain a subject of the French king, he would probably be admonished by a *letter*."

During our sail, Dr. Johnson asked about the use of the dirk, with which he imagined the Highlanders cut their meat. He was told, they had a knife and fork besides, to eat with. He asked, how did the women do ? and was answered, some of them had a knife and fork too ; but in general the men, when they had cut their meat, handed their knives and forks to the women, and they themselves eat with their fingers.

The old tutor of Macdonald always eat fish with his fingers, alleging that a knife and fork gave it a bad taste. I took the liberty to observe to Dr. Johnson, that he did so. " Yes," said he ; " but it is because I am short-sighted, and afraid of bones, for which reason I am not fond of eating many kinds of fish, because I must use my fingers."

Dr. M'Pherson's *Dissertations on Scottish Antiquities*, which he had looked at when at Corrichatachin, being mentioned, he remarked, that " you might read half an hour, and ask yourself what you had been reading : there were so many words to so little matter, that there was no getting through the book."

As soon as we reached the shore, we took leave of Kingsburgh, and mounted our horses. We passed through a wild moor, in many places so soft that we were obliged to walk, which was very fatiguing to Dr. Johnson. Once he had advanced on horseback to a very bad step. There was a steep declivity on his left, to which he was so near, that there was not room for him to dismount in the usual way. He tried to alight on the other side, as if he had been a *young buck* indeed, but in the attempt he fell at his length upon the ground ; from which, however, he got up immediately without being hurt. During this dreary ride, we were sometimes relieved by a view of branches of the sea, that universal medium of connection amongst mankind. A guide, who had been sent with us from Kingsburgh, explored the way (much in the same manner as, I suppose, is pursued in the wilds of America,) by observing certain marks known only to the inhabitants. We arrived at Dunvegan late in the afternoon. The great size of the castle, which is partly old and partly new, and is built upon a rock close to the sea, while the land around it presents nothing but wild, moorish, hilly, and craggy appearances, gave a rude magnificence to the scene. Having dismounted, we

ascended a flight of steps, which was made by the late
Macleod, for the accommodation of persons coming
to him by land, there formerly being, for security, no
other access to the castle but from the sea ; so that
visitors who came by the land were under the necessity
of getting into a boat, and sailed round to the only place
where it could be approached. We were introduced
into a stately dining-room, and received by Lady Macleod, mother of the laird, who, with his friend Talisker,
having been detained on the road, did not arrive till
some time after us.

We found the lady of the house a very polite and
sensible woman, who had lived for some time in London, and had there been in Dr. Johnson's company.
After we had dined, we repaired to the drawing-room,
where some of the young ladies of the family, with
their mother, were at tea. This room had formerly
been the bed-chamber of Sir Roderick Macleod, one
of the old Lairds ; and he chose it, because, behind it,
there was a considerable cascade, the sound of which
disposed him to sleep. Above his bed was this inscription : " Sir Rorie M'Leod of Dunvegan, Knight.
GOD send good rest ! "—Rorie is the contraction of
Roderick. He was called Rorie More, that is, great
Rorie, not from his size, but from his spirit.—Our
entertainment here was in so elegant a style, and reminded my fellow-traveller so much of England, that
he became quite joyous. He laughed, and said, " Boswell, we came in at the wrong end of this island."—
" Sir, (said I,) it was best to keep this for the last."—
He answered, " I would have it both first and last."

Tuesday, 14th September

Dr. Johnson said in the morning, " Is not this a fine
lady ? "—There was not a word now of his " impa-

tience to be in civilized life ; "—though indeed I should beg pardon,—he found it here. We had slept well, and lain long. After breakfast we surveyed the castle, and the garden. Mr. Bethune, the parish minister,— Magnus M'Leod, of Claggan, brother to Talisker, and M'Leod, of Bay, two substantial gentlemen of the clan, dined with us. We had admirable venison, generous wine ; in a word, all that a good table has. This was really the hall of a chief. Lady M'Leod had been much obliged to my father, who had settled by arbitration, a variety of perplexed claims between her and her relation, the Laird of Brodie, which she now repaid by particular attention to me.—M'Leod started the subject of making women do penance in the church for fornication.—JOHNSON. " It is right, sir. Infamy is attached to the crime, by universal opinion, as soon as it is known. I would not be the man who would discover it, if I alone knew it, for a woman may reform ; nor would I commend a parson who divulges a woman's first offence ; but being once divulged, it ought to be infamous. Consider, of what importance to society the chastity of women is. Upon that all the property in the world depends. We hang a thief for stealing a sheep ; but the unchastity of a woman transfers sheep, and farm and all, from the right owner. I have much more reverence for a common prostitute than for a woman who conceals her guilt. The prostitute is known. She cannot deceive : she cannot bring a strumpet into the arms of an honest man, without his knowledge."—BOSWELL. " There is, however, a great difference between the licentiousness of a single woman, and that of a married woman."—JOHNSON. " Yes, sir ; there is a great difference between stealing a shilling, and stealing a thousand pounds ; between simply taking a man's purse, and murdering him first, and then taking it. But when one begins to be vicious, it is easy to go on. Where single women are licentious, you rarely find faithful married women."—BOSWELL. "And yet we are told that in some nations in India, the distinction is strictly observed."—JOHNSON. "Nay, don't give us India. That puts me in mind of Montesquieu, who is really a fellow of genius too in many respects; whenever he wants to support a strange opinion, he quotes you the practice of Japan or of some other distant country, of which he knows nothing. To support polygamy, he tells you of the island of Formosa, where there are ten women born for one man. He had but to suppose another island, where there are ten men born for one woman, and so make a marriage between them."

At supper, Lady Macleod mentioned Dr. Cadogan's book on the gout.—JOHNSON. "It is a good book in general, but a foolish one in particulars. It is good in general, as recommending temperance, and exercise and cheerfulness. In that respect it is only Dr. Cheyne's book told in a new way; and there should come out such a book every thirty years, dressed in the mode of the times. It is foolish, in maintaining that the gout is not hereditary, and that one fit of it, when gone, is like a fever when gone."—Lady Macleod objected that the author does not practice what he teaches.—JOHNSON. "I cannot help that, madam. That does not make his book the worse. People are influenced more by what a man says, if his practice is suitable to it,—because they are blockheads. The more intellectual people are, the readier will they attend to what a man tells them. If it is just, they will follow it, be his practice what it will. No man practises so well as he writes. I have, all my life long, been lying till noon; yet I tell all young men, and tell them with great sincerity, that nobody who does not rise early will ever do any good. Only consider! You read a book; you are convinced by it; you do not know the authour. Suppose you afterwards know him, and find that he does not practice what he teaches ; are you to give up your former conviction ? At this rate you would be kept in a state of equilibrium, when reading every book, till you knew how the authour practised."—" But," said Lady M'Leod, " you would think better of Dr. Cadogan, if he acted according to his principles."—JOHNSON. " Why, madam, to be sure, a man who acts in the face of light, is worse than a man who does not know so much ; yet I think no man should be the worse thought of for publishing good principles. There is something noble in publishing truth, though it condemns one's self."— I expressed some surprize at Cadogan's recommending good humour, as if it were quite in our own power to attain it.—JOHNSON. " Why, sir, a man grows better humoured as he grows older. He improves by experience. When young, he thinks himself of great consequence, and every thing of importance. As he advances in life, he learns to think himself of no consequence, and little things of little importance ; and so he becomes more patient, and better pleased. All good-humour and complaisance are acquired. Naturally a child seizes directly what it sees, and thinks of pleasing itself only. By degrees, it is taught to please others, and to prefer others ; and that this will ultimately produce the greatest happiness. If a man is not convinced of that, he never will practice it. Common language speaks the truth as to this : we say, a person is well bred. As it is said, that all material motion is primarily in a right line, and is never *per circuitum*, never in another form, unless by some particular cause ; so it may be said intellectual motion is."—Lady M'Leod asked, if no man was naturally good ?—JOHNSON. " No, madam, no more than a wolf."—BOSWELL. " Nor no woman, sir ? "—JOHNSON. " No, sir."—Lady M'Leod started at this, saying, in a low voice, " This is worse than Swift."

M'Leod of Ulinish had come in the afternoon. We

were a jovial company at supper. The Laird, surrounded by so many of his clan, was to me a pleasing sight. They listened with wonder and pleasure, while Dr. Johnson harangued. I am vexed that I cannot take down his full strain of eloquence.

Wednesday, 15th September

The gentlemen of the clan went away early in the morning to the harbour of Lochbradale, to take leave of some of their friends who were going to America. It was a very wet day. We looked at Rorie More's horn, which is a large cow's horn, with the mouth of it ornamented with silver curiously carved. It holds rather more than a bottle and a half. Every Laird of M'Leod, it is said, must, as a proof of his manhood, drink it off full of claret, without laying it down.—From Rorie More many of the branches of the family are descended ; in particular, the Talisker branch ; so that his name is much talked of. We also saw his bow, which hardly any man now can bend, and his Glaymore, which was wielded with both hands, and is of a prodigious size. We saw here some old pieces of iron armour, immensely heavy. The broadsword now used, though called the Glaymore, (*i.e.* the great sword, is much smaller than that used in Rorie More's time. There is hardly a target now to be found in the Highlands. After the disarming act, they made them serve as covers to their butter-milk barrels ; a kind of change, like beating spears into pruning-hooks.

Sir George Mackenzie's Works (the folio edition) happened to lie in a window in the dining-room. I asked Dr. Johnson to look at the *Characteres Advocatorum*. He allowed him power of mind, and that he understood very well what he tells ; but said, that there was too much declamation, and that the Latin was not correct. He found fault with *appropinquabant,* in the character of Gilmour. I tried him with the opposition between *gloria* and *palma,* in the comparison between Gilmour and Nisbet, which Lord Hailes, in his Catalogue of the Lords of Session, thinks difficult to be understood. The words are, " *penes illum gloria, penes hunc palma.*"—In a short Account of the Kirk of Scotland, which I published some years ago, I applied these words to the two contending parties, and explained them thus : " The popular party has most eloquence ; Dr. Robertson's party most influence."— I was very desirous to hear Dr. Johnson's explication.—JOHNSON. " I see no difficulty. Gilmour was admired for his parts ; Nisbet carried his cause by his skill in law. *Palma* is victory."—I observed, that the character of Nicholson, in this book, resembled that of Burke : for it is said, in one place, " *in omnes lusos & jocos se sæpe resolvebat ;* and, in another, " *sed accipitris more e conspectu aliquando astantium sublimi se protrahens volatu, in prædam miro impetu descendebat.*" —JOHNSON. " No, sir ; I never heard Burke make a good joke in my life."—BOSWELL. " But, sir, you will allow he is a hawk."—Dr. Johnson, thinking that I meant this of his joking, said, " No, sir, he is not the hawk there. He is the beetle in the mire."—I still adhered to my metaphor,—" But he *soars* as the hawk."—JOHNSON. " Yes, sir ; but he catches nothing."—M'Leod asked, what is the particular excellence of Burke's eloquence ?—JOHNSON. " Copiousness and fertility of allusion ; a power of diversifying his matter, by placing it in various relations. Burke has great information, and great command of language ; though, in my opinion, it has not in every respect the highest elegance."—BOSWELL. " Do you think, sir, that Burke has read Cicero much ? "—JOHNSON. " I don't believe it, sir. Burke has great knowledge, great fluency of words, and great promptness of ideas, so that he can speak with great illustration on any subject that comes before him. He is neither like Cicero, nor like Demosthenes, nor like any one else, but speaks as well as he can."

In the 65th page of the first volume of Sir George Mackenzie, Dr. Johnson pointed out a paragraph beginning with *Aristotle,* and told me there was an error in the text, which he bade me try to discover. I was lucky enough to hit it at once. As the passage is printed, it is said that the devil answers *even* in *engines.* I corrected it to—*ever* in *ænigmas.* " Sir, (said he,) you are a good critick. This would have been a great thing to do in the text of an ancient authour."

Thursday, 16th September

Last night much care was taken of Dr. Johnson, who was still distressed by his cold. He had hitherto most strangely slept without a night-cap. Miss M'Leod made him a large flannel one, and he was prevailed with to drink a little brandy when he was going to bed. He has great virtue, in not drinking wine or any fermented liquor, because, as he acknowledged to us, he could not do it in moderation.—Lady M'Leod would hardly believe him, and said, " I am sure, sir, you would not carry it too far."—JOHNSON. " Nay, madam, it carried me. I took the opportunity of a long illness to leave it off. It was then prescribed to me not to drink wine ; and having broken off the habit, I have never returned to it."

In the argument on Tuesday night, about natural goodness, Dr. Johnson denied that any child was better than another, but by difference of instruction ; though, in consequence of greater attention being paid to instruction by one child than another, and of a variety of imperceptible causes, such as instruction being counteracted by servants, a notion was conceived, that of two children, equally well educated, one was naturally much worse than another. He owned, this morning, that one might have a greater aptitude to learn than another, and that we inherit dispositions from our parents. " I inherited, (said he,) a vile melancholy from my father, which has made me mad all my life, at least not sober." —Lady M'Leod wondered he should tell this.—" Madam, (said I,) he knows that with that madness he is superior to other men."

I have often been astonished with what exactness and perspicuity he will explain the process of any art. He this morning explained to us all the operation of coining, and, at night, all the operation of brewing, so very clearly, that Mr. M'Queen said, when he heard the first, he thought he had been bred in the Mint ; when he heard the second, that he had been bred a brewer.

I was elated by the thought of having been able to entice such a man to this remote part of the world. A ludicrous, yet just image presented itself to my mind, which I expressed to the company. I compared myself to a dog who has got hold of a large piece of meat, and runs away with it to a corner, where he may devour it in peace, without any fear of others taking it from him. " In London, Reynolds, Beauclerk, and all of them, are contending who shall enjoy Dr. Johnson's conversation. We are feasting upon it, undisturbed, at Dunvegan."

It was still a storm of wind and rain. Dr. Johnson however walked out with M'Leod, and saw Rorie More's cascade in full perfection. Colonel M'Leod, instead of being all life and gaiety, as I have seen him, was at present grave, and somewhat depressed by his anxious concern about M'Leod's affairs, and by finding some gentlemen of the clan by no means disposed to act a generous or affectionate part to their Chief in his distress, but bargaining with him as with a stranger. However, he was agreeable and polite, and Dr. Johnson said, he was a very pleasing man.—My fellow-traveller and I talked of going to Sweden ; and, while we were settling our plan, I expressed a pleasure in the prospect of seeing the king.—JOHNSON. " I doubt, sir, if he would speak to us."—Colonel M'Leod said, " I am sure Mr. Boswell would speak to *him*." But, seeing me a little disconcerted by his remark, he politely added, " and with great propriety."—Here let me offer a short defence of that propensity in my disposition, to which this gentleman alluded. It has procured me much happiness. I hope it does not deserve so hard a name as either forwardness or impudence. If I know myself, it is nothing more than an eagerness to share the society of men distinguished either by their rank or their talents, and a diligence to attain what I desire. If a man is praised for seeking knowledge, though mountains and seas are in his way, may he not be pardoned, whose ardour, in the pursuit of the same object, leads him to encounter difficulties as great, though of a different kind ?

After the ladies were gone from table, we talked of the Highlanders not having sheets ; and this led us to consider the advantage of wearing linen.—JOHNSON. " All animal substances are less cleanly than vegetables. Wool, of which flannel is made, is an animal substance ; flannel therefore is not so cleanly as linen. I remember I used to think tar dirty ; but when I knew it to be only a preparation of the juice of the pine, I thought so no longer. It is not disagreeable to have the gum that oozes from a plumb-tree upon your fingers, because it is vegetable ; but if you have any candle-grease, any tallow upon your fingers, you are uneasy till you rub it off.—I have often thought, that, if I kept a seraglio, the ladies should all wear linen gowns,—or cotton ;—I mean stuffs made of vegetable substances. I would have no silk; you cannot tell when it is clean: It will be very nasty before it is perceived to be so. Linen detects its own dirtiness."

To hear the grave Dr. Samuel Johnson, " that majestick teacher of moral and religious wisdom," while sitting solemn in an arm-chair in the Isle of Sky, talk, *ex cathedra*, of his keeping a seraglio, and acknowledge that the supposition had *often* been in his thoughts, struck me so forcibly with ludicrous contrast, that I could not but laugh immoderately. He was too proud to submit, even for a moment, to be the object of ridicule, and instantly retaliated with such keen sarcastick wit, and such a variety of degrading images, of every one of which I was the object, that, though I can bear such attacks as well as most men, I yet found myself so much the sport of all the company, that I would gladly expunge from my mind every trace of this severe retort.

Talking of our friend Langton's house in Lincolnshire, he said, " the old house of the family was burnt. A temporary building was erected in its room ; and to this day they have been always adding as the family increased. It is like a shirt made for a man when he was a child, and enlarged always as he grows older."

We talked to-night of Luther's allowing the Landgrave of Hesse two wives, and that it was with the consent of the wife to whom he was first married.— JOHNSON. " There was no harm in this, so far as she was only concerned, because *volenti non fit injuria*. But it was an offence against the general order of society, and against the law of the Gospel, by which one man and one woman are to be united. No man can have two wives, but by preventing somebody else from having one."

Friday, 17th September

After dinner yesterday, we had a conversation upon cunning. M'Leod said that he was not afraid of cunning people; but would let them play their tricks about him like monkeys. "But, (said I,) they'll scratch;" and Mr. M'Queen added, "they'll invent new tricks, as soon as you find out what they do."—JOHNSON. "Cunning has effect from the credulity of others, rather than from the abilities of those who are cunning. It requires no extraordinary talents to lie and deceive."—This led us to consider whether it did not require great abilities to be very wicked.—JOHNSON. "It requires great abilities to have the *power* of being very wicked; but not to *be* very wicked. A man who has the power, which great abilities procure him, may use it well or ill; and it requires more abilities to use it well, than to use it ill. Wickedness is always easier than virtue; for it takes the short cut to every thing. It is much easier to steal a hundred pounds, than to get it by labour, or any other way. Consider only what act of wickedness requires great abilities to commit it, when once the person who is to do it has the power; for *there* is the distinction. It requires great abilities to conquer an army, but none to massacre it after it is conquered."

The weather this day was rather better than any that we had since we came to Dunvegan. Mr. M'Queen had often mentioned a curious piece of antiquity near this, which he called a temple of the Goddess Anaitis. Having often talked of going to see it, he and I set out after breakfast, attended by his servant, a fellow quite like a savage. I must observe here, that in Sky there seems to be much idleness; for men and boys follow you, as colts follow passengers upon a road. The usual figure of a Sky-boy, is a *lown* with bare legs and feet, a dirty *kilt*, ragged coat and waistcoat, a bare head, and a stick in his hand, which, I suppose, is partly to help the lazy rogue to walk, partly to serve as a kind of a defensive weapon. We walked what is called two miles, but is probably four, from the castle, till we came to the sacred place. The country around is a black dreary moor on all sides, except to the sea-coast, towards which there is a view through a valley; and the farm of Bay shews some good land. The place itself is green ground, being well drained, by means of a deep glen on each side, in both of which there runs a rivulet with a good quantity of water, forming several cascades, which make a considerable appearance and sound. The first thing we came to was an earthen mound, or dyke, extending from the one precipice to the other. A little farther on was a strong stone-wall, not high, but very thick, extending in the same manner. On the outside of it were the ruins of two houses, one on each side of the entry or gate to it. The wall is built all along of uncemented stones, but of so large a size as to make a very firm and durable rampart. It has been built all about the consecrated ground, except where the precipice is steep enough to form an enclosure of itself. The sacred spot contains more than two acres. There are within it the ruins of many houses, none of them large,—a *cairn*,—and many graves marked by clusters of stones. Mr. M'Queen insisted that the ruin of a small building, standing east and west, was actually the temple of the Goddess Anaitis, where her statue was kept, and from whence processions were made to wash it in one of the brooks. There is, it must be owned, a hollow road visible for a good way from the extrance; but Mr. M'Queen, with the keen eye of an antiquary, traced it much farther than I could perceive it. There is not above a foot and a half in height of the walls now remaining; and the whole extent of the building was never, I imagine, greater than an ordinary

Highland house. Mr. M'Queen has collected a great
deal of learning on the subject of the temple of Anaitis
and I had endeavoured, in my Journal, to state such
particulars as might give some idea of it, and of the
surrounding scenery; but from the great difficulty
of describing visible objects, I found my account so
unsatisfactory, that my readers would probably have
exclaimed

> " And write about it, *Goddess*, and about it; "

and therefore I have omitted it.

When we got home, and were again at table with
Dr. Johnson, we first talked of portraits. He agreed
in thinking them valuable in families. I wished to
know which he preferred, fine portraits, or those of
which the merit was resemblance.—JOHNSON. " Sir,
their chief excellence is being like."—BOSWELL. " Are
you of that opinion as to the portraits of ancestors
whom one has never seen? "—JOHNSON. " It then becomes of more consequence that they should be like,
and I would have them in the dress of the times, which
makes a piece of history. One should like to see how
Rorie More looked. Truth, sir, is of the greatest value
in these things."—Mr. M'Queen observed, that if you
think it of no consequence whether portraits are like,
if they are but well painted, you may be indifferent
whether a piece of history is true or not, if well
told.

Dr. Johnson said at breakfast to-day, " that it was
but of late that historians bestowed pains and attention
in consulting records, to attain to accuracy. Bacon
in writing his *History of Henry VII.* does not seem
to have consulted any, but to have just taken what he
found in other histories, and blended it with what he
learnt by tradition." He agreed with me that there
should be a chronicle kept in every considerable family

to preserve the characters and transactions of successive generations.

After dinner I started the subject of the temple of Anaitis. Mr. M'Queen had laid stress on the name given to the place by the country people,—*Ainnit*; and added, " I knew not what to make of this piece of antiquity, till I met with the *Anaitidis delubrum* in Lydia, mentioned by Pausanias and the elder Pliny."— Dr. Johnson, with his usual acuteness, examined Mr. M'Queen as to the meaning of the word *Ainnit*, in Erse ; and it proved to be a *water-place*, or a place near water, " which," said Mr. M'Queen, " agrees with all the descriptions of the temples of that goddess, which were situated near rivers, that there might be water to wash the statue."—JOHNSON. " Nay, sir, the argument from the name is gone. The name is exhausted by what we see. We have no occasion to go to a distance for what we can pick up under our feet. Had it been an accidental name, the similarity between it and Anaitis might have had something in it ; but it turns out to be a mere physiological name."— Macleod said, Mr. M'Queen's knowledge of etymology had destroyed his conjecture.—JOHNSON. " Yes, sir ; Mr. M'Queen is like the eagle mentioned by Waller, who was shot with an arrow feather'd from his own wing."—Mr. M'Queen would not, however, give up his conjecture.—JOHNSON. " You have one possibility for you, and all possibilities against you. It is possible it may be the temple of Anaitis. But it is also possible that it may be a fortification ;—or it may be a place of Christian worship, as the first Christians often chose remote and wild places, to make an impression on the mind :—or, if it was a heathen temple, it may have been built near a river, for the purpose of lustration ; and there is such a multitude of divinities, to whom it may have been dedicated, that the chance of its being a temple of Anaitis is

hardly any thing. It is like throwing a grain of sand
upon the sea-shore to-day, and thinking you may find
it to-morrow. No, sir, this temple, like many an ill-
built edifice, tumbles down before it is roofed in.''—
In his triumph over the reverend antiquarian, he indulged himself in a conceit ; for, some vestige of the
altar of the goddess being much insisted on in support
of the hypothesis, he said, '' Mr. M'Queen is fighting
pro aris *et focis.''*

It was wonderful how well time passed in a remote
castle, and in dreary weather. After supper, we talked
of Pennant. It was objected that he was superficial.
Dr. Johnson defended him warmly. He said, '' Pennant has greater variety of enquiry than almost any man,
and has told us more than perhaps one in ten thousand
could have done, in the time that he took. He has not
said what he was to tell ; so you cannot find fault with
him, for what he has not told. If a man comes to look
for fishes, you cannot blame him if he does not attend to
fowls.''—'' But,'' said Colonel M'Leod, '' he mentions
the unreasonable rise of rents in the Highlands, and
says, ' the gentlemen are for emptying the bag, without
filling it ; ' for that is the phrase he uses. Why does
he not tell how to fill it ? ''—JOHNSON. '' Sir, there is
no end of negative criticism. He tells what he ob-
serves, and as much as he chooses. If he tells what
is not true, you may find fault with him ; but, though
he tells that the land is not well cultivated, he is not
obliged to tell how it may be well cultivated. If I
tell that many of the Highlanders go bare-footed, I am
not obliged to tell how they may get shoes. Pennant
tells a fact. He need go no farther, except he pleases.
He exhausts nothing ; and no subject whatever has yet
been exhausted. But Pennant has surely told a great
deal. Here is a man six feet high, and you are angry
because he is not seven.''—Notwithstanding this eloquent *Oratio pro Pennantio*, which they who have read

this gentleman's *Tours*, and recollect the Savage and the Shopkeeper at Monboddo, will probably impute to the spirit of contradiction, I still think that he had better have given more attention to fewer things, than have thrown together such a number of imperfect accounts.

Saturday, 18th September

Before breakfast, Dr. Johnson came up to my room, to forbid me to mention that this was his birth-day; but I told him I had done it already; at which he was displeased; I suppose from wishing to have nothing particular done on his account. Lady M'Leod and I got into a warm dispute. She wanted to build a house upon a farm which she has taken, about five miles from the castle, and to make gardens and other ornaments there; all of which I approved of; but insisted that the seat of the family should always be upon the rock of Dunvegan.—JOHNSON. " Ay, in time we'll build all round this rock. You may make a very good house at the farm; but it must not be such as to tempt the Laird of M'Leod to go thither to reside. Most of the great families of England have a secondary residence, which is called a jointure-house: let the new house be of that kind."—The lady insisted that the rock was very inconvenient; that there was no place near it where a good garden could be made; that it must always be a rude place; that it was a Herculean labour to make a dinner here.—I was vexed to find the alloy of modern refinement in a lady who had so much old family spirit.—" Madam, (said I,) if once you quit this rock, there is no knowing where you may settle. You move five miles first;—then to St. Andrews, as the late Laird did;—then to Edinburgh;—and so on till you end at Hampstead, or in France. No, no; keep to the rock : it is the very jewel of the estate. It looks as if it had been let down from heaven by the four corners, to be the residence of a Chief. Have all the comforts and conveniencies of life upon it, but never leave Rorie More's cascade."—" But, (said she,) is it not enough if we keep it ? Must we never have more convenience than Rorie More had ? he had his beef brought to dinner in one basket, and his bread in another. Why not as well be Rorie More all over, as live upon his rock ? And should not we tire, in looking perpetually on this rock ? It is very well for you, who have a fine place, and every thing easy, to talk thus, and think of chaining honest folks to a rock. You would not live upon it yourself."—" Yes, madam, (said I,) I would live upon it, were I Laird of M'Leod, and should be unhappy if I were not upon it."—JOHN-SON. (with a strong voice, and most determined manner,) " Madam, rather than quit the old rock, Boswell would live in the pit ; he would make his bed in the dungeon." —I felt a degree of elation, at finding my resolute feudal enthusiasm thus confirmed by such a sanction. The lady was puzzled a little. She still returned to her pretty farm,—rich ground,—fine garden.—" Madam, (said Dr. Johnson,) were they in Asia, I would not leave the rock."—My opinion on this subject is still the same. An ancient family residence ought to be a primary object ; and though the situation of Dunvegan be such that little can be done here in gardening, or pleasure-ground, yet, in addition to the veneration acquired by the lapse of time, it has many circumstances of natural grandeur, suited to the seat of a Highland Chief : it has the sea,—islands,—rocks,—hills,—a noble cascade ; and when the family is again in opulence, something may be done by art.

Mr. Donald M'Queen went away to-day, in order to preach at Bracadale next day. We were so comfortably situated at Dunvegan, that Dr. Johnson could hardly be moved from it.   I proposed to him that we should leave it on Monday. " No, sir, (said he,) I will not go before Wednesday.   I will have some more of this good." —However, as the weather was at this season so bad, and so very uncertain, and we had a great deal to do yet, Mr. M'Queen and I prevail'd with him to agree to set out on Monday, if the day should be good.   Mr. M'Queen, though it was inconvenient for him to be absent from his harvest, engaged to wait on Monday at Ulinish for us.   When he was going away, Dr. Johnson said, " I shall ever retain a great regard for you ; " then asked him if he had the *Rambler*.—Mr. M'Queen said, " No ; but my brother has it."—JOHNSON. " Have you the *Idler ?* "—M'QUEEN. " No, sir."—JOHNSON. " Then I will order one for you at Edinburgh, which you will keep in remembrance of me."—Mr. M'Queen was much pleased with this.   He expressed to me, in the strongest terms, his admiration of Dr. Johnson's wonderful know-ledge, and every other quality for which he is distin-guished.   I asked Mr. M'Queen, if he was satisfied with being a minister in Sky.   He said he was ; but he owned that his forefathers having been so long there, and his having been born there, made a chief ingredient in forming his contentment.   I should have mentioned, that on our left hand, between Portree and Dr. Macleod's house, Mr. M'Queen told me there had been a college of the Knights Templars ; that tradition said so ; and that there was a ruin remaining of their church, which had been burnt : but I confess Dr. Johnson has weakened my belief in remote tradition.   In the dispute about Anaitis, Mr. M'Queen said, Asia Minor was peopled by Scythians, and, as they were the ancestors of the Celts, the same religion might be in Asia Minor and Sky.— JOHNSON. " Alas ! sir, what can a nation that has not letters tell of its original.   I have always difficulty to be patient when I hear authors gravely quoted, as giving accounts of savage nations, which accounts they had from the savages themselves. What can the M'Craas tell about themselves a thousand years ago? There is no tracing the connection of ancient nations, but by language; and therefore I am always sorry when any language is lost, because languages are the pedigree of nations. If you find the same language in distant countries, you may be sure that the inhabitants of each have been the same people; that is to say, if you find the languages a good deal the same; for a word here and there being the same, will not do. Thus Butler, in his *Hudibras*, remembering that Penguin, in the Straits of Magellan, signifies a bird with a white head, and that the same word has, in Wales, the signification of a white-headed wench, (*pen* head, and *guin* white,) by way of ridicule, concludes that the people of those Straits are Welch."

A young gentleman of the name of M'Lean, nephew to the Laird of the isle of Muck, came this morning; and, just as we sat down to dinner, came the Laird of the isle of Muck himself, his lady, sister to Talisker, two other ladies their relations, and a daughter of the late M'Leod of Hamer, who wrote a treatise on the second sight, under the designation of *Theophilus Insulanus*. It was somewhat droll to hear this Laird called by his title. *Muck* would have sounded ill; so he was called *Isle of Muck*, which went off with great readiness. The name, as now written, is unseemly, but is not so bad in the original Erse, which is *Mouach*, signifying the Sows' Island. Buchanan calls it *Insula Porcorum*. It is so called from its form. Some call it Isle of *Monk*. The Laird insists that this is the proper name. It was formerly church-land belonging to Icolmkill, and a hermit lived in it. It is two miles long, and about three quarters of a mile broad. The Laird said, he had seven score of souls upon it. Last year he had eighty persons inoculated, mostly children, but some of them eighteen years of age. He agreed with the surgeon to come and do it, at half a crown a head.—It is very fertile in corn, of which they export some ; and its coasts abound in fish. A taylor comes there six times in a year. They get a good blacksmith from the isle of Egg.

Sunday, 19th September

It was rather worse weather than any that we had yet. At breakfast Dr. Johnson said, " Some cunning men choose fools for their wives, thinking to manage them, but they always fail. There is a spaniel fool and a mule fool. The spaniel fool may be made to do by beating. The mule fool will neither do by words or blows ; and the spaniel fool often turns mule at last : and suppose a fool to be made do pretty well, you must have the continual trouble of making her do. Depend upon it, no woman is the worse for sense and knowledge."—Whether afterwards he meant merely to say a polite thing, or to give his opinion, I could not be sure ; but he added, " Men know that women are an over-match for them, and therefore they choose the weakest or most ignorant. If they did not think so, they never could be afraid of women knowing as much as themselves."—In justice to the sex, I think it but candid to acknowledge, that, in a subsequent conversation, he told me that he was serious in what he had said.

He came to my room this morning before breakfast, to read my Journal, which he has done all along. He often before said, " I take great delight in reading it." To-day he said, " You improve : it grows better and better."—I observed, there was a danger of my getting a habit of writing in a slovenly manner.—" Sir," said he, " it is not written in a slovenly manner. It might be printed, were the subject fit for printing."—While Mr. Beaton preached to us in the dining-room, Dr.

Johnson sat in his own room, where I saw lying before him a volume of Lord Bacon's works, the *Decay of Christian Piety*, Monboddo's *Origin of Language*, and Sterne's Sermons.—He asked me to-day, how it happened that we were so little together : I told him, my Journal took up much time. Yet, on reflection, it appeared strange to me, that although I will run from one end of London to another, to pass an hour with him, I should omit to seize any spare time to be in his company, when I am settled in the same house with him. But my Journal is really a task of much time and labour, and he forbids me to contract it.

I omitted to mention, in its place, that Dr. Johnson told Mr. M'Queen that he had found the belief of the second sight universal in Sky, except among the clergy, who seemed determined against it. I took the liberty to observe to Mr. M'Queen, that the clergy were actuated by a kind of vanity. " The world, (say they,) takes us to be credulous men in a remote corner. We'll shew them that we are more enlightened than they think." The worthy man said, that his disbelief of it was from his not finding sufficient evidence ; but I could perceive that he was prejudiced against it.

After dinner to-day, we talked of the extraordinary fact of Lady Grange's being sent to St. Kilda, and confined there for several years, without any means of relief. Dr. Johnson said, if M'Leod would let it be known that he had such a place for naughty ladies, he might make it a very profitable island.—We had, in the course of our tour, heard of St. Kilda poetry. Dr. Johnson observed, " it must be very poor, because they have very few images."—BOSWELL. " There may be a poetical genius shewn in combining these, and in making poetry of them."—JOHNSON. " Sir, a man cannot make fire but in proportion as he has fuel. He cannot coin guineas but in proportion as he has gold."—At tea he talked of his intending to go to Italy in 1775. M'Leod said, he would like Paris better.—JOHNSON. " No, sir ; there are none of the French literati now alive, to visit whom I would cross a sea. I can find in Buffon's book all that he can say."

After supper he said, " I am sorry that prize-fighting is gone out ; every art should be preserved, and the art of defence is surely important. It is absurd that our soldiers should have swords, and not be taught the use of them. Prize-fighting made people accustomed not to be alarmed at seeing their own blood, or feeling a little pain from a wound. I think the heavy glaymore was an ill-contrived weapon. A man could only strike once with it. It employed both his hands, and he must of course be soon fatigued with wielding it ; so that if his antagonist could only keep playing a while, he was sure of him. I would fight with a dirk against Rorie More's sword. I could ward off a blow with a dirk, and then run in upon my enemy. When within that heavy sword, I have him ; he is quite helpless, and I could stab him at my leisure, like a calf.—It is thought by sensible military men, that the English do not enough avail themselves of their superior strength of body against the French ; for that must always have a great advantage in pushing with bayonets. I have heard an officer say, that if women could be made to stand, they would do as well as men in a mere interchange of bullets from a distance : but, if a body of men should come close up to them, then to be sure they must be overcome ; now, (said he,) in the same manner the weaker-bodied French must be overcome by our strong soldiers."

The subject of duelling was introduced.—JOHNSON. " There is no case in England where one or other of the combatants *must* die : if you have overcome your adversary by disarming him, that is sufficient, though you should not kill him ; your honour, or the honour of your family, is restored, as much as it can be by a duel. It is cowardly to force your antagonist to renew the combat, when you know that you have the advantage of him by superior skill. You might just as well go and cut his throat while he is asleep in his bed. When a duel begins, it is supposed there may be an equality; because it is not always skill that prevails. It depends much on presence of mind; nay on accidents. The wind may be in a man's face. He may fall. Many such things may decide the superiority.—A man is sufficiently punished, by being called out, and subjected to the risk that is in a duel."—But on my suggesting that the injured person is equally subjected to risk, he fairly owned he could not explain the rationality of duelling.

Monday, 20th September

When I awaked, the storm was higher still. It abated about nine, and the sun shone; but it rained again very soon, and it was not a day for travelling. At breakfast, Dr. Johnson told us, " there was once a pretty good tavern in Catharine-street in the Strand, where very good company met in an evening, and each man called for his own half-pint of wine, or gill, if he pleased; they were frugal men, and nobody paid but for what he himself drank. The house furnished no supper; but a woman attended with mutton-pies, which any body might purchase. I was introduced to this company by Cumming the Quaker, and used to go there sometimes when I drank wine. In the last age, when my mother lived in London, there were two sets of people, those who gave the wall, and those who took it; the peaceable and the quarrelsome. When I returned to Lichfield, after having been in London, my mother asked me, whether I was one of those who gave the wall, or those who took it. Now, it is fixed that every man keeps to the right; or, if one is taking the wall, another yields it, and it is never a dispute."—He was very severe on a lady, whose name was mentioned. He said, he would have sent her to St. Kilda. That she was as bad as negative badness could be, and stood in the way of what was good : that insipid beauty would not go a great way ; and that such a woman might be cut out of a cabbage, if there was a skilful artificer.

M'Leod was too late in coming to breakfast. Dr. Johnson said, laziness was worse than the toothache. —BOSWELL. " I cannot agree with you, sir ; a bason of cold water, or a horse whip, will cure laziness."— JOHNSON. " No, sir ; it will only put off the fit ; it will not cure the disease. I have been trying to cure my laziness all my life, and could not do it."—BOSWELL. " But if a man does in a shorter time what might be the labour of a life, there is nothing to be said against him."—JOHNSON (perceiving at once that I alluded to him and his Dictionary). " Suppose that flattery to be true, the consequence would be, that the world would have no right to censure a man ; but that will not justify him to himself."

After breakfast, he said to me, " A Highland Chief should now endeavour to do every thing to raise his rents, by means of the industry of his people. Formerly, it was right for him to have his house full of idle fellows ; they were his defenders, his servants, his dependants, his friends. Now they may be better employed. The system of things is now so much altered, that the family cannot have influence but by riches, because it has no longer the power of ancient feudal times. An individual of a family may have it ; but it cannot now belong to a family, unless you could have a perpetuity of men with the same views. M'Leod has four times the land that the Duke of Bedford has. I think, with his spirit, he may in time make himself the greatest man in the king's dominions ; for land may always be improved to a certain degree. I would never have any man sell land, to throw money into the funds, as is often done, or to try any other species of trade. Depend upon it, this rage of trade will destroy itself. You and I shall not see it; but the time will come when there will be an end of it. Trade is like gaming. If a whole company are gamesters, play must cease; for there is nothing to be won. When all nations are traders, there is nothing to be gained by trade, and it will stop first where it is brought to the greatest perfection. Then the proprietors of land only will be the great men."—I observed, it was hard that M'Leod should find ingratitude in so many of his people.—JOHNSON. " Sir, gratitude is a fruit of great cultivation; you do not find it among gross people."—I doubt of this. Nature seems to have implanted gratitude in all living creatures. The lion, mentioned by Aulus Gellius, had it. It appears to me that culture, which brings luxury and selfishness with it, has a tendency rather to weaken than promote this affection.

Dr. Johnson said this morning, when talking of our setting out, that he was in the state in which Lord Bacon represents kings. He desired the end, but did not like the means. He wished much to get home, but was unwilling to travel in Sky.—" You are like kings too in this, sir, (said I,) that you must act under the direction of others."

Tuesday, 21st September

The uncertainty of our present situation having prevented me from receiving any letters from home for some time, I could not help being uneasy. Dr. Johnson had an advantage over me, in this respect, he having no wife or child to occasion anxious apprehension in his mind.—It was a good morning; so we resolved to set out. But, before quitting this castle, where we have been so well entertained, let me give a short description of it.

Along the edge of the rock, there are the remains of a wall, which is now covered with ivy. A square court is formed by buildings of different ages, particularly some towers, said to be of great antiquity ; and at one place there is a row of false cannon of stone. There is a very large unfinished pile, four stories high, which we were told was here when Leod, the first of this family, came from the Isle of Man, married the heiress of the M'Crails, the ancient possessors of Dunvegan, and afterwards acquired by conquest as much land as he had got by marriage. He surpassed the house of Austria ; for he was *felix* both *bella gerere* et *nubere*. John Breck M'Leod, the grandfather of the late laird, began to repair the castle, or rather to complete it : but he did not live to finish his undertaking. Not doubting, however, that he should do it, he, like those who have had their epitaphs written before they died, ordered the following inscription, composed by the minister of the parish, to be cut upon a broad stone above one of the lower windows, where it still remains to celebrate what was not done, and to serve as a memento of the uncertainty of life, and the presumption of man :

" Joannes Macleod Beganoduni Dominus gentis suæ Philarchus, Durinesiæ Haraiæ Vaternesiæ, &c. : Baro D. Floræ Macdonald matrimoniali vinculo conjugatus turrem hanc Beganodunensem proavorum habitaculum longe vetustissimum diu penitus labefectatam Anno æræ vulgaris MDCLXXXVI instauravit.

> " Quem stabilire juvat proavorum tecta vetusta,
> Omne scelus fugiat, justitiamque colat.
> Vertit in aerias turres magalia virtus,
> Inque casas humiles tecta superba nefas."

M'Leod and Talisker accompanied us. We passed by the parish church of Durinish. The church-yard is not enclosed, but a pretty murmuring brook runs along one side of it.   In it is a pyramid erected to the memory of Thomas Lord Lovat, by his son Lord Simon, who suffered on Tower-hill.   It is of freestone, and, I suppose, about thirty feet high.   There is an inscription on a piece of white marble inserted in it, which I suspect to have been the composition of Lord Lovat himself, being much in his pompous style :

" This pyramid was erected by SIMON LORD FRASER of LOVAT, in honour of Lord THOMAS his Father, a Peer of Scotland, and Chief of the great and ancient Clan of the FRASERS.   Being attacked for his birthright by the family of ATHOLL, then in power and favour with KING WILLIAM, yet, by the valour and fidelity of his clan, and the assistance of the CAMPBELLS, the old friends and allies of his family, he defended his birthright with such greatness and fermety of soul, and such valour and activity, that he was an honour to his name, and a good pattern to all brave Chiefs of clans.   He died in the month of May, 1699, in the 63rd year of his age, in Dunvegan, the house of the LAIRD of MAC LEOD, whose sister he had married : by whom he had the above SIMON LORD FRASER, and several other children.   And, for the great love he bore to the family of MAC LEOD, he desired to be buried near his wife's relations, in the place where two of her uncles lay.   And his son LORD SIMON, to shew to posterity his great affection for his mother's kindred, the brave MAC LEODS, chooses rather to leave his father's bones with them, than carry them to his own burial-place, near Lovat."

I have preserved this inscription, though of no great value, thinking it characteristical of a man who has made some noise in the world.   Dr. Johnson said, it was poor stuff, such as Lord Lovat's butler might have written.

I observed, in this church-yard, a parcel of people assembled at a funeral, before the grave was dug.   The coffin, with the corpse in it, was placed on the ground, while the people alternately assisted in making a grave. One man, at a little distance, was busy cutting a long turf for it, with the crooked spade which is used in Sky; a very aukward instrument. The iron part of it is like a plough-coulter. It has a rude tree for a handle, in which a wooden pin is placed for the foot to press upon. A traveller might, without further enquiry, have set this down as the mode of burying in Sky. I was told, however, that the usual way is to have a grave previously dug.

I observed to-day, that the common way of carrying home their grain here is in loads on horseback. They have also a few sleds, or *cars*, as we call them in Ayrshire, clumsily made, and rarely used.

We got to Ulinish about six o'clock, and found a very good farm-house, of two stories. Mr. M'Leod of Ulinish, the sheriff-substitute of the island, was a plain honest gentleman, a good deal like an English justice of peace; not much given to talk, but sufficiently sagacious, and somewhat droll. His daughter, though she was never out of Sky, was a very well-bred woman. —Our reverend friend, Mr. Donald M'Queen, kept his appointment, and met us here.

Talking of Phipps's voyage to the North Pole, Dr. Johnson observed, that it " was conjectured that our former navigators have kept too near land, and so have found the sea frozen far north, because the land hinders the free motion of the tide; but, in the wide ocean, where the waves tumble at their full convenience, it is imagined that the frost does not take effect."

Wednesday, 22nd September

In the morning I walked out, and saw a ship, the *Margaret* of Clyde, pass by with a number of emigrants on board. It was a melancholy sight.—After breakfast, we went to see what was called a subterraneous house, about a mile off. It was upon the side of a rising-ground. It was discovered by a fox's having taken up his abode in it, and in chacing him, they dug into it. It was very narrow and low, and seemed about forty feet in length. Near it, we found the foundations of several small huts, built of stone.—Mr. M'Queen, who is always for making every thing as ancient as possible, boasted that it was the dwelling of some of the first inhabitants of the island, and observed, what a curiosity it was to find here a specimen of the houses of the Aborigines, which he believed could be found no where else ; and it was plain that they lived without fire.—Dr. Johnson remarked, that they who made this were not in the rudest state ; for that it was more difficult to make *it* than to build a house ; therefore certainly those who made it were in possession of houses, and had this only as a hiding-place.—It appeared to me, that the vestiges of houses, just by it, confirmed Dr. Johnson's opinion.

From an old tower, near this place, is an extensive view of Loch-Braccadil, and, at a distance, of the isles of Barra and South Uist ; and on the land-side, the Cuillin, a prodigious range of mountains, capped with rocky pinnacles in a strange variety of shapes. They resemble the mountains near Corté in Corsica, of which there is a very good print. They make part of a great range for deer, which, though entirely devoid of trees, is in these countries called a *forest*.

In the afternoon, Ulinish carried us in his boat to an island possessed by him, where we saw an immense cave, much more deserving the title of *antrum immane* than that of the Sybil described by Virgil, which I likewise have visited. It is one hundred and eighty feet long, about thirty feet broad, and at least thirty feet high. This cave, we were told, had a remarkable echo ; but we found none. They said it was owing

to the great rains having made it damp. Such are
the excuses by which the exaggeration of Highland
narratives is palliated.—There is a plentiful garden at
Ulinish, (a great rarity in Sky,) and several trees ;
and near the house is a hill, which has an Erse name,
signifying " the hill of strife," where, Mr. M'Queen
informed us, justice was of old administered. It is like
the *mons placiti* of Scone, or those hills which are called
laws, such as Kelly Law, North-Berwick Law, and
several others. It is singular that this spot should
happen now to be the sheriff's residence.

We had a very cheerful evening, and Dr. Johnson
talked a good deal on the subject of literature.—Speaking of the noble family of Boyle, he said, that all the
Lord Orrerys, till the present, had been writers. The
first wrote several plays ; the second was Bentley's antagonist ; the third wrote the *Life of Swift*, and several
other things ; his son Hamilton wrote some papers in
the *Adventurer* and *World*. He told us, he was well
acquainted with Swift's Lord Orrery. He said, he
was a feeble-minded man ; that, on the publication
of Dr. Delany's *Remarks* on his book, he was so much
alarmed that he was afraid to read them. Dr. Johnson comforted him, by telling him they were both
in the right ; that Delany had seen most of the good
side of Swift,—Lord Orrery most of the bad.—M'Leod
asked, if it was not wrong in Orrery to expose the de-
fects of a man with whom he lived in intimacy.—JOHN-
SON. " Why no, sir, after the man is dead ; for then it
is done historically." He added, " If Lord Orrery had
been rich, he would have been a very liberal patron.
His conversation was like his writings, neat and elegant,
but without strength. He grasped at more than his
abilities could reach ; tried to pass for a better talker,
a better writer, and a better thinker than he was. There
was a quarrel between him and his father, in which his
father was to blame ; because it arose from the son's not

allowing his wife to keep company with his father's mistress. The old lord shewed his resentment in his will, —leaving his library from his son, and assigning, as his reason, that he could not make use of it."

I mentioned the affectation of Orrery, in ending all his letters on the *Life of Swift* in studied varieties of phrase, and never in the common mode of "*I am*," &c. an observation which I remember to have been made several years ago by old Mr. Sheridan. This species of affectation in writing, as a foreign lady of distinguished talents once remarked to me, is almost peculiar to the English. I took up a volume of Dryden, containing the *Conquest of Granada*, and several other plays, of which all the dedications had such studied conclusions. Dr. Johnson said, such conclusions were more elegant, and, in addressing persons of high rank, (as when Dryden dedicated to the Duke of York,) they were likewise more respectful. I agreed that *there* it was much better : it was making his escape from the Royal presence with a genteel sudden timidity, in place of having the resolution to stand still, and make a formal bow.

Lord Orrery's unkind treatment of his son in his will, led us to talk of the dispositions a man should have when dying. I said, I did not see why a man should act differently with respect to those of whom he thought ill when in health, merely because he was dying.—JOHNSON. "I should not scruple to speak against a party, when dying ; but should not do it against an individual.—It is told of Sixtus Quintus, that on his death-bed, in the intervals of his last pangs, he signed death-warrants."—Mr. M'Queen said, he should not do so ; he would have more tenderness of heart.—JOHNSON. "I believe I should not either ; but Mr. M'Queen and I are cowards. It would not be from tenderness of heart ; for the heart is as tender when a man is in health as when he is sick, though his resolution may be stronger. Sixtus Quintus was a sovereign as well as a priest ; and, if the criminals deserved death, he was doing his duty to the last. You would not think a judge died ill, who should be carried off by an apoplectick fit while pronouncing sentence of death. Consider a class of men whose business it is to distribute death :—soldiers, who die scattering bullets.—Nobody thinks they die ill on that account."

Talking of Biography, he said, he did not think that the life of any literary man in England had been well written. Beside the common incidents of life, it should tell us his studies, his mode of living, the means by which he attained to excellence, and his opinion of his own works. He told us, he had sent Derrick to Dryden's relations, to gather materials for his *Life;* and he believed Derrick had got all that he himself should have got ; but it was nothing. He added, he had a kindness for Derrick, and was sorry he was dead.

His notion as to the poems published by Mr. M'Pherson, as the works of Ossian, was not shaken here. Mr. M'Queen always evaded the point of authenticity, saying only that Mr. M'Pherson's pieces fell far short of those he knew in Erse, which were said to be Ossian's. —JOHNSON. " I hope they do. I am not disputing that you may have poetry of great merit ; but that M'Pherson's is not a translation from ancient poetry. You do not believe it. I say before you, you do not believe it, though you are very willing that the world should believe it."—Mr. M'Queen made no answer to this.— Dr. Johnson proceeded, " I look upon M'Pherson's *Fingal* to be as gross an imposition as ever the world was troubled with. Had it been really an ancient work, a true specimen how men thought at that time, it would have been a curiosity of the first rate. As a modern production, it is nothing."—He said, he could never get the meaning of an Erse song explained to him. They told him, the chorus was generally unmeaning.

" I take it, (said he,) Erse songs are like a song which I
remember : it was composed in Queen Elizabeth's time,
on the Earl of Essex ; and the burthen was

" ' Radaratoo, radarate, radara tadara tandore.' "

" But surely," said Mr. M'Queen, " there were words
to it, which had meaning."—JOHNSON. " Why, yes,
sir ; I recollect a stanza, and you shall have it :

" ' O ! then bespoke the prentices all,
    Living in London, both proper and tall,
    For Essex's sake they would fight all.
        Radaratoo, radarate, radara, tadara, tandore.' "

When Mr. M'Queen began again to expatiate on the
beauty of Ossian's poetry, Dr. Johnson entered into no
further controversy, but, with a pleasant smile, only
cried, " Ay, ay ; Radaratoo radarate."

Thursday, 23rd September

I took *Fingal* down to the parlour in the morning,
and tried a test proposed by Mr. Roderick M'Leod,
son to Ulinish. Mr. M'Queen had said he had some
of the poem in the original. I desired him to mention
any passage in the printed book, of which he could
repeat the original. He pointed out one in page 50
of the quarto edition, and read the Erse, while Mr.
Roderick M'Leod and I looked on the English ;—
and Mr. M'Leod said, that it was pretty like what Mr.
M'Queen had recited. But when Mr. M'Queen read
a description of Cuchullin's sword in Erse, together
with a translation of it in English verse, by Sir James
Foulis, Mr. M'Leod said, that was much more like
than Mr. M'Pherson's translation of the former passage.
Mr. M'Queen then repeated in Erse a description of

one of the horses in Cuchillin's car. Mr. M'Leod said,
Mr. M'Pherson's English was nothing like it.

When Dr. Johnson came down, I told him that I
had now obtained some evidence concerning Fingal;
for that Mr. M'Queen had repeated a passage in the
original Erse, which Mr. M'Pherson's translation was
pretty like ; and reminded him that he himself had
once said, he did not require Mr. M'Pherson's Ossian
to be more like the original than Pope's Homer.—
JOHNSON. " Well, sir, this is just what I always maintained. He has found names, and stories, and phrases,
nay passages in old songs, and with them has blended
his own compositions, and so made what he gives to
the world as the translation of an ancient poem."—
If this was the case, I observed, it was wrong to publish it as a poem in six books.—JOHNSON. " Yes, sir ;
and to ascribe it to a time too when the Highlanders
knew nothing of *books*, and nothing of *six* ;—or perhaps
were got the length of counting six. We have been
told, by Condamine, of a nation that could count no
more than four. This should be told to Monboddo ;
it would help him. There is as much charity in helping
a man down-hill, as in helping him up-hill."—BOSWELL.
" I don't think there is as much charity."—JOHNSON.
" Yes, sir, if his *tendency* be downwards. Till he is at
the bottom, he flounders ; get him once there, and he
is quiet. Swift tells, that Stella had a trick, which she
learned from Addison, of encouraging a man in absurdity,
instead of endeavouring to extricate him."

Mr. M'Queen's answers to the inquiries concerning
Ossian were so unsatisfactory, that I could not help
observing, that, were he examined in a court of justice,
he would find himself under a necessity of being more
explicit.—JOHNSON. " Sir, he has told Blair a little
too much, which is published ; and he sticks to it.
He is so much at the head of things here, that he has
never been accustomed to be closely examined ; and

so he goes on quite smoothly."—BOSWELL. "He has never had any body to work him."—JOHNSON. "No, sir ; and a man is seldom disposed to work himself ; though he ought to work himself, to be sure."—Mr. M'Queen made no reply.

Having talked of the strictness with which witnesses are examined in courts of justice, Dr. Johnson told us, that Garrick, though accustomed to face multitudes, when produced as a witness in Westminster-hall, was so disconcerted by a new mode of publick appearance, that he could not understand what was asked. It was a cause where an actor claimed a *free benefit ;* that is to say, a benefit without paying the expence of the house ; but the meaning of the term was disputed. Garrick was asked, " Sir, have you a free benefit ? "—" Yes."—" Upon what terms have you it ? "—" Upon—the terms—of—a free benefit." —He was dismissed as one from whom no information could be obtained.—Dr. Johnson is often too hard on our friend Mr. Garrick. When I asked him, why he did not mention him in the Preface to his Shakspeare, he said, " Garrick has been liberally paid for any thing he has done for Shakspeare. If I should praise him, I should much more praise the nation who paid him. He has not made Shakspeare better known ; he cannot illustrate Shakspeare : So I have reasons enough against mentioning him, were reasons necessary. There should be reasons *for* it."—I spoke of Mrs. Montague's very high praises of Garrick.—JOHNSON. " Sir, it is fit she should say so much, and I should say nothing. Reynolds is fond of her book, and I wonder at it ; for neither I, nor Beauclerk, nor Mrs. Thrale, could get through it."

Last night Dr. Johnson gave us an account of the whole process of tanning,—and of the nature of milk, and the various operations upon it, as making whey, &c. His variety of information is surprising ; and it gives one much satisfaction to find such a man bestowing his attention on the useful arts of life. Ulinish was much struck with his knowledge; and said, " He is a great orator, sir; it is musick to hear this man speak."—A strange thought struck me, to try if he knew any thing of an art, or whatever it should be called, which is no doubt very useful in life, but which lies far out of the way of a philosopher and poet; I mean the trade of a butcher. I enticed him into the subject, by connecting it with the various researches into the manners and customs of uncivilized nations, that have been made by our late navigators into the South Seas.—I began with observing, that Mr. (now Sir Joseph) Banks tells us, that the art of slaughtering animals was not known in Otaheite, for, instead of bleeding to death their dogs, (a common food with them,) they strangle them. This he told me himself; and I supposed that their hogs were killed in the same way. Dr. Johnson said, " This must be owing to their not having knives,—though they have sharp stones with which they can cut a carcase in pieces tolerably." By degrees, he shewed that he knew something even of butchery. " Different animals (said he) are killed differently. An ox is knocked down, and a calf stunned; but a sheep has its throat cut, without any thing being done to stupify it. The butchers have no view to the ease of the animals, but only to make them quiet, for their own safety and convenience. A sheep can give them little trouble.— Hales is of opinion, that every animal should be blooded, without having any blow given to it, because it bleeds better."—BOSWELL. " That would be cruel."—JOHNSON. " No, sir; there is not much pain, if the jugular vein be properly cut."—Pursuing the subject, he said, the kennels of Southwark ran with blood two or three days in the week; that he was afraid there were slaughter-houses in more streets in London than one supposes;

(speaking with a kind of horrour of butchering;) and yet, he added, "any of us would kill a cow, rather than not have beef."—I said we *could* not.—"Yes, (said he,) any one may. The business of a butcher is a trade indeed, that is to say, there is an apprenticeship served to it; but it may be learnt in a month."

I mentioned a club in London, at the Boar's Head in Eastcheap, the very tavern where Falstaff and his joyous companions met; the members of which all assume Shakspeare's characters. One is Falstaff, another Prince Henry, another Bardolph, and so on.— JOHNSON. "Don't be of it, sir. Now that you have a name, you must be careful to avoid many things, not bad in themselves, but which will lessen your character. This every man who has a name must observe. A man who is not publickly known may live in London as he pleases, without any notice being taken of him; but it is wonderful how a person of any consequence is watched. There was a member of parliament, who wanted to prepare himself to speak on a question that was to come on in the House; and he and I were to talk it over together. He did not wish it should be known that he talked with me; so he would not let me come to his house, but came to mine. Some time after he had made his speech in the house, Mrs. Cholmondeley, a very airy lady, told me, ' Well, you could make nothing of him!' naming the gentleman; which was a proof that he was watched.—I had once some business to do for government, and I went to Lord North's. Precaution was taken that it should not be known. It was dark before I went; yet a few days after I was told, ' Well, you have been with Lord North.' That the door of the prime minister should be watched, is not strange; but that a member of parliament should be watched, or that my door should be watched, is wonderful."

We set out this morning on our way to Talisker,

in Ulinish's boat, having taken leave of him and his family. Mr. Donald M'Queen still favoured us with his company, for which we were much obliged to him. As we sailed along Dr. Johnson got into one of his fits of railing at the Scots. He owned that they had been a very learned nation for a hundred years, from about 1550 to about 1650; but that they afforded the only instance of a people among whom the arts of civil life did not advance in proportion with learning; that they had hardly any trade, any money, or any elegance, before the Union; that it was strange that, with all the advantages possessed by other nations, they had not any of those conveniencies and embellishments which are the fruit of industry, till they came in contact with a civilized people. "We have taught you, (said he,) and we'll do the same in time to all barbarous nations,—to the Cherokees,—and at last to the Ouran-Outangs;" laughing with as much glee as if Monboddo had been present.—BOSWELL. "We had wine before the Union."—JOHNSON. "No, sir; you had some weak stuff, the refuse of France, which would not make you drunk."—BOSWELL. "I assure you, sir, there was a great deal of drunkenness."—JOHNSON. "No, sir; there were people who died of dropsies, which they contracted in trying to get drunk."

I must here glean some of his conversation at Ulinish, which I have omitted. He repeated his remark, that a man in a ship was worse than a man in a jail. "The man in a jail, (said he,) has more room, better food, and commonly better company, and is in safety."—"Ay; but, (said Mr. M'Queen,) the man in the ship has the pleasing hope of getting to shore."—JOHNSON. "Sir, I am not talking of a man's getting to shore; but of a man while he is in a ship: and then, I say, he is worse than a man while he is in a jail. A man in a jail *may* have the 'pleasing hope' of getting out. A man confined for only a limited time, actually *has* it."—M'Leod mentioned his schemes for carrying on fisheries with spirit, and that he would wish to understand the construction of boats. I suggested that he might go to a dock-yard and work, as Peter the Great did.—JOHNSON. "Nay, sir, he need not work. Peter the Great had not the sense to see that the mere mechanical work may be done by any body, and that there is the same art in constructing a vessel, whether the boards are well or ill wrought. Sir Christopher Wren might as well have served his time to a bricklayer, and first, indeed, to a brickmaker."

There is a beautiful little island in the Loch of Dunvegan, called Isa. M'Leod said, he would give it to Dr. Johnson, on condition of his residing on it three months in the year; nay one month. Dr. Johnson was highly amused with the fancy. I have seen him please himself with little things, even with mere ideas like the present. He talked a great deal of this island; —how he would build a house there,—how he would fortify it,—how he would have cannon,—how he would plant,—how he would sally out, and *take* the isle of Muck;—and then he laughed with uncommon glee, and could hardly leave off. I have seen him do so at a small matter that struck him, and was a sport to no one else. Mr. Langton told me, that one night he did so while the company were all grave about him:— only Garrick, in his significant smart manner darting his eyes around, exclaimed, "*Very* jocose, to be sure!" —M'Leod encouraged the fancy of Dr. Johnson's becoming owner of an island; told him, that it was the practice in this country to name every man by his lands; and begged leave to drink to him in that mode: "Island Isa, your health!"—Ulinish, Talisker, Mr. M'Queen, and I, all joined in our different manners, while Dr. Johnson bowed to each, with much good humour.

We had good weather, and a fine sail this day. The shore was varied with hills, and rocks, and corn-fields, and bushes, which are here dignified with the name of natural *wood*. We landed near the house of Ferneley, a farm possessed by another gentleman of the name of M'Leod, who, expecting our arrival, was waiting on the shore, with a horse for Dr. Johnson. The rest of us walked.—At dinner, I expressed to M'Leod the joy which I had in seeing him on such cordial terms with his clan. " Government (said he) has deprived us of our ancient power ; but it cannot deprive us of our domestick satisfactions. I would rather drink punch in one of their houses, (meaning the houses of his people,) than be enabled by their hardships, to have claret in my own."—This should be the sentiment of every Chieftain. All that he can get by raising his rents, is more luxury in his own house. Is it not better to share the profits of his estate, to a certain degree, with his kinsmen, and thus have both social intercourse and patriarchal influence ?

We had a very good ride, for about three miles, to Talisker, where Colonel M'Leod introduced us to his lady. We found here Mr. Donald M'Lean, the young Laird of Col, (nephew to Talisker,) to whom I delivered the letter with which I had been favoured by his uncle, Professor M'Leod, at Aberdeen. He was a little lively young man. We found he had been a good deal in England, studying farming, and was resolved to improve the value of his father's lands, without oppressing his tenants, or losing the ancient Highland fashions.

Talisker is a better place than one commonly finds in Sky. It is situated in a rich bottom. Before it is a wide expanse of sea, on each hand of which are immense rocks ; and, at some distance in the sea, three are three columnal rocks rising to sharp points. The billows break with prodigious force and noise on the coast of Talisker. There are here a good many well-grown trees. Talisker is an extensive farm. The possessor of it has, for several generations, been the next heir to M'Leod, as there has been but one son always in that family. The court before the house is most injudiciously paved with the round blueish-grey pebbles which are found upon the sea-shore; so that you walk as if upon cannon-balls driven into the ground.

After supper, I talked of the assiduity of the Scottish clergy, in visiting and privately instructing their parishioners, and observed how much in this they excelled the English clergy. Dr. Johnson would not let this pass. He tried to turn it off by saying, "There are different ways of instructing. Our clergy pray and preach."—M'Leod and I pressed the subject, upon which he grew warm, and broke forth: "I do not believe your people are better instructed. If they are, it is the blind leading the blind; for your clergy are not instructed themselves." Thinking he had gone a little too far, he checked himself, and added, "When I talk of the ignorance of your clergy, I talk of them as a body: I do not mean that there are not individuals who are learned (looking at Mr. M'Queen). I suppose there are such among the clergy in Muscovy. The clergy of England have produced the most valuable books in support of religion, both in theory and practice. What have your clergy done, since you sunk into presbyterianism? Can you name one book of any value, on a religious subject, written by them?"—We were silent. —"I'll help you. Forbes wrote very well; but I believe he wrote before episcopacy was quite extinguished."— And then pausing a little, he said, "Yes, you have Wishart AGAINST Repentance."—BOSWELL. "But, sir, we are not contending for the superior learning of our clergy, but for their superior assiduity."—He bore us down again, with thundering against their ignorance, and said to me, "I see you have not been well taught; for you have not charity."—He had been in some measure forced into this warmth, by the exulting air which I assumed; for, when he began, he said, "Since you *will* drive the nail ! "—He again thought of good Mr. M'Queen, and, taking him by the hand, said, " Sir, I did not mean any disrespect to you."

Here I must observe, that he conquered by deserting his ground, and not meeting the argument as I had put it. The assiduity of the Scottish clergy is certainly greater than that of the English. His taking up the topick of their not having so much learning, was, though ingenious, yet a fallacy in logick. It was as if there should be a dispute whether a man's hair is well dressed, and Dr. Johnson should say, " Sir, his hair cannot be well dressed ; for he has a dirty shirt. No man who has not clean linen has his hair well dressed."—When some days afterwards he read this passage, he said, " No, sir ; I did not say that a man's hair could not be well dressed because he has not clean linen, but because he is bald."

He used one argument against the Scottish clergy being learned, which I doubt was not good. " As we believe a man dead till we know that he is alive ; so we believe men ignorant till we know that they are learned." Now our maxim in law is, to presume a man alive, till we know he is dead. However, indeed, it may be answered, that we must first know he has lived ; and that we have never known the learning of the Scottish clergy. Mr. M'Queen, though he was of opinion that Dr. Johnson had deserted the point really in dispute, was much pleased with what he said, and owned to me, he thought it very just ; and Mrs. M'Leod was so much captivated by his eloquence, that she told me " I was a good advocate for a bad cause."

Friday, 24th September

This was a good day. Dr. Johnson told us, at breakfast, that he rode harder at a fox chace than any body.

" The English (said he) are the only nation who ride
hard a-hunting. A Frenchman goes out upon a managed
horse, and capers in the field, and no more thinks of
leaping a hedge than of mounting a breach. Lord
Powerscourt laid a wager, in France, that he would
ride a great many miles in a certain short time. The
French academicians set to work, and calculated that,
from the resistance of the air, it was impossible. His
lordship however performed it."

Our money being nearly exhausted, we sent a bill for
thirty pounds, drawn on Sir William Forbes and Co. to
Lochbraccadale, but our messenger found it very difficult
to procure cash for it ; at length, however, he got us
value from the master of a vessel which was to carry
away some emigrants. There is a great scarcity of
specie in Sky. Mr. M'Queen said he had the utmost
difficulty to pay his servants' wages, or to pay for any
little thing which he has to buy. The rents are paid
in bills, which the drovers give. The people consume
a vast deal of snuff and tobacco, for which they must
pay ready money ; and pedlers, who come about selling
goods, as there is not a shop in the island, carry away
the cash. If there were encouragement given to fisheries and manufactures, there might be a circulation of
money introduced. I got one-and-twenty shillings in
silver at Portree, which was thought a wonderful
store.

Talisker, Mr. M'Queen, and I, walked out, and looked
at no less than fifteen different waterfalls near the
house, in the space of about a quarter of a mile. We
also saw Cuchillin's well, said to have been the favourite
spring of that ancient hero. I drank of it. The water
is admirable. On the shore are many stones full of
crystallizations in the heart.

Though our obliging friend, Mr. M'Lean, was but the
young laird, he had the title of Col constantly given
him. After dinner he and I walked to the top of Priesh-

well, a very high rocky hill, from whence there is a view of Barra,—the Long Island,—Bernera,—the Loch of Dunvegan,—part of Rum—part of Rasay, and a vast deal of the isle of Sky. Col, though he had come into Sky with an intention to be at Dunvegan, and pass a considerable time in the island, most politely resolved first to conduct us to Mull, and then to return to Sky. This was a very fortunate circumstance; for he planned an expedition for us of more variety than merely going to Mull. He proposed we should see the islands of Egg, Muck, Col, and Tyr-yi. In all these islands he could shew us every thing worth seeing; and in Mull he said he should be as if at home, his father having lands there, and he a farm.

Dr. Johnson did not talk much to-day, but seemed intent in listening to the schemes of future excursion, planned by Col. Dr. Birch, however, being mentioned, he said, he had more anecdotes than any man. I said, Percy had a great many; that he flowed with them like one of the brooks here.—JOHNSON. " If Percy is like one of the brooks here, Birch was like the river Thames. Birch excelled Percy in that, as much as Percy excels Goldsmith."—I mentioned Lord Hailes as a man of anecdote. He was not pleased with him, for publishing only such memorials and letters as were unfavourable for the Stuart family. " If, (said he), a man fairly warns you, ' I am to give all the ill; do you find the good;' he may: but if the object which he professes be to give a view of a reign, let him tell all the truth. I would tell the truth of the two Georges, or of that scoundrel, king William.—Granger's *Biographical History* is full of curious anecdote, but might have been better done. The dog is a Whig. I do not like much to see a Whig in any dress; but I hate to see a Whig in a parson's gown."

Saturday, 25th September

It was resolved that we should set out, in order to return to Slate, to be in readiness to take boat whenever there should be a fair wind. Dr. Johnson remained in his chamber writing a letter, and it was long before we could get him into motion. He did not come to breakfast, but had it sent to him. When he had finished his letter, it was twelve o'clock, and we should have set out at ten. When I went up to him, he said to me, " Do you remember a song which begins,

> ' Every island is a prison
>   Strongly guarded by the sea ;
> Kings and princes, for that reason,
>   Prisoners are, as well as we.' "

I suppose he had been thinking of our confined situation. He would fain have gone in a boat from hence, instead of riding back to Slate. A scheme for it was proposed. He said, " We'll not be driven tamely from it : "—but it proved impracticable.

We took leave of M'Leod and Talisker, from whom we parted with regret. Talisker, having been bred to physick, had a tincture of scholarship in his conversation, which pleased Dr. Johnson, and he had some very good books ; and being a colonel in the Dutch service, he and his lady, in consequence of having lived abroad, had introduced the ease and politeness of the continent into this rude region.

Young Col was now our leader. Mr. M'Queen was to accompany us half a day more. We stopped at a little hut, where we saw an old woman grinding with the *quern*, the ancient Highland instrument, which it is said was used by the Romans, but which, being very slow in its operation, is almost entirely gone into disuse.

The walls of the cottages in Sky, instead of being

one compacted mass of stones, are often formed by two exterior surfaces of stone, filled up with earth in the middle, which makes them very warm. The roof is generally bad. They are thatched, sometimes with straw, sometimes with heath, sometimes with fern. The thatch is secured by ropes of straw, or of heath ; and, to fix the ropes, there is a stone tied to the end of each. These stones hang round the bottom of the roof, and make it look like a lady's hair in papers ; but I should think that, when there is wind, they would come down, and knock people on the head.

We dined at the inn at Sconser, where I had the pleasure to find a letter from my wife. Here we parted from our learned companion, Mr. Donald M'Queen. Dr. Johnson took leave of him very affectionately, saying, " Dear sir, do not forget me ! "—We settled, that he should write an account of the Isle of Sky, which Dr. Johnson promised to revise. He said, Mr. M'Queen should tell all that he could ; distinguishing what he himself knew, what was traditional, and what conjectural.

We sent our horses round a point of land, that we might shun some very bad road ; and resolved to go forward by sea. It was seven o'clock when we got into our boat. We had many showers, and it soon grew pretty dark. Dr. Johnson sat silent and patient. Once he said, as he looked on the black coast of Sky,—black, as being composed of rocks seen in the dusk,—" This is very solemn." Our boatmen were rude singers, and seemed so like wild Indians, that a very little imagination was necessary to give one an impression of being upon an American river. We landed at Strolimus, from whence we got a guide to walk before us, for two miles, to Corrichatachin. Not being able to procure a horse for our baggage, I took one portmanteau before me, and Joseph another. We had but a single star to light us on our way. It was about eleven when we arrived.

8

We were most hospitably received by the master and mistress, who were just going to bed, but, with unaffected ready kindness, made a good fire, and at twelve o'clock at night had supper on the table.

James Macdonald, of Knockow, Kingsburgh's brother, whom we had seen at Kingsburgh, was there. He shewed me a bond granted by the late Sir James Macdonald, to old Kingsburgh, the preamble of which does so much honour to the feelings of that much-lamented gentleman, that I thought it worth transcribing. It was as follows :

" I, Sir James Macdonald, of Macdonald, Baronet, now, after arriving at my perfect age, from the friendship I bear to Alexander Macdonald of Kingsburgh, and in return for the long and faithful services done and performed by him to my deceased father, and to myself during my minority, when he was one of my Tutors and Curators ; being resolved, now that the said Alexander Macdonald is advanced in years, to contribute my endeavours for making his old age placid and comfortable,"—therefore he grants him an annuity of fifty pounds sterling.

Dr. Johnson went to bed soon. When one bowl of punch was finished, I rose, and was near the door, in my way up stairs to bed ; but Corrichatachin said, it was the first time Col had been in his house, and he should have his bowl ;—and would not I join in drinking it ? The heartiness of my honest landlord, and the desire of doing social honour to our very obliging conductor, induced me to sit down again. Col's bowl was finished ; and by that time we were well warmed. A third bowl was soon made, and that too was finished. We were cordial, and merry to a high degree ; but of what passed I have no recollection, with any accuracy. I remember calling Corrichatachin by the familiar appellation of Corri, which his friends do. A fourth

bowl was made, by which time Col, and young M'Kinnon,
Corrichatachin's son, slipped away to bed. I continued
a little with *Corri* and *Knockow;* but at last I left
them. It was near five in the morning when I got
to bed.

Sunday, 26th September

I awaked at noon, with a severe head-ach. I was
much vexed that I should have been guilty of such a
riot, and afraid of a reproof from Dr. Johnson. I
thought it very inconsistent with that conduct which
I ought to maintain, while the companion of the
Rambler. About one he came into my room, and
accosted me, " What, drunk yet ? "—His tone of
voice was not that of severe upbraiding; so I was
relieved a little.—" Sir, (said I,) they kept me up."
—He answered, " No, you kept them up, you drunken
dog : "—This he said with good-humoured *English*
pleasantry. Soon afterwards, Corrichatachin, Col, and
other friends assembled round my bed. *Corri* had
a brandy-bottle and glass with him, and insisted I
should take a dram.—" Ay, (said Dr. Johnson,) fill
him drunk again. Do it in the morning, that we may
laugh at him all day. It is a poor thing for a fellow
to get drunk at night, and sculk to bed, and let his
friends have no sport."—Finding him thus jocular, I
became quite easy; and when I offered to get up, he
very good-naturedly said, " You need be in no such
hurry now."—I took my host's advice, and drank
some brandy, which I found an effectual cure for my
head-ach. When I rose, I went into Dr. Johnson's
room, and taking up Mrs. M'Kinnon's Prayer-book, I
opened it at the twentieth Sunday after Trinity, in the
epistle for which I read, " And be not drunk with wine,
wherein there is excess." Some would have taken this
as a divine interposition.

Mrs. M'Kinnon told us at dinner, that old Kingsburgh, her father, was examined at Mugstot, by General Campbell, as to the particulars of the dress of the person who had come to his house in woman's clothes, along with Miss Flora M'Donald ; as the General had received intelligence of that disguise. The particulars were taken down in writing, that it might be seen how far they agreed with the dress of the *Irish girl* who went with Miss Flora from the Long Island. Kingsburgh, she said, had but one song, which he always sung when he was merry over a glass. She dictated the words to me, which are foolish enough :

> Green sleeves and pudding pies,
> Tell me where my mistress lies,
> And I'll be with her before she rise,
> Fiddle and aw' together.
>
> May our affairs abroad succeed,
> And may our king come home with speed,
> And all pretenders shake for dread,
> And let *his* health go round.
>
> To all our injured friends in need,
> This side and beyond the Tweed !—
> Let all pretenders shake for dread,
> And let *his* health go round.
> Green sleeves, &c.

While the examination was going on, the present Talisker, who was there as one of M'Leod's militia, could not resist the pleasantry of asking Kingsburgh, in allusion to his only song, " Had she green sleeves ? " Kingsburgh gave him no answer. Lady Margaret M'Donald was very angry at Talisker for joking on such a serious occasion, as Kingsburgh was really in danger of his life.—Mrs. M'Kinnon added that Lady Margaret was quite adored in Sky. That when she travelled through the island, the people ran in crowds before her, and took the stones off the road, lest her horse should stumble and she be hurt. Her husband,

Sir Alexander, is also remembered with great regard. We were told that every week a hogshead of claret was drunk at his table.

This was another day of wind and rain ; but good cheer and good society helped to beguile the time. I felt myself comfortable enough in the afternoon. I then thought that my last night's riot was no more than such a social excess as may happen without much moral blame ; and recollected that some physicians maintained, that a fever produced by it was, upon the whole, good for health : so different are our reflections on the same subject, at different periods ; and such the excuses with which we palliate what we know to be wrong.

Monday, 27th September

Mr. Donald M'Leod, our original guide, who had parted from us at Dunvegan, joined us again to-day. The weather was still so bad that we could not travel. I found a closet here, with a good many books, beside those that were lying about. Dr. Johnson told me, he found a library in his room at Talisker ; and observed, that it was one of the remarkable things of Sky, that there were so many books in it.

Though we had here great abundance of provisions, it is remarkable that Corrichatachin has literally no garden : not even a turnip, a carrot or a cabbage.— After dinner, we talked of the crooked spade used in Sky, already described, and they maintained that it was better than the usual garden-spade, and that there was an art in tossing it, by which those who were accustomed to it could work very easily with it.—" Nay, (said Dr. Johnson,) it may be useful in land where there are many stones to raise ; but it certainly is not a good instrument for digging good land. A man may toss it, to be sure ; but he will toss a light spade much better : its weight makes it an incumbrance. A man *may* dig any land with it ; but he has no occasion for such a weight in digging good land. You may take a field piece to shoot sparrows ; but all the sparrows you can bring home will not be worth the charge."—He was quite social and easy amongst them ; and, though he drank no fermented liquor, toasted Highland beauties with great readiness. His conviviality engaged them so much, that they seemed eager to shew their attention to him, and vied with each other in crying out, with a strong Celtick pronunciation, " Toctor Shonson, Toctor Shonson, your health ! "

This evening one of our married ladies, a lively pretty little woman, good-humouredly sat down upon Dr. Johnson's knee, and, being encouraged by some of the company, put her arms round his neck, and kissed him.—" Do it again, (said he,) and let us see who will tire first."—He kept her on his knee some time, while he and she drank tea. He was now like a *buck* indeed. All the company were much entertained to find him so easy and pleasant. To me it was highly comick, to see the grave philosopher,—the Rambler,—toying with a Highland beauty !—But what could he do ? He must have been surly, and weak too, had he not behaved as he did. He would have been laughed at, and not more respected, though less loved.

He read to-night, to himself, as he sat in company, a great deal of my Journal, and said to me, " The more I read of this, I think the more highly of you."—The gentlemen sat a long time at their punch, after he and I had retired to our chambers. The manner in which they were attended struck me as singular :—The bell being broken, a smart lad lay on a table in the corner of the room, ready to spring up and bring the kettle, whenever it was wanted. They continued drinking, and singing Erse songs, till near five in the morning, when they all came into my room, where some of them had beds. Unluckily for me, they found a bottle of punch in a corner, which they drank ; and Corrichatachin went for another, which they also drank. They made many apologies for disturbing me. I told them, that, having been kept awake by their mirth, I had once thoughts of getting up, and joining them again. Honest Corrichatachin said, " To have had you done so, I would have given a cow."

Tuesday, 28th September

The weather was worse than yesterday. I felt as if imprisoned. Dr. Johnson said, it was irksome to be detained thus : yet he seemed to have less uneasiness, or more patience, than I had. What made our situation worse here was, that we had no rooms that we could command ; for the good people had no notion that a man could have any occasion but for a mere sleeping-place ; so, during the day, the bed chambers were common to all the house. Servants eat in Dr. Johnson's ; and mine was a kind of general rendezvous of all under the roof, children and dogs not excepted. As the gentlemen occupied the parlour, the ladies had no place to sit in, during the day, but Dr. Johnson's room. I had always some quiet time for writing in it, before he was up ; and, by degrees, I accustomed the ladies to let me sit in it after breakfast, at my Journal, without minding me.

Dr. Johnson was this morning for going to see as many islands as we could ; not recollecting the uncertainty of the season, which might detain us in one place for many weeks. He said to me, " I have more the spirit of adventure than you."—For my part, I was anxious to get to Mull, from whence we might almost any day reach the main land.

Dr. Johnson mentioned, that the few ancient Irish

gentlemen yet remaining have the highest pride of
family ; that Mr. Sandford, a friend of his, whose
mother was Irish, told him, that O'Hara (who was
true Irish, both by father and mother) and he, and Mr.
Ponsonby, son to the Earl of Besborough, the greatest
man of the three, but of an English family, went to see
one of those ancient Irish, and that he distinguished
them thus : " O'Hara, you are welcome ! Mr. Sandford, your mother's son is welcome ! Mr. Ponsonby,
you may sit down."

He talked both of threshing and thatching. He said,
it was very difficult to determine how to agree with
a thresher. " If you pay him by the day's wages, he
will thresh no more than he pleases ; though, to be
sure, the negligence of a thresher is more easily detected
than that of most labourers, because he must always
make a sound while he works. If you pay him by the
piece, by the quantity of grain which he produces, he
will thresh only while the grain comes freely, and,
though he leaves a good deal in the ear, it is not worth
while to thresh the straw over again ; nor can you fix
him to do it sufficiently, because it is so difficult to
prove how much less a man threshes than he ought to
do. Here then is a dilemma : but, for my part, I
would engage him by the day : I would rather trust
his idleness than his fraud." He said, a roof thatched
with Lincolnshire reeds would last seventy years, as
he was informed when in that county ; and that he
told this in London to a great thatcher, who said, he
believed it might be true.—Such are the pains that
Dr. Johnson takes to get the best information on every
subject.

He proceeded : " It is difficult for a farmer in England to find day-labourers, because the lowest manu-
facturers can always get more than a day-labourer. It
is of no consequence how high the wages of manu-
facturers are ; but it would be of very bad consequence

to raise the wages of those who procure the immediate necessaries of life, for that would raise the price of provisions. Here then is a problem for politicians. It is not reasonable that the most useful body of men should be the worst paid ; yet it does not appear how it can be ordered otherwise. It were to be wished, that a mode for its being otherwise were found out. In the mean time, it is better to give temporary assistance by charitable contributions to poor labourers, at times when provisions are high, than to raise their wages ; because, if wages are once raised, they will never get down again."

Happily the weather cleared up between one and two o'clock, and we got ready to depart ; but our kind host and hostess would not let us go without taking a *snatch*, as they called it ; which was in truth a very good dinner. While the punch went round, Dr. Johnson kept a close whispering conference with Mrs. M'Kinnon, which, however, was loud enough to let us hear that the subject of it was the particulars of Prince Charles's escape. The company were entertained and pleased to observe it. Upon that subject, there was something congenial between the soul of Dr. Samuel Johnson, and that of an isle of Sky farmer's wife. It is curious to see people, how far soever removed from each other in the general system of their lives, come close together on a particular point which is common to each. We were merry with Corrichatachin, on Dr. Johnson's whispering with his wife. She, perceiving this, humourously cried, " I am in love with him. What is it to live and not to love ? " Upon her saying something, which I did not hear, or cannot recollect, he seized her hand eagerly, and kissed it.

As we were going, the Scottish phrase of " *honest man !* " which is an expression of kindness and regard, was again and again applied by the company to Dr. Johnson. I was also treated with much civility ; and

I must take some merit from my assiduous attention to him, and from my contriving that he shall be easy wherever he goes, that he shall not be asked twice to eat or drink any thing, (which always disgusts him) that he shall be provided with water at his meals, and many such little things, which, if not attended to would fret him. I also may be allowed to claim some merit in leading the conversation : I do not mean leading, as in an orchestra, by playing the first fiddle ; but leading as one does in examining a witness,—starting topics, and making him pursue them. He appears to me like a great mill, into which a subject is thrown to be ground. It requires, indeed, fertile minds to furnish materials for this mill. I regret whenever I see it unemployed ; but sometimes I feel myself quite barren, and having nothing to throw in.—I know not if this mill be a good figure ; though Pope makes his mind a mill for turning verses.

We set out about four. Young Corrichatachin went with us. We had a fine evening, and arrived in good time at Ostig, the residence of Mr. Martin M'Pherson, minister of Slate. It is a pretty good house, built by his father, upon a farm near the church. We were received here with much kindness by Mr. and Mrs. M'Pherson, and his sister, Miss M'Pherson, who pleased Dr. Johnson much, by singing Erse songs, and playing on the guitar. He afterwards sent her a present of his *Rasselas*. In his bed-chamber was a press stored with books, Greek, Latin, French, and English, most of which had belonged to the father of our host, the learned Dr. M'Pherson ; who, though his *Dissertations* have been mentioned in a former page as unsatisfactory, was a man of distinguished talents. Dr. Johnson looked at a Latin paraphrase of the song of Moses, written by him, and published in the *Scots Magazine* for 1747, and said, " It does him honour ; he has a great deal of Latin, and good Latin."—Dr. M'Pherson published also in the same magazine, June 1739, an original Latin ode, which he wrote from the isle of Barra, where he was minister for some years. It is very poetical, and exhibits a striking proof how much all things depend upon comparison : for Barra, it seems, appeared to him so much worse than Sky, his *natale solum*, that he languished for its " blessed mountains," and thought himself buried alive amongst barbarians where he was.—My readers will probably not be displeased to have a specimen of this ode :

> "Hei mihi ! quantos patior dolores,
> Dum procul specto juga ter beata ;
> Dum feræ Barræ steriles arenas
> Solus oberro.

> "Ingemo, indignor, crucior, quod inter
> Barbaros Thulen lateam colentes ;
> Torpeo languens, morior sepultus,
> Carcere cœco."

After wishing for wings to fly over to his dear country, which was in his view, from what he calls *Thule*, as being the most western isle of Scotland, except St. Kilda ; after describing the pleasures of society, and the miseries of solitude, he at last, with becoming propriety, has recourse to the only sure relief of thinking men,—*Sursum corda*,—the hope of a better world, and disposes his mind to resignation :

> "Interim fiat, tua, rex, voluntas :
> Erigor sursum quoties subit spes
> Certa migrandi Solymam supernam,
> Numinis aulam."

He concludes in a noble strain of orthodox piety :

> "Vita tum demum vocitanda vita est.
> Tum licet gratos socios habere,
> Seraphim et sanctos TRIADEM verendam
> Concelebrantes."

Wednesday, 29th September

After a very good sleep, I rose more refreshed than I had been for some nights. We were now at but a little distance from the shore, and saw the sea from our windows, which made our voyage seem nearer. Mr. M'Pherson's manners and address pleased us much. He appeared to be a man of such intelligence and taste as to be sensible of the extraordinary powers of his illustrious guest. He said to me, " Dr. Johnson is an honour to mankind ; and, if the expression may be used, is an honour to religion."

Col, who had gone yesterday to pay a visit at Camuscross, joined us this morning at breakfast. Some other gentlemen also came to enjoy the entertainment of Dr. Johnson's conversation.—The day was windy and rainy, so that we had just seized a happy interval for our journey last night. We had good entertainment here, better accommodation than at Corrichatachin, and time enough to ourselves. The hours slipped along imperceptibly. We talked of Shenstone. Dr. Johnson said, he was a good layer-out of land, but would not allow him to approach excellence as a poet. He said, he believed he had tried to read all his Love Pastorals, but did not get through them. I repeated the stanza,

> She gazed as I slowly withdrew ;
> My path I could hardly discern ;
> So sweetly she bade me adieu,
> I thought that she bade me return.

He said, " That seems to be pretty." I observed that Shenstone, from his short maxims in prose, appeared to have some power of thinking ; but Dr. Johnson would not allow him that merit. He agreed, however, with Shenstone, that it was wrong in the brother of one of his correspondents to burn his letters ; " for, (said he,)

Shenstone was a man whose correspondence was an
honour."—He was this afternoon full of critical severity,
and dealt about his censures on all sides. He said,
Hammond's Love Elegies were poor things. He spoke
contemptuously of our lively and elegant, though too
licentious, Lyrick bard, Hanbury Williams, and said,
" he had no fame, but from boys who drank with him."

While he was in this mood, I was unfortunate enough,
simply perhaps, but I could not help thinking, unde-
servedly, to come within " the whiff and wind of his
fell sword." I asked him, if he had ever been accustomed to wear a night-cap. He said " No." I asked,
if it was best not to wear one.—JOHNSTON. " Sir, I had
this custom by chance, and perhaps no man shall ever
know whether it is best to sleep with or without a night-
cap."—Soon afterwards he was laughing at some
deficiency in the Highlands, and said, " One might as
well go without shoes and stockings."—Thinking to
have a little hit at his own deficiency, I ventured to
add,—" or without a night-cap, sir." But I had better
have been silent ; for he retorted directly. " I do not
see the connection there (laughing). Nobody before
was ever foolish enough to ask whether it was best to
wear a night-cap or not. This comes of being a little
wrong-headed."—He carried the company along with
him : and yet the truth is, that if he had always worn
a night-cap, as is the common practice, and found the
Highlanders did not wear one, he would have wondered
at their barbarity ; so that my hit was fair enough.

Thursday, 30th September

There was as great a storm of wind and rain as I
have almost ever seen, which necessarily confined us
to the house ; but we were fully compensated by Dr.
Johnson's conversation. He said, he did not grudge

Burke's being the first man in the House of Commons, for he was the first man every where ; but he grudged that a fellow who makes no figure in company, and has a mind as narrow as the neck of a vinegar cruet, should make a figure in the House of Commons, merely by having the knowledge of a few forms, and being furnished with a little occasional information. He told us, the first time he saw Dr. Young was at the house of Mr. Richardson, the author of *Clarissa*. He was sent for, that the doctor might read to him his *Conjectures on original Composition*, which he did, and Dr. Johnson made his remarks ; and he was surprized to find Young receive as novelties, what he thought very common maxims. He said, he believed Young was not a great scholar, nor had studied regularly the art of writing ; that there were very fine things in his *Night Thoughts*, though you could not find twenty lines together without some extravagance. He repeated two passages from his *Love of Fame*,—the characters of Brunetta and Stella, which he praised highly. He said Young pressed him much to come to Wellwyn. He always intended it, but never went. He was sorry when Young died. The cause of quarrel between Young and his son, he told us, was, that his son insisted Young should turn away a clergyman's widow, who lived with him, and who, having acquired great influence over the father, was saucy to the son. Dr. Johnson said, she could not conceal her resentment at him, for saying to Young, that " an old man should not resign himself to the management of any body."—I asked him, if there was any improper connection between them.—" No, sir, no more than between two statues. —He was past fourscore, and she a very coarse woman. She read to him, and, I suppose, made his coffee, and frothed his chocolate, and did such things as an old man wishes to have done for him."

Dr. Doddridge being mentioned, he observed that

" he was the author of one of the finest epigrams in
the English language. It is in Orton's Life of him.
The subject is his family-motto,—*Dum vivimus, viva-
mus*; which, in its primary signification, is, to be
sure, not very suitable to a Christian divine; but he
paraphrased it thus:

> ' Live, while you live, the *epicure* would say,
> And seize the pleasures of the present day.
> Live, while you live, the sacred *preacher* cries,
> And give to GOD each moment as it flies.
> Lord, in my views let both united be;
> I live in *pleasure*, when I live to *thee*.' "

I asked if it was not strange that government should
permit so many infidel writings to pass without censure.
—JOHNSON. " Sir, it is mighty foolish. It is for want of
knowing their own power. The present family on the
throne came to the crown against the will of nine tenths
of the people. Whether those nine tenths were right
or wrong, it is not our business now to inquire. But
such being the situation of the royal family, they were
glad to encourage all who would be their friends.
Now you know every bad man is a Whig; every man
who has loose notions. The church was all against this
family. They were, as I say, glad to encourage any
friends; and therefore, since their accession, there is
no instance of any man being kept back on account of
his bad principles; and hence this inundation of impiety." I observed that Mr. Hume, some of whose
writings were very unfavourable to religion, was, however, a Tory.—JOHNSON. " Sir, Hume is a Tory by
chance, as being a Scotchman; but not upon a principle
of duty; for he has no principle. If he is any thing, he
is a Hobbist."

There was something not quite serene in his humour
to-night, after supper; for he spoke of hastening away
to London, without stopping much at Edinburgh. I
reminded him, that he had General Oughton and many

others to see.—JOHNSON. " Nay, I shall neither go in jest, nor stay in jest. I shall do what is fit."—BOSWELL. " Ay, sir, but all I desire is, that you will let me tell you when it is fit."—JOHNSON. " Sir, I shall not consult you."—BOSWELL. " If you are to run away from us, as soon as you get loose, we will keep you confined in an island."—He was, however, on the whole, very good company. Mr. Donald M'Leod expressed very well the gradual impression made by Dr. Johnson on those who are so fortunate as to obtain his acquaintance. " When you see him first, you are struck with awful reverence ;—then you admire him ;— and then you love him cordially."

I read this evening some part of Voltaire's History of the War in 1741, and of Lord Kames against Hereditary Indefeasible Right. This is a very slight circumstance, with which I should not trouble my reader, but for the sake of observing, that every man should keep minutes of whatever he reads. Every circumstance of his studies should be recorded ; what books he has consulted ; how much of them he has read ; at what times ; how often the same authors ; and what opinions he formed of them, at different periods of his life.— Such an account would much illustrate the history of his mind.

Friday, 1st October

I shewed to Dr. Johnson verses in a magazine, on his Dictionary, composed of uncommon words taken from it :

" Little of *Anthropopathy* has he," &c.

He read a few of them, and said, " I am not answerable for all the words in my Dictionary."—I told him, that Garrick kept a book of all who had either praised, or abused him.—On the subject of his own reputation, he said, " Now that I see it has been so current a topick, I wish I had done so too ; but it could not well be done now, as so many things are scattered in news-papers." —He said he was angry at a boy of Oxford, who wrote in his defence against Kenrick ; because it was doing him hurt to answer Kenrick. He was told afterwards, the boy was to come to him to ask a favour. He first thought to treat him rudely, on account of his meddling in that business ; but then he considered, he had meant to do him all the service in his power, and he took another resolution ; he told him he would do what he could for him, and did so ; and the boy was satisfied. He said, he did not know how his pamphlet was done, as he had read very little of it. The boy made a good figure at Oxford, but died. He remarked, that attacks on authors did them much service. " A man who tells me my play is very bad, is less my enemy than he who lets it die in silence. A man, whose business it is to be talked of, is much helped by being attacked." —Garrick, I observed, had been often so helped.— JOHNSON. " Yes, sir ; though Garrick had more opportunities than almost any man, to keep the publick in mind of him, by exhibiting himself to such numbers, he would not have had so much reputation, had he not been so much attacked. Every attack produces a defence ; and so attention is engaged. There is no sport in mere praise, when people are all of a mind." —BOSWELL. " Then Hume is not the worse for Beattie's attack ? "—JOHNSON. " He is, because Beattie has confuted him. I do not say, but that there may be some attacks which will hurt an author. Though Hume suffered from Beattie, he was the better for other attacks." (He certainly could not include in that number those of Dr. Adams, and Mr. Tytler.) —BOSWELL. " Goldsmith is the better for attacks." —JOHNSON. " Yes, sir ; but he does not think so yet. When Goldsmith and I published, each of us something, at the same time, we were given to understand that we might review each other. Goldsmith was for accepting the offer. I said, No ; set Reviewers at defiance.—It was said to old Bentley, upon the attacks against him, ' Why, they'll write you down.' ' No, sir,' he replied ; ' depend upon it, no man was ever written down but by himself.' " He observed to me afterwards, that the advantages authours derived from attacks, were chiefly in subjects of taste, where you cannot confute, as so much may be said on either side. —He told me he did not know who was the authour of the *Adventures of a Guinea*, but that the bookseller had sent the first volume to him in manuscript, to have his opinion if it should be printed ; and he thought it should.

The weather being now somewhat better, Mr. James M'Donald, factor to Sir Alexander M'Donald in Slate, insisted that all the company at Ostig should go to the house at Armidale, which Sir Alexander had left, having gone with his lady to Edinburgh, and be his guests, till we had an opportunity of sailing to Mull. We accordingly got there to dinner ; and passed our day very cheerfully, being no less than fourteen in number.

Saturday, 2nd October

Dr. Johnson said, that " a Chief and his Lady should make their house like a court. They should have a certain number of the gentlemen's daughters to receive their education in the family, to learn pastry and such things from the housekeeper, and manners from my lady. That was the way in the great families in Wales ; at Lady Salisbury's, Mrs. Thrale's grandmother's, and at Lady Philips's. I distinguish the families by the ladies, as I speak of what was properly their province. There were always six young ladies at Sir John Philips's : when one was married, her place was filled up. There was a large school-room, where they learnt needle-work and other things."—I observed, that, at some courts in Germany, there were academies for the pages, who are the sons of gentlemen, and receive their education without any expense to their parents. Dr. Johnson said, that manners were best learnt at those courts. " You are admitted with great facility to the prince's company, and yet must treat him with much respect. At a great court, you are at such a distance that you get no good." —I said, " Very true : a man sees the court of Versailles, as if he saw it on a theatre."—He said, " The best book that ever was written upon good breeding, *Il Corteggiano*, by Castiglione, grew up at the little court of Urbino, and you should read it."—I am glad always to have his opinion of books. At Mr. M'Pherson's, he commended *Whitby's Commentary*, and said, he had heard him called rather lax ; but he did not perceive it. He had looked at a novel, called *The Man of the World*, at Rasay, but thought there was nothing in it. He said to-day, while reading my Journal, " This will be a great treasure to us some years hence."

Talking of a very penurious gentleman of our acquaintance, he observed, that he exceeded *L'Avare* in the play. I concurred with him, and remarked that he would do well, if introduced in one of Foote's farces ; that the best way to get it done, would be to bring Foote to be entertained at his house for a week, and then it would be *facit indignatio*.—JOHNSON. " Sir, I wish he had him. I, who have eaten his bread, will not give him to him ; but I should be glad he came honestly by him."

He said, he was angry at Thrale, for sitting at General Oglethorpe's without speaking. He censured a man for degrading himself to a non-entity. I observed, that Goldsmith was on the other extreme ; for he spoke at all ventures.—JOHNSON. " Yes, sir ; Goldsmith, rather than not speak, will talk of what he knows himself to be ignorant, which can only end in exposing him."—" I wonder, (said I,) if he feels that he exposes himself. If he was with two taylors "—" Or with two founders, (said Dr. Johnson, interrupting me,) he would fall a talking on the method of making cannon, though both of them would soon see that he did not know what metal a cannon is made of."—We were very social and merry in his room this forenoon. In the evening the company danced as usual. We performed, with much activity, a dance which, I suppose, the emigration from Sky has occasioned. They call it *America*. Each of the couples, after the common *involutions* and *evolutions*, successively whirls round in a circle, till all are in motion ; and the dance seems intended to shew how emigration catches, till a whole neighbourhood is set afloat.—Mrs. M'Kinnon told me, that last year when a ship sailed from Portree for America, the people on shore were almost distracted when they saw their relations go off ; they lay down on the ground, tumbled, and tore the grass with their teeth.—This year there was not a tear shed. The people on shore seemed to think that they would soon follow. This indifference is a mortal sign for the country.

We danced to-night to the musick of the bagpipe, which made us beat the ground with prodigious force. I thought it better to endeavour to conciliate the kindness of the people of Sky, by joining heartily in their amusements, than to play the abstract scholar. I looked on this Tour to the Hebrides as a copartnership between Dr. Johnson and me. Each was to do all he could to promote its success ; and I have some reason to flatter myself, that my gayer exertions were of service to us. Dr. Johnson's immense fund of knowledge and wit was a wonderful source of admiration and delight to them ; but they had it only at times ; and they required to have the intervals agreeably filled up, and even little elucidations of his learned text. I was also fortunate enough frequently to draw him forth to talk, when he would otherwise have been silent. The fountain was at times locked up, till I opened the spring. —It was curious to hear the Hebridians, when any dispute happened while he was out of the room, saying, " Stay till Dr. Johnson comes : say that to *him* ! "

Yesterday Dr. Johnson said, " I cannot but laugh, to think of myself roving among the Hebrides at sixty. I wonder where I shall rove at fourscore ! "—This evening he disputed the truth of what is said, as to the people of St. Kilda catching cold whenever strangers come. " How can there (said he) be a physical effect without a physical cause ? "—He added, laughing, " the arrival of a ship full of strangers would kill them ; for, if one stranger gives them one cold, two strangers must give them two colds ; and so in proportion."— I wondered to hear him ridicule this, as he had praised M'Aulay for putting it in his book : saying, that it was manly in him to tell a fact, however strange, if he himself believed it. He said, the evidence was not adequate to the improbability of the thing ; that if a physician, rather disposed to be incredulous, should go to St. Kilda, and report the fact, then he would begin to look about him. They said, it was annually proved by M'Leod's steward, on whose arrival all the inhabitants caught cold. He jocularly remarked, " the steward always comes to demand something from them ; and so they fall a coughing. I suppose the people in Sky all take a cold, when——(naming a certain person) comes."—They said, he came only in summer.—JOHNSON. " That is out of tenderness to you. Bad weather and he, at the same time, would be too much."

Sunday, 3rd October

Joseph reported that the wind was still against us. Dr. Johnson said, " A wind, or not a wind ? that is the question ; " for he can amuse himself at times with a little play of words, or rather sentences. I remember when he turned his cup at Aberbrothick, where we drank tea, he muttered, *Claudite jam rivos, pueri.* I must again and again apologize to fastidious readers, for recording such minute particulars. They prove the scrupulous fidelity of my Journal. Dr. Johnson said it was a very exact picture of a portion of his life.

While we were chatting in the indolent stile of men who were to stay here all this day at least, we were suddenly roused at being told that the wind was fair, that a little fleet of herring-busses was passing by for Mull, and that Mr. Simpson's vessel was about to sail. Hugh M'Donald, the skipper, came to us, and was impatient that we should get ready, which we soon did. Dr. Johnson, with composure and solemnity, repeated the observation of Epictetus, that, " as man has the voyage of death before him—whatever may be his employment, he should be ready at the master's call ; and an old man should never be far from the shore, lest he should not be able to get himself ready." He rode, and I and the other gentlemen walked, about an English mile to the shore, where the vessel lay. Dr. Johnson said, he should never forget Sky, and returned thanks for all civilities. We were carried to the vessel in a small boat which she had, and we set sail very briskly about one o'clock. I was much pleased with the motion for many hours. Dr. Johnson grew sick, and retired under cover, as it rained a good deal. I kept above, that I might have fresh air, and finding myself not affected by the motion of the vessel, I exulted in being a stout seaman, while Dr. Johnson was quite in a state of annihilation. But I was soon humbled ; for after imagining that I could go with ease to America or the East-Indies, I became very sick, but kept above board, though it rained hard.

As we had been detained so long in Sky by bad

weather, we gave up the scheme that Col had planned for us of visiting several islands, and contented ourselves with the prospect of seeing Mull, and Icolmkill and Inchkenneth, which lie near to it.

Mr. Simpson was sanguine in his hopes for awhile, the wind being fair for us. He said, he would land us at Icolmkill that night. But when the wind failed, it was resolved we should make for the sound of Mull, and land in the harbour of Tobermorie. We kept near the five herring vessels for some time ; but afterwards four of them got before us, and one little wherry fell behind us. When we got in full view of the point of Ardnamurchan, the wind changed, and was directly against our getting into the sound. We were then obliged to tack, and get forward in that tedious manner. As we advanced, the storm grew greater, and the sea very rough. Col then began to talk of making for Egg, or Canna, or his own island. Our skipper said, he would get us into the Sound. Having struggled for this a good while in vain, he said, he would push forward till we were near the land of Mull, where we might cast anchor, and lie till the morning ; for although, before this, there had been a good moon, and I had pretty distinctly seen not only the land of Mull, but up the Sound, and the country of Morven as at one end of it, the night was now grown very dark. Our crew consisted of one M'Donald, our skipper, and two sailors, one of whom had but one eye ; Mr. Simpson himself, Col, and Hugh M'Donald his servant, all helped. Simpson said, he would willingly go for Col, if young Col or his servant would undertake to pilot us to a harbour ; but, as the island is low land, it was dangerous to run upon it in the dark. Col and his servant appeared a little dubious. The scheme of running for Canna seemed then to be embraced ; but Canna was ten leagues off, all out of our way ; and they were afraid to attempt the harbour of Egg. All these different

plans were successively in agitation. The old skipper
still tried to make for the land of Mull; but then it
was considered that there was no place there where
we could anchor in safety. Much time was lost in
striving against the storm. At last it became so rough,
and threatened to be so much worse, that Col and his
servant took more courage, and said they would undertake to hit one of the harbours in Col.—" Then let us
run for it in GOD's name," said the skipper; and instantly we turned towards it. The little wherry which
had fallen behind us, had hard work. The master
begged that, if we made for Col, we should put out a
light to him. Accordingly one of the sailors waved a
glowing peat for some time. The various difficulties
that were started, gave me a good deal of apprehension,
from which I was relieved, when I found we were to
run for a harbour before the wind. But my relief was
but of short duration; for I soon heard that our sails
were very bad, and were in danger of being torn in
pieces, in which case we should be driven upon the
rocky shore of Col. It was very dark, and there was
a heavy and incessant rain. The sparks of the burning
peat flew so much about, that I dreaded the vessel
might take fire. Then, as Col was a sportsman, and
had powder on board, I figured that we might be blown
up. Simpson and he appeared a little frightened, which
made me more so; and the perpetual talking, or rather
shouting, which was carried on in Erse, alarmed me
still more. A man is always suspicious of what is saying in an unknown tongue; and, if fear be his passion
at the time, he grows more afraid. Our vessel often
lay so much on one side, that I trembled lest she should
be overset, and indeed they told me afterwards, that
they had run her sometimes to within an inch of the
water, so anxious were they to make what haste they
could before the night should be worse. I now saw
what I never saw before, a prodigious sea, with immense

billows coming upon a vessel, so as that it seemed hardly possible to escape. There was something grandly horrible in the sight. I am glad I have seen it once. Amidst all these terrifying circumstances, I endeavoured to compose my mind. It was not easy to do it ; for all the stories that I had heard of the dangerous sailing among the Hebrides, which is proverbial, came full upon my recollection. When I thought of those who were dearest to me, and would suffer severely, should I be lost, I upbraided myself, as not having a sufficient cause for putting myself in such danger. Piety afforded me comfort ; yet I was disturbed by the objections that have been made against a particular providence, and by the arguments of those who maintain that it is in vain to hope that the petitions of an individual, or even of congregations, can have any influence with the Deity ; objections which have been often made, and which Dr. Hawkesworth has lately revived, in his Preface to the *Voyages to the South Seas;* but Dr. Ogden's excellent doctrine on the efficacy of intercession prevailed.

It was half an hour after eleven before we set ourselves in the course for Col. As I saw them all busy doing something, I asked Col, with which earnestness, what I could do. He, with a happy readiness, put into my hand a rope, which was fixed to the top of one of the masts, and told me to hold it till he bade me pull. If I had considered the matter, I might have seen that this could not be of the least service ; but his object was to keep me out of the way of those who were busy working the vessel, and at the same time to divert my fear, by employing me, and making me think that I was of use. Thus did I stand firm to my post, while the wind and rain beat upon me, always expecting a call to pull my rope.

The man with one eye steered ; old M'Donald, and Col and his servant, lay upon the fore-castle, looking sharp out for the harbour. It was necessary to carry much *cloth*, as they termed it, that is to say, much sail, in order to keep the vessel off the shore of Col. This made violent plunging in a rough sea. At last they spied the harbour of Lochiern, and Col cried, "Thank GOD, we are safe!" We ran up till we were opposite to it, and soon afterwards we got into it, and cast anchor.

Dr. Johnson had all this time been quiet and unconcerned. He had lain down on one of the beds, and having got free from sickness, was satisfied. The truth is, he knew nothing of the danger we were in; but, fearless and unconcerned, might have said, in the words which he has chosen for the motto to his *Rambler*,

Quo me cunque rapit tempestas, deferor hospes.

Once, during the doubtful consultations, he asked whither we were going; and upon being told that it was not certain whether to Mull or Col, he cried, "Col for my money!"—I now went down, with Col and Mr. Simpson, to visit him. He was lying in philosophick tranquillity with a greyhound of Col's at his back, keeping him warm. Col is quite the *Juvenis qui gaudet canibus*. He had, when we left Talisker, two greyhounds, two terriers, a pointer, and a large Newfoundland water-dog. He lost one of his terriers by the road, but had still five dogs with him. I was very ill, and very desirous to get to shore. When I was told that we could not land that night, as the storm had now increased, I looked so miserably, as Col afterwards informed me, that what Shakspeare has made the Frenchman say of the English soldiers, when scantily dieted, "Piteous they will look, like drowned mice!" might, I believe, have been well applied to me. There was in the harbour, before us, a Campbelltown vessel, the *Betty*, Kenneth Morison master, taking in kelp, and bound for Ireland. We sent our boat to beg beds for two gentlemen, and that the master would send his boat, which was larger than ours. He accordingly did so, and Col and I were accommodated in his vessel till the morning.

Monday, 4th October

About eight o'clock we went in the boat to Mr. Simpson's vessel, and took in Dr. Johnson. He was quite well, though he had tasted nothing but a dish of tea since Saturday night. On our expressing some surprise at this, he said, that, " when he lodged in the Temple, and had no regular system of life, he had fasted for two days at a time, during which he had gone about visiting, though not at the hours of dinner or supper ; that he had drunk tea, but eaten no bread ; that this was no intentional fasting, but happened just in the course of a literary life."

There was a little miserable publick-house close upon the shore, to which we should have gone, had we landed last night : but this morning Col resolved to take us directly to the house of Captain Lauchlan M'Lean, a descendant of his family, who had acquired a fortune in the East-Indies, and taken a farm in Col. We had about an English mile to go to it. Col and Joseph, and some others, ran to some little horses, called here *Shelties*, that were running wild on a heath, and catched one of them. We had a saddle with us, which was clapped upon it, and a straw-halter was put on its head. Dr. Johnson was then mounted, and Joseph very slowly and gravely led the horse. I said to Dr. Johnson, " I wish, sir, *the club* saw you in this attitude."

It was a very heavy rain, and I was wet to the skin. Captain M'Lean had but a poor temporary house, or rather hut ; however, it was a very good haven to us. There was a blazing peat-fire, and Mrs. M'Lean, daughter of the minister of the parish, got us tea. I felt still the motion of the sea. Dr. Johnson said, it was not in imagination, but a continuation of motion on the fluids, like that of the sea itself after the storm is over.

There were some books on the board which served as a chimney-piece. Dr. Johnson took up Burnet's *History of his own Times*. He said, " The first part of it is one of the most entertaining books in the English language ; it is quite dramatick : while he went about every where, saw every where, and heard every where. By the first part, I mean so far as it appears that Burnet himself was actually engaged in what he has told ; and this may be easily distinguished." Captain M'Lean censured Burnet, for his high praise of Lauderdale in a dedication, when he shews him in his history to have been so bad a man.—JOHNSON. " I do not myself think that a man should say in a dedication what he could not say in a history. However, allowance should be made ; for there is a great difference. The known style of a dedication is flattery : it professes to flatter. There is the same difference between what a man says in a dedication, and what he says in a history, as between a lawyer's pleading a cause, and reporting it."

The day passed away pleasantly enough. The wind became fair for Mull in the evening, and Mr. Simpson resolved to sail next morning : but having been thrown into the island of Col, we were unwilling to leave it un- examined, especially as we considered that the Campbell- town vessel would sail for Mull in a day or two, and therefore we determined to stay.

Tuesday, 5th October

I rose, and wrote my Journal till about nine ; and then went to Dr. Johnson, who sat up in bed and talked and laughed. I said, it was curious to look back ten years, to the time when we first thought of visiting the

Hebrides. How distant and improbable the scheme then appeared ! Yet here we were actually among them.—" Sir, (said he,) people may come to do any thing almost, by talking of it. I really believe, I could talk myself into building a house upon island Isa, though I should probably never come back again to see it. I could easily persuade Reynolds to do it ; and there would be no great sin in persuading him to do it. Sir, he would reason thus : ' What will it cost me to be there once in two or three summers ?—Why, perhaps, five hundred pounds ; and what is that, in comparison of having a fine retreat, to which a man can go, or to which he can send a friend ? ' He would never find out that he may have this within twenty miles of London. —Then I would tell him, that he may marry one of the Miss M'Leods, a lady of great family.—Sir, it is surprising how people will go to a distance for what they may have at home. I knew a lady who came up from Lincolnshire to Knightsbridge with one of her daughters and gave five guineas a week for a lodging and a warm bath ; that is, mere warm water. That, you know, could not be had in Lincolnshire ! She said, it was made either too hot or too cold there."

After breakfast, Dr. Johnson and I, and Joseph, mounted horses, and Col and the captain walked with us about a short mile across the island. We paid a visit to the Reverend Mr. Hector M'Lean. His parish consists of the islands of Col and Tyr-yi. He was about seventy-seven years of age, a decent ecclesiastick, dressed in a full suit of black clothes, and a black wig. He appeared like a Dutch pastor, or one of the assembly of divines at Westminster. Dr. Johnson observed to me afterwards, " that he was a fine old man, and was as well-dressed, and had as much dignity in his appearance as the dean of a cathedral." We were told, that he had a valuable library, though but poor accommodation for it, being obliged to keep his books in large chests

It was curious to see him and Dr. Johnson together. Neither of them heard very distinctly ; so each of them talked in his own way, and at the same time. Mr. M'Lean said, he had a confutation of Bayle, by Leibnitz.— JOHNSON. " A confutation of Bayle, sir ! What part of Bayle do you mean ? The greatest part of his writings is not confutable : it is historical and critical."— Mr. M'Lean said, " the irreligious part ; " and proceeded to talk of Leibnitz's controversy with Clarke, calling Leibnitz a great man.—JOHNSON. " Why, sir, Leibnitz persisted in affirming that Newton called space *sensorium numinis*, notwithstanding he was corrected, and desired to observe that Newton's words were QUASI *sensorium numinis*. No, sir ; Leibnitz was as paltry a fellow as I know. Out of respect to Queen Caroline, who patronised him, Clarke treated him too well."

During the time that Dr. Johnson was thus going on, the old minister was standing with his back to the fire, cresting up erect, pulling down the front of his periwig, and talking what a great man Leibnitz was. To give an idea of the scene, would require a page with two columns ; but it ought rather to be represented by two good players. The old gentleman said, Clarke was very wicked, for going so much into the Arian system. " I will not say he was wicked," said Dr. Johnson ; " he might be mistaken."—M'LEAN. " He was wicked, to shut his eyes against the Scriptures ; and worthy men in England have since confuted him to all intents and purposes."—JOHNSON. " I know not *who* has confuted him to *all intents* and *purposes*."—Here again there was a double talking, each continuing to maintain his own argument, without hearing exactly what the other said.

I regretted that Dr. Johnson did not practice the art of accommodating himself to different sorts of people. Had he been softer with this venerable old man, we might have had more conversation ; but his forcible spirit, and impetuosity of manner, may be said to spare

neither sex nor age. I have seen even Mrs. Thrale
stunned ; but I have often maintained, that it is better
he should retain his own manner. Pliability of address
I conceive to be inconsistent with that majestick power
of mind which he possesses, and which produces such
noble effects. A lofty oak will not bend like a supple
willow.

He told me afterwards, he liked firmness in an old
man, and was pleased to see Mr. M'Lean so orthodox.
"At his age, it is too late for a man to be asking himself questions as to his belief."

We rode to the northern part of the island, where
we saw the ruins of a church or chapel. We then proceeded to a place called Grissipol, or the rough Pool.

At Grissipol we found a good farm house, belonging
to the Laird of Col, and possessed by Mr. M'Sweyn.
On the beach here there is a singular variety of curious
stones. I picked up one very like a small cucumber.
By the by, Dr. Johnson told me, that Gay's line in the
Beggar's Opera, "As men should serve a cucumber,"
&c., has no waggish meaning, with reference to men
flinging away cucumbers as too *cooling*, which some have
thought ; for it has been a common saying of physicians
in England, that a cucumber should be well sliced, and
dressed with pepper and vinegar, and then thrown out,
as good for nothing.—Mr. M'Sweyn's predecessors had
been in Sky from a very remote period, upon the estate
belonging to M'Leod ; probably before M'Leod had it.
The name is certainly Norwegian, from *Sueno*, King of
Norway. The present Mr. M'Sweyn left Sky upon the
late M'Leod's raising his rents. He then got this farm
from Col.

He appeared to be near fourscore ; but looked as
fresh, and was as strong as a man of fifty. His son
Hugh looked older ; and, as Dr. Johnson observed,
had more the manners of an old man than he. I had
often heard of such instances, but never saw one before.

Mrs. M'Sweyn was a decent old gentlewoman. She was dressed in tartan, and could speak nothing but Erse. She said, she taught Sir James M'Donald Erse, and would teach me soon. I could now sing a verse of the song *Hatyin foam'eri*, made in honour of Allan, the famous Captain of Clanranald, who fell at Sherrifmuir ; whose servant, who lay on the field watching his master's dead body, being asked next day who that was, answered, " He was a man yesterday."

We were entertained here with a primitive heartiness. Whisky was served round in a shell, according to the ancient Highland custom. Dr. Johnson would not partake of it ; but, being desirous to do honour to the modes " of other times," drank some water out of the shell.

In the forenoon Dr. Johnson said, " it would require great resignation to live in one of these islands."— BOSWELL. " I don't know, sir ; I have felt myself at times in a state of almost mere physical existence, satisfied to eat, drink, and sleep, and walk about, and enjoy my own thoughts ; and I can figure a continuation of this."—JOHNSON. " Ay, sir ; but if you were shut up here, your own thoughts would torment you : you would think of Edinburgh or London, and that you could not be there."

We set out after dinner for Breacacha, the family seat of the Laird of Col, accompanied by the young laird, who had now got a horse, and by the younger Mr. M'Sweyn, whose wife had gone thither before us, to prepare every thing for our reception, the laird and his family being absent at Aberdeen. It is called Breacacha, or the Spotted Field, because in summer it is enamelled with clover and daisies, as young Col told me. We passed by a place where there is a very large stone, I may call it a *rock ;*—" a vast weight for Ajax." The tradition is, that a giant threw such another stone at his mistress, up to the top of a hill, at a small distance ; and that she in return, threw this mass down to him.   It was all in sport.

Malo me petit lasciva puella.

As we advanced, we came to a large extent of plain ground. I had not seen such a place for a long time. Col and I took a gallop upon it by way of race.   It was very refreshing to me, after having been so long taking short steps in hilly countries.   It was like stretching a man's legs after being cramped in a short bed. We also passed close by a large extent of sand-hills, near two miles square. Dr. Johnson said, " he never had the image before. It was horrible, if barren-ness and danger could be so."   I heard him, after we were in the house of Breacacha, repeating to himself, as he walked about the room,

" And smother'd in the dusty whirlwind, dies."

Probably he had been thinking of the whole of the simile in *Cato*, of which that is the concluding line ; the sandy desert had struck him so strongly.   The sand has of late been blown over a good deal of meadow ; and the people of the island say, that their fathers remembered much of the space which is now covered with sand, to have been under tillage.   Col's house is situated on a bay called Breacacha Bay.   We found here a neat new-built gentleman's house, better than any we had been in since we were at Lord Errol's.   Dr. John-son relished it much at first, but soon remarked to me, that " there was nothing becoming a Chief about it : it was a mere tradesman's box."   He seemed quite at home, and no longer found any difficulty in using the Highland address ; for, as soon as we arrived, he said, with a spirited familiarity, " Now, Col, if you could get us a dish of tea."—Dr. Johnson and I had each an ex-

9

cellent bed-chamber. We had a dispute which of us had the best curtains. His were rather the best, being of linen ; but I insisted that my bed had the best posts, which was undeniable. "Well, (said he,) if you *have* the best *posts*, we will have you tied to them and whipped."—I mention this slight circumstance, only to shew how ready he is, even in mere trifles, to get the better of his antagonist, by placing him in a ludicrous view. I have known him sometimes use the same art, when hard pressed in serious disputation. Goldsmith, I remember, to retaliate for many a severe defeat which he has suffered from him, applied to him a lively saying in one of Cibber's comedies, which puts this part of his character in a strong light.—" There is no arguing with Johnson ; for, *if his pistol misses fire, he knocks you down with the but-end of it.*"

Wednesday, 6th October

After a sufficiency of sleep, we assembled at breakfast. We were just as if in barracks. Every body was master. We went and viewed the old castle of Col, which is not far from the present house, near the shore, and founded on a rock. It has never been a larger feudal residence, and has nothing about it that requires a particular description. Like other old inconvenient buildings of the same age, it exemplified Gray's picturesque lines,

> " Huge windows that exclude the light,
> And passages that lead to nothing."

It may however be worth mentioning, that on the second story we saw a vault, which was, and still is, the family prison. There was a woman put into it by the laird, for theft, within these ten years ; and any offender would be confined there yet; for, from the necessity of the thing, as the island is remote from any power established by law, the laird must exercise his jurisdiction to a certain degree.

We were shewn, in a corner of this vault, a hole, into which Col said greater criminals used to be put. It was now filled up with rubbish of different kinds. He said, it was of a great depth. "Ay, (said Dr. Johnson, smiling,) all such places, that *are filled up*, were of a great depth." He is very quick in shewing that he does not give credit to careless or exaggerated accounts of things. After seeing the castle, we looked at a small hut near it. It is called Teigh Franchich, *i.e.* the Frenchman's House. Col could not tell us the history of it. A poor man with a wife and children now lived in it. We went into it, and Dr. Johnson gave them some charity. There was but one bed for all the family, and the hut was very smoky. When he came out, he said to me, "*Et hoc secundum sententiam philosophorum est esse beatus.*"—BOSWELL. "The philosophers, when they placed happiness in a cottage, supposed cleanliness and no smoke."—JOHNSON. "Sir, they did not think about either."

We walked a little in the laird's garden, in which endeavours have been used to rear some trees; but, as soon as they got above the surrounding wall, they died. Dr. Johnson recommended sowing the seeds of hardy trees, instead of planting.

Col and I rode out this morning, and viewed a part of the island. In the course of our ride, we saw a turnip-field, which he had hoed with his own hands. He first introduced this kind of husbandry into the Western Islands. We also looked at an appearance of lead, which seemed very promising. It has been long known; for I found letters to the late laird, from Sir John Areskine and Sir Alexander Murray, respecting it.

After dinner came Mr. M'Lean, of Corneck, brother to Isle of Muck, who is a cadet of the family of Col. He possesses the two ends of Col, which belong to the Duke of Argyll. Corneck had lately taken a lease of them at a very advanced rent, rather than let the Campbells get a footing in the island, one of whom had offered nearly as much as he. Dr. Johnson well observed, that, " landlords err much when they calculate merely what their land *may* yield. The rent must be in a proportionate ratio of what the land may yield, and of the power of the tenant to make it yield. A tenant cannot make by his land, but according to the corn and cattle which he has. Suppose you should give him twice as much land as he has, it does him no good, unless he gets also more stock. It is clear then, that the Highland landlords, who let their substantial tenants leave them, are infatuated ; for the poor small tenants cannot give them good rents, from the very nature of things. They have not the means of raising more from their farms." Corneck, Dr. Johnson said, was the most distinct man that he had met with in these isles ; he did not shut his eyes, or put his fingers in his ears, which he seemed to think was a good deal the mode with most of the people whom we have seen of late.

Thursday, 7th October

Captain M'Lean joined us this morning at breakfast. There came on a dreadful storm of wind and rain, which continued all day, and rather increased at night. The wind was directly against our getting to Mull. We were in a strange state of abstraction from the world : we could neither hear from our friends, nor write to them. Col had brought Daille *on the Fathers*, Lucas *on Happiness*, and More's *Dialogues*, from the Reverend Mr. M'Lean's, and Burnet's *History of his*

own Times, from Captain M'Lean's ; and he had of his
own some books of farming, and Gregory's *Geometry*.
Dr. Johnson read a good deal of Burnet, and of Gregory, and I observed he made some geometrical notes in
the end of his pocket-book. I read a little of Young's
Six Weeks Tour through the Southern Counties; and
Ovid's *Epistles*, which I had bought at Inverness, and
which helped to solace many a weary hour.

We were to have gone with Dr. Johnson this morning to see the mine ; but were prevented by the storm.
While it was raging, he said, " We may be glad we
are not *damnati ad metalla*."

Friday, 8th October

Dr. Johnson appeared to-day very weary of our
present confined situation. He said, " I want to be
on the main land, and go on with existence. This is
a waste of life."

I shall here insert, without regard to chronology,
some of his conversation at different times.

" There was a man some time ago, who was well
received for two years, among the gentlemen of Nor-
thamptonshire, by calling himself my brother. At
last he grew so impudent as by his influence to get
tenants turned out of their farms. Allen the Printer,
who is of that county, came to me, asking, with much
appearance of doubtfulness, if I had a brother ; and
upon being assured I had none alive, he told me of the
imposition, and immediately wrote to the country, and
the fellow was dismissed. It pleased me to hear that
so much was got by using my name. It is not every
name that can carry double ; do both for a man's self
and his brother (laughing). I should be glad to see
the fellow. However, I could have done nothing
against him. A man can have no redress for his name

being used, or ridiculous stories being told of him in the news-papers, except he can shew that he has suffered damage.—Some years ago a foolish piece was published, said to be written ' by S. Johnson.' Some of my friends wanted me to be very angry about this. I said, it would be in vain ; for the answer would be, ' S. Johnson may be Simon Johnson, or Simeon Johnson, or Solomon Johnson ; ' and even if the full name, Samuel Johnson, had been used, it might be said ; ' it is not you ; it is a much cleverer fellow.'

" Beauclerk and I, and Langton, and Lady Sydney Beauclerk, mother to our friend, were one day driving in a coach by Cuper's Gardens, which were then unoccupied. I, in sport, proposed that Beauclerk and Langton, and myself should take them ; and we amused ourselves with scheming how we should all do our parts. Lady Sydney grew angry, and said, ' an old man should not put such things in young people's heads.' She had no notion of a joke, sir ; had come late into life, and had a mighty unpliable understanding.

" Carte's *Life of the Duke of Ormond* is considered as a book of authority ; but it is ill-written. The matter is diffused in too many words ; there is no animation, no compression, no vigour. Two good volumes in duodecimo might be made out of the two in folio."

Talking of our confinement here, I observed, that our discontent and impatience could not be considered as very unreasonable ; for that we were just in the state of which Seneca complains so grievously, while in exile in Corsica. " Yes, (said Dr. Johnson,) and he was not farther from home than we are." The truth is, he was much nearer.

There was a good deal of rain to-day, and the wind was still contrary. Corneck attended me, while I amused myself in examining a collection of papers belonging to the family of Col. The first laird was a younger son of the Chieftain M'Lean, and got the middle part of Col for his patrimony. Dr. Johnson having given a very particular account of the connection between this family and a branch of the family of Camerons, called M'Lonich, I shall only insert the following document, (which I found in Col's cabinet,) as a proof of its continuance, even to a late period :

" To the Laird of Col

" Dear Sir,

" The long-standing tract of firm affectionate friendship 'twixt your worthy predecessors and ours affords us such assurance, as that we may have full relyance on your favour and undoubted friendship, in recommending the bearer, Ewen Cameron, our cousin, son to the deceast Dugall M'Connill of Innermaillie, sometime in Glenpean, to your favour and conduct, who is a man of undoubted honesty and discretion, only that he has the misfortune of being alledged to have been accessory to the killing of one of M'Martin's family about fourteen years ago, upon which alledgeance the M'Martins are now so sanguine on revenging, that they are fully resolved for the deprivation of his life ; to the preventing of which you are relyed on by us, as the only fit instrument, and a most capable person. Therefore your favour and protection is expected and intreated, during his good behaviour ; and failing of which behaviour, you'll please to use him as a most insignificant person deserves.

" Sir, he had, upon the alledgeance foresaid, been transported, at Lochiel's desire, to France, to gratify the M'Martins, and upon his return home, about five years ago, married : But now he is so much threatened by the M'Martins, that he is not secure enough to stay where he is, being Ardmurchan, which occasions this trouble to you. Wishing prosperity and happiness to attend still yourself, worthy Lady, and good family, we are, in the most affectionate manner,

"Dear Sir,
"Your most obliged, affectionate,
and most humble servants,
"DUGALL CAMERON, of Strone.
"DUGALL CAMERON, of Barr.
"DUGALL CAMERON, of Inveriskvouilline.
"DUGALL CAMERON, of Invinvalie."

"STRONE, 11th March, 1737."

Ewen Cameron was protected, and his son has now a farm from the Laird of Col, in Mull.

The family of Col was very loyal in the time of the great Montrose, from whom I found two letters in his own hand-writing. The first is as follows:

"FOR MY VERY LOVING FRIEND THE LAIRD OF COALL.

"SIR,
"I MUST heartily thank you for all your willing-ness and good affection to his Majesty's service, and particularly the sending alongs of your son, to who I will heave ane particular respect, hopeing also that you will still continue ane goode instrument for the advance-ing ther of the King's service, for which, and all your former loyal carriages, be confident you shall find the effects of his Maⁱˢ favour, as they can be witnessed you by

"Your very faithful friende,
"MONTROSE."

"STRETHEARNE, 20 Janˉ. 1646."

The other is,

"FOR THE LAIRD OF COL.

"SIR,
"HAVING occasion to write to your fields, I cannot

be forgetful of your willingness and good affection to his Majesty's service. I acknowledge to you, and thank you heartily for it, assuring, that in what lies in my power, you shall find the good. Mean while, I shall expect that you will continue your loyal endeavours, in wishing those slack people that are about you, to appear more obedient than they do, and loyal in their prince's service ; whereby I assure you, you shall find me ever

" Your faithful friend,
" MONTROSE."

" PETTY, 17 *April*, 1646."

I found some uncouth lines on the death of the present laird's father, intituled " Nature's Elegy upon the Death of Donald Maclean of Col." They are not worth insertion. I shall only give what is called his Epitaph, which Dr. Johnson said, " was not so very bad."

" Nature's minion, Virtue's wonder,
Art's corrective here lyes under."

I asked, what " Art's corrective " meant. " Why, sir, (said he,) that the laird was so exquisite, that he set Art right, when she was wrong."

I found several letters to the late Col, from my father's old companion at Paris, Sir Hector M'Lean, one of which was written at the time of settling the colony in Georgia. It dissuades Col from letting people go there, and assures him there will soon be an opportunity of employing them better at home. Hence it appears that emigration from the Highlands, though not in such numbers at a time as of late, has always been practised. Dr. Johnson observed, that, " the Lairds, instead of improving their country, diminished their people."

There are several districts of sandy desart in Col

There are forty-eight lochs of fresh water; but many of them are very small,—mere pools. About one half of them, however, have trout and eel. There is a great number of horses in the island, mostly of a small size. Being over-stocked, they sell some in Tir-yi, and on the main land. Their black cattle, which are chiefly rough-haired, are reckoned remarkably good. The climate being very mild in winter, they never put their beasts in any house. The lakes are never frozen so as to bear a man; and snow never lies above a few hours. They have a good many sheep, which they eat mostly themselves, and sell but a few. They have goats in several places. There are no foxes; no serpents, toads, or frogs, nor any venomous creature. They have otters and mice here; but had no rats till lately that an American vessel brought them. There is a rabbit-warren on the north-east of the island, belonging to the Duke of Argyle. Young Col intends to get some hares, of which there are none at present. There are no black-cock, muir-fowl, nor partridges; but there are snipe, wild-duck, wild-geese, and swans, in winter; wild-pidgeons, plover, and great number of starlings; of which I shot some, and found them pretty good eating. Woodcocks come hither, though there is not a tree upon the island. There are no rivers in Col; but only some brooks, in which there is a great variety of fish. In the whole isle there are but three hills, and none of them considerable, for a Highland country. The people are very industrious. Every man can tan. They get oak, and birch-bark, and lime, from the main land. Some have pits; but they commonly use tubs. I saw brogues very well tanned; and every man can make them. They all make candles of the tallow of their beasts, both moulded and dipped; and they all make oil of the livers of fish. The little fish called Cuddies produce a great deal. They sell some oil out of the island, and they use it much for light in their houses, in little iron lamps, most of which they have from England ; but of late their own blacksmith makes them. He is a good workman ; but he has no employment in shoeing horses, for they all go unshod here, except some of a better kind belonging to young Col, which were now in Mull. There are two carpenters in Col ; but most of the inhabitants can do something as boat-carpenters. They can all dye. Heath is used for yellow ; and for red, a moss which grows on stones. They make broad-cloth, and tartan, and linen, of their own wool and flax, sufficient for their own use ; as also stockings. Their bonnets come from the main land. Hard-ware and several small articles are brought annually from Greenock, and sold in the only shop in the island, which is kept near the house, or rather hut, used for publick worship, there being no church in the island. —The inhabitants of Col have increased considerably within these thirty years, as appears from the parish registers. There are but three considerable tacksmen on Col's part of the island : the rest is let to small tenants, some of whom pay so low a rent as four, three, or even two guineas. The highest is seven pounds, paid by a farmer, whose son goes yearly on foot to Aberdeen for education, and in summer returns, and acts as a school-master in Col. Dr. Johnson said, " There is something noble in a young man's walking two hundred miles and back again, every year, for the sake of learning."

This day a number of people came to Col, with complaints of each others' trespasses. Corneck, to prevent their being troublesome, told them, that the lawyer from Edinburgh was here, and if they did not agree, he would take them to task. They were alarmed at this ; said, they had never been used to go to law, and hoped Col would settle matters himself.—In the evening Corneck left us.

Saturday, 9th October

As, in our present confinement, any thing that had even the name of curious was an object of attention, I proposed that Col should show me the great stone, mentioned in a former page, as having been thrown by a giant to the top of a mountain. Dr. Johnson, who did not like to be left alone, said he would accompany us as far as riding was practicable. We ascended a part of the hill on horseback, and Col and I scrambled up the rest. A servant held our horses, and Dr. Johnson placed himself on the ground, with his back against a large fragment of rock. The wind being high, he let down the cocks of his hat, and tied it with his handkerchief under his chin. While we were employed in examining the stone, which did not repay our trouble in getting to it, he amused himself with reading *Gataker on Lots and on the Christian Watch*, a very learned book, of the last age, which had been found in the garret of Col's house, and which he said was a treasure here. When we descried him from above, he had a most eremitical appearance ; and on our return told us, he had been so much engaged by Gataker, that he had never missed us. His avidity for variety of books, while we were in Col, was frequently expressed ; and he often complained that so few were within his reach. Upon which I observed to him, that it was strange he should complain of want of books, when he could at any time make such good ones.

We next proceeded to the lead mine. In our way we came to a strand of some extent, where we were glad to take a gallop, in which my learned friend joined with great alacrity. Dr. Johnson, mounted on a large bay mare without shoes, and followed by a foal, which had some difficulty in keeping up with him, was a singular spectacle.

After examining the mine, we returned through a very uncouth district, full of sand hills ; down which, though apparent precipices, our horses carried us with safety, the sand always gently sliding away from their feet. Vestiges of houses were pointed out to us, which Col, and two others who had joined us, asserted had been overwhelmed with sand blown over them. But, on going close to one of them, Dr. Johnson shewed the absurdity of the notion, by remarking, that " it was evidently only a house abandoned, the stones of which had been taken away for other purposes ; for the large stones, which form the lower part of the walls, were still standing higher than the sand. If *they* were not blown over, it was clear nothing higher than they could be blown over." This was quite convincing to me ; but it made not the least impression on Col and the others, who were not to be argued out of a Highland tradition.

We did not sit down to dinner till between six and seven. We lived plentifully here, and had a true welcome. In such a season, good firing was of no small importance. The peats were excellent, and burned cheerfully. Those at Dunvegan, which were damp, Dr. Johnson called " a sullen fuel."—Here a Scottish phrase was singularly applied to him. One of the company having remarked that he had gone out on a stormy evening, and brought in a supply of peats from the stack, old Mr. M'Sweyn said, " that was *main honest !* "

Blenheim being occasionally mentioned, he told me he had never seen it : he had not gone formerly ; and he would not go now, just as a common spectator, for his money : he would not put it in the power of some man about the Duke of Marlborough to say, " Johnson was here ; I knew him, but I took no notice of him." He said, he should be very glad to see it, if properly invited, which in all probability would never be the case, as it was not worth his while to seek for it.—I observed, that he might be easily introduced there by a common friend of ours, nearly related to the duke. He answered, with an uncommon attention to delicacy of feeling, " I doubt whether our friend be on such a footing with the duke as to carry any body there ; and I would not give him the uneasiness of seeing that I knew he was not, or even of being himself reminded of it."

Sunday, 10th October

There was this day the most terrible storm of wind and rain that I ever remember. It made such an awful impression on us all, as to produce, for some time, a kind of dismal quietness in the house. The day was passed without much conversation : only, upon my observing that there must be something bad in a man's mind, who does not like to give leases to his tenants, but wishes to keep them in a perpetual wretched dependence on his will, Dr. Johnson said, " You are right : it is a man's duty to extend comfort and security among as many people as he can. He should not wish to have his tenants mere *Ephemeræ*,—mere beings of an hour."—BOSWELL. " But, sir, if they have leases, is there not some danger that they may grow insolent ? I remember you yourself once told me, an English tenant was so independent, that, if provoked, he would *throw* his rent at his landlord."—JOHNSON. " Depend upon it, sir, it is the landlord's own fault, if it is thrown at him. A man may always keep his tenants in dependence enough, though they have leases. He must be a good tenant indeed, who will not fall behind in his rent, if his landlord will let him ; and if he does fall behind, his landlord has him at his mercy. Indeed, the poor man is always much at the mercy of the rich ; no matter whether landlord or tenant. If the tenant lets his landlord have a little rent before-hand, or has lent him money, then the landlord is in his power.

There cannot be a greater man than a tenant who has
lent money to his landlord ; for he has under subjection
the very man to whom he should be subjected."

Monday, 11th October

We had some days ago engaged the Campbell-town
vessel to carry us to Mull, from the harbour where she
lay. The morning was fine, and the wind fair and
moderate ; so we hoped at length to get away.

Mrs. M'Sweyn, who officiated as our landlady here,
had never been on the main land. On hearing this,
Dr. Johnson said to me, before her, " This is rather
being behind-hand with life. I would at least go and
see Glenelg."—BOSWELL. " You yourself, sir, have
never seen, till now, any thing but your native island."
—JOHNSON. " But, sir, by seeing London, I have seen
as much of life as the world can shew."—BOSWELL.
" You have not seen Pekin."—JOHNSON. " What is
Pekin ? Ten thousand Londoners would drive all the
people of Pekin : they would drive them like deer."

We set out about eleven for the harbour ; but, before
we reached it, so violent a storm came on, that we were
obliged again to take shelter in the house of Captain
M'Lean, where we dined, and passed the night.

Tuesday, 12th October

After breakfast, we made a second attempt to get to
the harbour ; but another storm soon convinced us that
it would be in vain. Captain M'Lean's house being
in some confusion, on account of Mrs. M'Lean being
expected to lie-in, we resolved to go to Mr. M'Sweyn's,
where we arrived very wet, fatigued, and hungry. In
this situation, we were somewhat disconcerted by being

told that we should have no dinner till late in the
evening ; but should have tea in the mean time. Dr.
Johnson opposed this arrangement ; but they persisted,
and he took the tea very readily. He said to me
afterwards, " You must consider, sir, a dinner here is
a matter of great consequence. It is a thing to be first
planned, and then executed. I suppose the mutton
was brought some miles off, from some place where
they knew there was a sheep killed."

Talking of the good people with whom we were, he
said, " Life has not got at all forward by a generation
in M'Sweyn's family : for the son is exactly formed
upon the father. What the father says, the son says ;
and what the father looks, the son looks."

There being little conversation to-night, I must
endeavour to recollect what I may have omitted on
former occasions.—When I boasted, at Rasay, of my
independency of spirit, and that I could not be bribed,
he said, " Yes, you may be bribed by flattery."—At
the Reverend Mr. M'Lean's, Dr. Johnson asked him,
if the people of Col had any superstitions. He said,
" No." The cutting peats at the increase of the moon
was mentioned as one ; but he would not allow it,
saying, it was not a superstition, but a whim. Dr.
Johnson would not admit the distinction. There were
many superstitions, he maintained, not connected with
religion ; and this was one of them.—On Monday we
had a dispute at the Captain's, whether sand-hills could
be fixed down by art. Dr. Johnson said, " How *the
devil* can you do it ? " but instantly corrected himself,
" How can you do it ? "—I never before heard him use
a phrase of that nature.

He has particularities which it is impossible to
explain. He never wears a night-cap, as I have already
mentioned : but he puts a handkerchief on his head in
the night —The day that we left Talisker, he bade us
ride on. He then turned the head of his horse back

towards Talisker, stopped for some time; then wheeled round to the same direction with ours, and then came briskly after us. He sets open a window in the coldest day or night, and stands before it. It may do with his constitution; but most people, amongst whom I am one, would say, with the frogs in the fable, " This may be sport to you; but it is death to us."—It is in vain to try to find a meaning in every one of his particularities, which, I suppose, are mere habits, contracted by chance; of which every man has some that are more or less remarkable. His speaking to himself, or rather repeating, is a common habit with studious men accustomed to deep thinking: and, in consequence of their being thus rapt, they will even laugh by themselves, if the subject which they are musing on is a merry one. Dr. Johnson is often uttering pious ejaculations, when he appears to be talking to himself; for sometimes his voice grows stronger, and parts of the Lord's Prayer are heard. I have sat beside him with more than ordinary reverence on such occasions.

In our Tour, I observed that he was disgusted whenever he met with coarse manners. He said to me, " I know not how it is, but I cannot bear low life: and I find others, who have as good a right as I to be fastidious, bear it better, by having mixed more with different sorts of men. You would think that I have mixed pretty well too."

He read this day a good deal of my Journal, written in a small book with which he had supplied me, and was pleased, for he said, " I wish thy books were twice as big." He helped me to fill up blanks which I had left in first writing it, when I was not quite sure of what he had said, and he corrected any mistakes that I had made. " They call me a scholar, (said he,) and yet how very little literature is there in my conversation."—BOSWELL. " That, sir, must be according to your company. You would not give literature to those who cannot taste it. Stay till we meet Lord Elibank."

We had at last a good dinner, or rather supper, and were very well satisfied with our entertainment.

Wednesday, 13th October

Col called me up, with intelligence that it was a good day for a passage to Mull; and just as we rose, a sailor from the vessel arrived for us. We got all ready with dispatch. Dr. Johnson was displeased at my bustling, and walking quickly up and down. He said, " It does not hasten us a bit. It is getting on horseback in a ship. All boys do it; and you are longer a boy than others." He himself has no alertness, or whatever it may be called; so he may dislike it, as *Oderunt hilarem tristes.*

Before we reached the harbour, the wind grew high again. However, the small boat was waiting, and took us on board. We remained for some time in uncertainty what to do: at last it was determined, that, as a good part of the day was over, and it was dangerous to be at sea at night, in such a vessel, and such weather, we should not sail till the morning tide, when the wind would probably be more gentle. We resolved not to go ashore again, but lie here in readiness. Dr. Johnson and I had each a bed in the cabbin. Col sat at the fire in the forecastle, with the captain, and Joseph, and the rest. I eat some dry oatmeal, of which I found a barrel in the cabbin. I had not done this since I was a boy. Dr. Johnson owned that he too was fond of it when a boy; a circumstance which I was highly pleased to hear from him, as it gave me an opportunity of observing that, notwithstanding his joke on the article of OATS, he was himself a proof that this kind of *food* was not peculiar to the people of Scotland.

Thursday, 14th October

When Dr. Johnson awaked this morning, he called, " Lanky ! " having, I suppose, been thinking of Langton ; but corrected himself instantly, and cried, " Bozzy ! " He has a way of contracting the names of his friends. Goldsmith feels himself so important now, as to be displeased at it. I remember one day, when Tom Davies was telling that Dr. Johnson said, " We are all in labour for a name to *Goldy's* play," Goldsmith cried, " I have often desired him not to call me *Goldy*."

Between six and seven we hauled our anchor, and set sail with a fair breeze ; and, after a pleasant voyage, we got safely and agreeably into the harbour of Tobermorie, before the wind rose, which it always has done, for some days, about noon.

Tobermorie is an excellent harbour. An island lies before it, and it is surrounded by a hilly theatre. The island is too low, otherwise this would be quite a secure port ; but, the island not being a sufficient protection, some storms blow very hard here. Not long ago, fifteen vessels were blown from their moorings. There are sometimes sixty or seventy sail here : to-day there were twelve or fourteen vessels. To see such a fleet was the next thing to seeing a town. The vessels were from different places ; Clyde, Campbelltown, Newcastle, &c. One was returning to Lancaster from Hamburgh. After having been shut up so long in Col, the sight of such an assemblage of moving habitations, containing such a variety of people, engaged in different pursuits, gave me much gaiety of spirit. When we had landed, Dr. Johnson said, " Boswell is now all alive. He is like Antæus ; he gets new vigour whenever he touches the ground."—I went to the top of a hill fronting the harbour, from whence I had a good view of it. We had here a tolerable inn. Dr. Johnson had owned to me this

morning, that he was out of humour. Indeed, he shewed
it a good deal in the ship ; for when I was expressing my
joy on the prospect of our landing in Mull, he said, he
had no joy, when he recollected that it would be five
days before he should get to the main land. I was
afraid he would now take a sudden resolution to give up
seeing Icolmkill. A dish of tea, and some good bread
and butter, did him service, and his bad humour went
off. I told him, that I was diverted to hear all the
people whom we had visited in our Tour, say, " Honest
man ! he's pleased with every thing ; he's always content ! "—" Little do they know," said I. He laughed,
and said, " You rogue ! "

We sent to hire horses to carry us across the island
of Mull to the shore opposite to Inchkenneth, the
residence of Sir Allan M'Lean, uncle to young Col,
and Chief of the M'Leans, to whose house we intended
to go the next day. Our friend Col went to visit his
aunt, the wife of Dr. Alexander M'Lean, a physician,
who lives about a mile from Tobermorie.

Dr. Johnson and I sat by ourselves at the inn, and
talked a good deal.—I told him, that I had found, in
Leandro Alberti's *Description of Italy*, much of what
Addison had given us in his *Remarks*. He said, " The
collection of passages from the Classicks has been made
by another Italian : it is, however, impossible to detect
a man as a plagiary in such a case, because all who set
about making such a collection must find the same passages ; but, if you find the same applications in another
book, then Addison's learning in his *Remarks* tumbles
down. It is a tedious book ; and, if it were not attached
to Addison's previous reputation, one would not think
much of it. Had he written nothing else, his name
would not have lived. Addison does not seem to have
gone deep in Italian literature : he shews nothing of
it in his subsequent writings. He shews a great deal
of French learning.—There is, perhaps, more know-

ledge circulated in the French language than in any other. There is more original knowledge in English."—"But the French (said I) have the art of accommodating literature."—JOHNSON. "Yes, sir; we have no such book as Moreri's Dictionary."—BOSWELL. "Their *Ana* are good."—JOHNSON. "A few of them are good; but we have one book of that kind better than any of them; Selden's *Table-talk*. As to original literature, the French have a couple of tragick poets who go round the world, Racine and Corneille, and one comick poet, Moliere."—BOSWELL. "They have Fenelon."—JOHNSON. "Why, sir, Telemachus is pretty well."—BOSWELL. "And Voltaire, sir."—JOHNSON. "He has not stood his trial yet. And what makes Voltaire chiefly circulate is collection; such as his *Universal History*."—BOSWELL. "What do you say to the Bishop of Meaux?"—JOHNSON. "Sir, nobody reads him."—He would not allow Massillon and Bourdaloue to go round the world. In general, however, he gave the French much praise for their industry.

He asked me whether he had mentioned, in any of the papers of the *Rambler*, the description in Virgil of the entrance into Hell, with an application to the press; "for (said he) I do not much remember them." I told him, "No." Upon which he repeated it:

> Vestibulum ante ipsum, primisque in faucibus orci,
> Luctus et ultrices posuere cubilia Curæ;
> Pallentesque habitant Morbi, tristisque Senectus,
> Et metus, et malesuada Fames, et turpis Egestas,
> Terribiles visu formæ; Lethumque, Laborque.

"Now, (said he), almost all these apply exactly to an authour; all these are the concomitants of a printing-house." I proposed to him to dictate an essay on it, and offered to write it. He said, he would not do it then, but perhaps would write one at some future period.

The Sunday evening that we sat by ourselves at Aberdeen, I asked him several particulars of his life from his early years, which he readily told me ; and I wrote them down before him. This day I proceeded in my inquiries, also writing them in his presence. I have them on detached sheets. I shall collect authentick materials for THE LIFE OF SAMUEL JOHNSON, LL.D. ; and, if I survive him, I shall be one who will most faithfully do honour to his memory. I have now a vast treasure of his conversation, at different times, since the year 1762, when I first obtained his acquaintance ; and, by assiduous inquiry, I can make up for not knowing him sooner.

A Newcastle ship-master, who happened to be in the house, intruded himself upon us. He was much in liquor, and talked nonsense about his being a man for *Wilkes and Liberty*, and against the ministry. Dr. Johnson was angry, that " a fellow should come into *our* company, who was fit for *no* company." He left us soon.

Col returned from his aunt, and told us, she insisted that we should come to her house that night. He introduced to us Mr. Campbell, the Duke of Argyle's factor in Tyr-yi. He was a genteel, agreeable man. He was going to Inveraray, and promised to put letters into the post-office for us. I now found that Dr. Johnson's desire to get on the main land, arose from his anxiety to have an opportunity of conveying letters to his friends.

After dinner, we proceeded to Dr. M'Lean's, which was about a mile from our inn. He was not at home, but we were received by his lady and daughter, who entertained us so well, that Dr. Johnson seemed quite happy. When we had supped, he asked me to give him some paper to write letters. I begged he would write short ones, and not expatiate, as we ought to set off early. He was irritated by this, and said, " What

must be done, must be done : the thing is past a joke."
—" Nay, sir, (said I,) write as much as you please ;
but do not blame me, if we are kept six days before we
get to the main land. You were very impatient in the
morning : but no sooner do you find yourself in good
quarters, than you forget that you are to move." I
got him paper enough, and we parted in good humour.

Let me now recollect whatever particulars I have
omitted.—In the morning I said to him, before we
landed at Tobermorie, " We shall see Dr. M'Lean, who
has written the History of the M'Leans."—JOHNSON.
" I have no great patience to stay to hear the history
of the M'Leans. I would rather hear the History of
the Thrales."—When on Mull, I said, " Well, sir, this
is the fourth of the Hebrides that we have been upon."
—JOHNSON. " Nay, we cannot boast of the number we
have seen. We thought we should see many more.
We thought of sailing about easily from island to island ;
and so we should, had we come at a better season ; but
we, being wise men, thought it would be summer all
the year where *we* were. However, sir, we have seen
enough to give us a pretty good notion of the system
of insular life."

Let me not forget, that he sometimes amused himself
with very slight reading ; from which, however, his
conversation showed that he contrived to extract some
benefit. At Captain M'Lean's he read a good deal in
The Charmer, a collection of songs.

Friday, 15th October

We this morning found that we could not proceed,
there being a violent storm of wind and rain, and the
rivers being impassable. When I expressed my discontent at our confinement, Dr. Johnson said, " Now
that I have had an opportunity of writing to the main

land, I am in no such haste." I was amused with his
being so easily satisfied ; for the truth was, that the
gentleman who was to convey our letters, as I was now
informed, was not to set out for Inveraray for some
time ; so that it was probable we should be there as
soon as he : however, I did not undeceive my friend,
but suffered him to enjoy his fancy.

Dr. Johnson asked, in the evening, to see Dr. M'Lean's
books. He took down Willis *de Anima Brutorum*, and
pored over it a good deal.

Miss M'Lean produced some Erse poems by John
M'Lean, who was a famous bard in Mull, and had
died only a few years ago. He could neither read nor
write. She read and translated two of them ; one, a
kind of elegy on Sir John M'Lean's being obliged to
fly his country in 1715 ; another, a dialogue between
two Roman Catholick young ladies, sisters, whether it
was better to be a nun or to marry. I could not perceive much poetical imagery in the translation. Yet
all of our company who understood Erse, seemed
charmed with the original. There may, perhaps, be
some choice of expression, and some excellence of
arrangement, that cannot be shewn in translation.

After we had exhausted the Erse poems, of which
Dr. Johnson said nothing, Miss M'Lean gave us several
tunes on a spinnet, which, though made so long ago as
in 1667, was still very well toned. She sung along with
it. Dr. Johnson seemed pleased with the musick, though
he owns he neither likes it, nor has hardly any percep-
tion of it. At Mr. M'Pherson's, in Slate, he told us, that
" he knew a drum from a trumpet, and a bagpipe from
a guittar, which was about the extent of his knowledge
of musick." To-night he said, that, " if he had learnt
musick, he should have been afraid he would have done
nothing else but play. It was a method of employing
the mind, without the labour of thinking at all, and with
some applause from a man's self."

We had the musick of the bagpipe every day, at Armidale, Dunvegan, and Col. Dr. Johnson appeared fond of it, and used often to stand for some time with his ear close to the great drone.

The penurious gentleman of our acquaintance, formerly alluded to, afforded us a topick of conversation to-night. Dr. Johnson said, I ought to write down a collection of the instances of his narrowness, as they almost exceeded belief. Col told us, that O'Kane, the famous Irish harper, was once at that gentleman's house. He could not find in his heart to give him any money, but gave him a key for a harp, which was finely ornamented with gold and silver, and with a precious stone, and was worth eighty or a hundred guineas. He did not know the value of it ; and when he came to know it, he would fain have had it back ; but O'Kane took care that he should not.—JOHNSON. " They exaggerate the value ; every body is so desirous that he should be fleeced. I am very willing it should be worth eighty or a hundred guineas ; but I do not believe it."—BOSWELL. " I do not think O'Kane was obliged to give it back."—JOHNSON. " No, sir. If a man with his eyes open, and without any means used to deceive him, gives me a thing, I am not to let him have it again when he grows wiser. I like to see how avarice defeats itself : how, when avoiding to part with money, the miser gives something more valuable."— Col said, the gentleman's relations were angry at his giving away the harp-key, for it had been long in the family.—JOHNSON. " Sir, he values a new guinea more than an old friend."

Col also told us, that the same person having come up with a serjeant and twenty men, working on the high road, he entered into discourse with the serjeant, and then gave him sixpence for the men to drink. The serjeant asked, " Who is this fellow ? " Upon being informed, he said, " If I had known who he was, I should have thrown it in his face."—JOHNSON. "There is much want of sense in all this. He had no business to speak with the serjeant. He might have been in haste, and trotted on. He has not learnt to be a miser; I believe we must take him apprentice."—BOSWELL. "He would grudge giving half a guinea to be taught." —JOHNSON. "Nay, sir, you must teach him *gratis*. You must give him an opportunity to practice your precepts."

Let me now go back, and glean *Johnsoniana*.—The Saturday before we sailed from Slate, I sat awhile in the afternoon with Dr. Johnson in his room, in a quiet serious frame. I observed, that hardly any man was accurately prepared for dying; but almost every one left something undone, something in confusion; that my father, indeed, told me he knew one man, (Carlisle of Limekilns,) after whose death all his papers were found in exact order; and nothing was omitted in his will.—JOHNSON. "Sir, I had an uncle who died so; but such attention requires great leisure, and great firmness of mind. If one was to think constantly of death, the business of life would stand still. I am no friend to making religion appear too hard. Many good people have done harm, by giving severe notions of it. In the same way, as to learning: I never frighten young people with difficulties; on the contrary, I tell them that they may very easily get as much as will do very well. I do not indeed tell them that they will be Bentleys."

The night we rode to Col's house, I said, "Lord Elibank is probably wondering what is become of us." —JOHNSON. "No, no; he is not thinking of us."— BOSWELL. "But recollect the warmth with which he wrote. Are we not to believe a man, when he says he has a great desire to see another? Don't you believe that I was very impatient for your coming to Scotland?"—JOHNSON. "Yes, sir; I believe you were;

and I was impatient to come to you. A young man feels so, but seldom an old man." I however convinced him that Lord Elibank, who has much of the spirit of a young man, might feel so.—He asked me if our jaunt had answered expectation. I said it had much exceeded it. I expected much difficulty with him, and had not found it. "And (he added) wherever we have come, we have been received like princes in their progress."

He said, he would not wish not to be disgusted in the Highlands ; for that would be to lose the power of distinguishing, and a man might then lie down in the middle of them. He wished only to conceal his disgust.

At Captain M'Lean's, I mentioned Pope's friend, Spence.—JOHNSON. "He was a weak conceited man."—BOSWELL. "A good scholar, sir ? "—JOHNSON. "Why, no, sir."—BOSWELL. "He was a pretty scholar."—JOHNSON. "You have about reached him."

Last night at the inn, when the factor in Tyr-yi spoke of his having heard that a roof was put on some part of the buildings at Icolmkill, I unluckily said, " It will be fortunate if we find a cathedral with a roof on it." I said this from a foolish anxiety to engage Dr. Johnson's curiosity more. He took me short at once. "What, sir ? how can you talk so ? If we shall *find* a cathedral roofed ! as if we were going to a *terra incognita :* when everything that is at Icolmkill is so well known. You are like some New-England-men who came to the mouth of the Thames. ' Come, (said they,) let us go up and see what sort of inhabit-ants there are here.' They talked, sir, as if they had been to go up the Susquehannah, or any other American river."

Saturday, 16th October

This day there was a new moon, and the weather changed for the better. Dr. Johnson said of Miss

M'Lean, " She is the most accomplished lady that I
have found in the Highlands. She knows French,
musick, and drawing, sews neatly, makes shell-work,
and can milk cows ; in short, she can do everything.
She talks sensibly, and is the first person whom I have
found, that can translate Erse poetry literally."—We
set out, mounted on little Mull horses. Mull corre-
sponded exactly with the idea which I had always
had of it ; a hilly country, diversified with heath and
grass, and many rivulets. Dr. Johnson was not in
very good humour. He said, it was a dreary country,
much worse than Sky. I differed from him. " O, sir,
(said he,) a most dolorous country ! "

   We had a very hard journey to-day. I had no bridle
for my sheltie, but only a halter ; and Joseph rode without a saddle. At one place, a loch having swelled over
the road, we were obliged to plunge through pretty deep
water. Dr. Johnson observed, how helpless a man
would be, were he travelling here alone, and should meet
with any accident ; and said, " he longed to get to a
country of saddles and bridles." He was more out of
humour to-day, than he has been in the course of our
Tour, being fretted to find that his little horse could
scarcely support his weight ;—and having suffered a
loss, which, though small in itself, was of some consequence to him, while travelling the rugged steeps of
Mull, where he was at times obliged to walk. The loss
that I allude to was that of the large oak-stick, which,
as I formerly mentioned, he had brought with him from
London. It was of great use to him in our wild peregrina-
tion ; for, ever since his last illness in 1766, he has had
a weakness in his knees, and has not been able to walk
easily. It had too the properties of a measure ; for
one nail was driven into it at the length of a foot ;
another at that of a yard. In return for the services
it had done him, he said, this morning, he would make
a present of it to some Museum ; but he little thought

he was so soon to lose it. As he preferred riding with
a switch, it was intrusted to a fellow to be delivered
to our baggage-man, who followed us at some distance,
but we never saw it more. I could not persuade him
out of a suspicion that it had been stolen. " No, no,
my friend, (said he,) it is not to be expected that any
man in Mull, who has got it, will part with it. Consider,
sir, the value of such a *piece of timber* here ! "

As we travelled this forenoon, we met Dr. M'Lean,
who expressed much regret at his having been so unfortunate as to be absent while we were at his house.

We were in hopes to get to Sir Allan Maclean's at
Inchkenneth, to-night ; but the eight miles, of which
our road was said to consist, were so very long, that
we did not reach the opposite coast of Mull till seven
at night, though we had set out about eleven in the
forenoon ; and when we did arrive there, we found
the wind strong against us. Col determined that we
should pass the night at M'Quarrie's, in the island of
Ulva, which lies between Mull and Inchkenneth ; and
a servant was sent forward to the ferry, to secure the
boat for us : but the boat was gone to the Ulva side,
and the wind was so high that the people could not
hear him call ; and the night so dark that they could
not see a signal. We should have been in a very bad
situation, had there not fortunately been lying in the
little sound of Ulva an Irish vessel, the *Bonnetta*, of
Londonderry, Captain M'Lure, master. He himself was
at M'Quarrie's ; but his men obligingly came with their
long-boat, and ferried us over.

M'Quarrie's house was mean ; but we were agreeably surprised with the appearance of the master,
whom we found to be intelligent, polite, and much a
man of the world. Though his clan is not numerous,
he is a very ancient Chief, and has a burial place
at Icolmkill. He told us, his family had possessed
Ulva for nine hundred years ; but I was distressed

to hear that it was soon to be sold for payment of his debts.

Captain M'Lure, whom we found here, was of Scotch extraction, and properly a M'Leod, being descended of some of the M'Leod's who went with Sir Normand of Bernera to the battle of Worcester; and after the defeat of the royalists, fled to Ireland, and, to conceal themselves, took a different name. He told me, there was a great number of them about Londonderry; some of good property. I said, they should now resume their real name. The Laird of M'Leod should go over, and assemble them, and make them all drink the large horn full, and from that time they should be M'Leods.—The captain informed us, he had named his ship the *Bonnetta*, out of gratitude to Providence; for once, when he was sailing to America with a good number of passengers, the ship in which he then sailed was becalmed for five weeks, and during all that time, numbers of the fish Bonnetta swam close to her, and were caught for food; he resolved therefore, that the ship he should next get, should be called the *Bonnetta*.

M'Quarrie told us a strong instance of the second sight. He had gone to Edinburgh, and taken a man-servant along with him. An old woman, who was in the house, said one day, " M'Quarrie will be at home to-morrow, and will bring two gentlemen with him;" and she said, she saw his servant return in red and green. He did come home next day. He had two gentlemen with him; and his servant had a new red and green livery, which M'Quarrie had bought for him at Edinburgh, upon a sudden thought, not having the least intention when he left home to put his servant in livery; so that the old woman could not have heard any previous mention of it. This, he assured us, was a true story.

M'Quarrie insisted that the *Mercheta Mulierum* mentioned in our old charters, did really mean the privilege which a lord of a manor, or a baron, had, to have the first night of all his vassal's wives. Dr. Johnson said, the belief of such a custom having existed was also held in England, where there is a tenure called *Borough English*, by which the eldest child does not inherit, from a doubt of his being the son of the tenant. M'Quarrie told us, that still, on the marriage of each of his tenants, a sheep is due to him; for which the composition is fixed at five shillings. I suppose, Ulva is the only place where this custom remains.

Talking of the sale of an estate of an ancient family, which was said to have been purchased much under its value by the confidential lawyer of that family, and it being mentioned that the sale would probably be set aside by a suit in equity, Dr. Johnson said, " I am very willing that this sale should be set aside, but I doubt much whether the suit will be successful; for the argument for avoiding the sale is founded on vague and indeterminate principles,—as that the price was too low, and that there was a great degree of confidence placed by the seller in the person who became the purchaser. Now, how low should a price be? or what degree of confidence should there be to make a bargain be set aside? a bargain, which is a wager of skill between man and man.—If, indeed, any fraud can be proved, that will do."

When Dr. Johnson and I were by ourselves at night, I observed of our host, " *aspectum generosum habet;* " —" *et generosum animum,*" he added.—For fear of being overheard in the small Highland houses, I often talked to him in such Latin as I could speak, and with as much of the English accent as I could assume, so as not to be understood, in case our conversation should be too loud for the space.

We had each an elegant bed in the same room; and here it was that a circumstance occurred, as to which he has been strangely misunderstood. From his description of his chamber, it has erroneously been supposed, that his bed being too short for him, his feet, during the night, were in the mire ; whereas he has only said, that when he undressed, he felt his feet in the mire : that is, the clay-floor of the room, on which he stood upon before he went into bed, was wet, in consequence of the windows being broken, which let in the rain.

Sunday, 17*th October*

Being informed that there was nothing worthy of observation in Ulva, we took boat, and proceeded to Inchkenneth, where we were introduced by our friend Col to Sir Allan M'Lean, the Chief of his clan, and to two young ladies, his daughters. Inchkenneth is a pretty little island, a mile long, and about half a mile broad, all good land.

As we walked up from the shore, Dr. Johnson's heart was cheered by the sight of a road marked with cart-wheels, as on the mainland ; a thing which we had not seen for a long time. It gave us a pleasure similar to that which a traveller feels, when, whilst wandering on what he fears is a desert island, he perceives the print of human feet.

Military men acquire excellent habits of having all conveniences about them. Sir Allan M'Lean, who had been long in the army, and had now a lease of the island, had formed a commodious habitation, though it consisted but of a few small buildings, only one story high. He had, in his little apartments, more things than I could enumerate in a page or two.

Among other agreeable circumstances, it was not the least, to find here a parcel of the *Caledonian Mercury*, published since we left Edinburgh ; which I read with that pleasure which every man feels who has been for some time secluded from the animated scenes of the busy world.

Dr. Johnson found books here. He bade me buy Bishop Gastrell's *Christian Institutes*, which was lying in the room. He said, " I do not like to read any thing on a Sunday, but what is theological ; not that I would scrupulously refuse to look at any thing which a friend should shew me in a newspaper ; but in general, I would read only what is theological.—I read just now some of Drummond's *Travels*, before I perceived what books were here. I then took up Derham's *Physico-Theology*."

Every particular concerning this island having been so well described by Dr. Johnson, it would be super-fluous in me to present the publick with the observa-tions that I made upon it, in my Journal.

I was quite easy with Sir Allan almost instantaneously. He knew the great intimacy that had been between my father and his predecessor, Sir Hector, and was himself of a very frank disposition.—After dinner, Sir Allan said he had got Dr. Campbell about an hundred sub-scribers to his *Britannia Elucidata*, (a work since pub-lished under the title of *A Political Survey of Great Britain*,) of whom he believed twenty were dead, the publication having been so long delayed.—JOHNSON. " Sir, I imagine the delay of publication is owing to this ;—that, after publication, there will be no more subscribers, and few will send the additional guinea to get their books : in which they will be wrong ; for there will be a great deal of instruction in the work. I think highly of Campbell. In the first place, he has very good parts. In the second place, he has very extensive reading ; not, perhaps, what is properly called learning, but history, politicks, and, in short, that popular knowledge which makes a man very useful. In the third place, he has learned much by what is called the *vox viva*. He talks with a great many people."

Speaking of this gentleman, at Rasay, he told us, that he one day called on him, and they talked of *Tull's Husbandry*. Dr. Campbell said something. Dr. Johnson began to dispute it. " Come, (said Dr. Campbell,) we do not want to get the better of one another : we want to encrease each other's ideas."— Dr. Johnson took it in good part, and the conversation then went on coolly and instructively.—His candour in relating this anecdote does him much credit, and his conduct on that occasion proves how easily he could be persuaded to talk from a better motive than " for victory."

Dr. Johnson here shewed so much of the spirit of a Highlander, that he won Sir Allan's heart : indeed, he has shewn it during the whole of our Tour.—One night, in Col, he strutted about the room with a broad sword and target, and made a formidable appearance ; and, another night, I took the liberty to put a large blue bonnet on his head. His age, his size, and his bushy grey wig, with this covering on it, presented the image of a venerable *Senachi :* and, however unfavourable to the Lowland Scots, he seemed much pleased to assume the appearance of an ancient Caledonian. We only regretted that he could not be prevailed with to partake of the social glass. One of his arguments against drinking, appears to me not convincing. He urged, that, " in proportion as drinking makes a man different from what he is before he has drunk, it is bad ; because it has so far affected his reason." But may it not be answered, that a man may be altered by it *for the better ;* that his spirits may be exhilarated, without his reason being affected ? On the general subject of drinking, however, I do not mean positively to take the other side. I am *dubius, non improbus.*

In the evening, Sir Allan informed us that it was the custom of his house to have prayers every Sunday ; and Miss M'Lean read the evening service, in which we all joined. I then read Ogden's second and ninth Sermons on Prayer, which, with their other distinguished excellence, have the merit of being short. Dr. Johnson said, that it was the most agreeable Sunday he had ever passed ; and it made such an impression on his mind, that he afterwards wrote the following Latin verses upon Inchkenneth :

INSULA SANCTI KENNETHI

Parva quidem regio, sed relligione priorum
  Nota, Caledonias panditur inter aquas ;
Voce ubi Cennethus populos domuisse feroces
  Dicitur, et vanos dedocuisse deos.
Huc ego delatus placido per cœrula cursu
  Scire locum volui quid daret ille novi.
Illic Leniades humili regnabat in aula,
  Leniades magnis nobilitatus avis :
Una duas habuit casa cum genitore puellas,
  Quas Amor undarum fingeret esse deas :
Non tamen inculti gelidis latuere sub antris,
  Accola Danubii qualia sævus habet ;
Mollia non deerant vacuæ solatia vitæ,
  Sive libros poscant otia, sive lyram.
Luxerat illa dies, legis gens docta supernæ
  Spes hominum ac curas cum procul esse jubet,
Ponti inter strepitus sacri non munera cultus
  Cessarunt ; pietas hic quoque cura fuit :
Quid quod sacrifici versavit femina libros,
  Legitimas faciunt pectora pura preces.
Quo vagor ulterius ? quod ubique requiritur hic est ;
  Hic secura quies, hic et honestus amor.

Monday, 18th October

We agreed to pass this day with Sir Allan, and he engaged to have every thing in order for our voyage to-morrow.

Being now soon to be separated from our amiable friend young Col, his merits were all remembered. At Ulva he had appeared in a new character, having given us a good prescription for a cold. On my mentioning him with warmth, Dr. Johnson said, " Col does every thing for us : we will erect a statue to Col."—" Yes, (said I,) and we will have him with his various attributes and characters, like Mercury, or any other of the heathen gods. We will have him as a pilot ; we will have him as a fisherman, as a hunter, as a husbandman, as a physician."

I this morning took a spade, and dug a little grave in the floor of a ruined chapel, near Sir Allan M'Lean's house, in which I buried some human bones I found there. Dr. Johnson praised me for what I had done, though he owned, he could not have done it. He shewed in the chapel at Rasay his horrour at dead men's bones. He shewed it again at Col's house. In the Charter-room there was a remarkable large shin-bone, which was said to have been a bone of John Garve, one of the lairds. Dr. Johnson would not look at it ; but started away.

At breakfast, I asked, " What is the reason that we are angry at a trader's having opulence ? "—JOHNSON. " Why, sir, the reason is, (though I don't undertake to prove that there is a reason,) we see no qualities in trade that should entitle a man to superiority. We are not angry at a soldier's getting riches, because we see that he possesses qualities which we have not. If a man returns from a battle, having lost one hand, and with the other full of gold, we feel that he deserves the gold ; but we cannot think that a fellow, by sitting all day at a desk, is entitled to get above us."— BOSWELL. " But, sir, may we not suppose a merchant to be a man of an enlarged mind, such as Addison in the *Spectator* describes Sir Andrew Freeport to have been ? "—JOHNSON. " Why, sir, we may suppose any fictitious character. We may suppose a philosophical day-labourer, who is happy in reflecting that, by his labour, he contributes to the fertility of the earth, and to the support of his fellow-creatures ; but we find no such philosophical day-labourer. A merchant may, perhaps, be a man of an enlarged mind; but there is nothing in trade connected with an enlarged mind."

I mentioned that I had heard Dr. Solander say he was a Swedish Laplander.—JOHNSON. "Sir, I don't believe he is a Laplander. The Laplanders are not much above four feet high. He is as tall as you; and he has not the copper colour of a Laplander."—BOSWELL. "But what motive could he have to make himself a Laplander?"—JOHNSON. "Why, sir, he must either mean the word Laplander in a very extensive sense, or may mean a voluntary degradation of himself. 'For all my being the great man that you see me now, I was originally a Barbarian;' as if Burke should say, 'I came over a wild Irishman,'—which he might say in his present state of exaltation."

Having expressed a desire to have an island like Inchkenneth, Dr. Johnson set himself to think what would be necessary for a man in such a situation. "Sir, I should build me a fortification, if I came to live here; for, if you have it not, what should hinder a parcel of ruffians to land in the night, and carry off every thing you have in the house, which, in a remote country, would be more valuable than cows and sheep? add to all this the danger of having your throat cut."—BOSWELL. "I would have a large dog."—JOHNSON. "So you may, sir; but a large dog is of no use but to alarm."—He, however, I apprehend, thinks too lightly of the power of that animal. I have heard him say, that he is afraid of no dog. "He would take him up by the hinder legs, which would render him quite helpless,—and then knock his head against a stone, and beat out his brains."—Topham Beauclerk told me, that at his house in the country, two large ferocious dogs were fighting. Dr. Johnson looked steadily at them for a little while; and then, as one would separate two little boys, who were foolishly hurting each other, he ran up to them, and cuffed their heads till he drove them asunder. But few men have his intrepidity, Herculean strength, or presence of mind. Most thieves or robbers would be afraid to encounter a mastiff.

I observed, that, when young Col talked of the lands belonging to his family, he always said, " *my* lands." For this he had a plausible pretence ; for he told me, there has been a custom in this family, that the laird resigns the estate to the eldest son when he comes of age, reserving to himself only a certain life-rent. He said, it was a voluntary custom ; but I think I found an instance in the charter-room, that there was such an obligation in a contract of marriage. If the custom was voluntary, it was only curious ; but if founded on obligation, it might be dangerous ; for I have been told, that in Otaheité, whenever a child is born, (a son, I think,) the father loses his right to the estate and honours, and that this unnatural, or rather absurd custom, occasions the murder of many children.

Young Col told us he could run down a greyhound ; " for, (said he,) the dog runs himself out of breath, by going too quick, and then I get up with him." I accounted for his advantage over the dog, by remarking that Col had the faculty of reason, and knew how to moderate his pace, which the dog had not sense enough to do. Dr. Johnson said, " He is a noble animal. He is as complete an islander as the mind can figure. He is a farmer, a sailor, a hunter, a fisher : he will run you down a dog : if any man has a *tail*, it is Col. He is hospitable ; and he has an intrepidity of talk, whether he understands the subject or not. I regret that he is not more intellectual."

Dr. Johnson observed, that there was nothing of which he would not undertake to persuade a Frenchman in a foreign country. " I'll carry a Frenchman to St. Paul's Church-yard, and I'll tell him, ' by our law you may walk half round the church ; but, if you walk round the whole, you will be punished capitally : ' and he will believe me at once. Now, no Englishman would readily swallow such a thing : he would go and inquire of somebody else."—The Frenchman's credulity, I observed, must be owing to his being accustomed to implicit submission ; whereas every Englishman reasons upon the laws of his country, and instructs his representatives, who compose the legislature.

This day was passed in looking at a small island adjoining Inchkenneth, which afforded nothing worthy of observation ; and in such social and gay entertainments as our little society could furnish.

Tuesday, 19th October

After breakfast we took leave of the young ladies, and of our excellent companion Col, to whom we had been so much obliged. He had now put us under the care of his Chief ; and was to hasten back to Sky. We parted from him with very strong feelings of kindness and gratitude ; and we hoped to have had some future opportunity of proving to him the sincerity of what we felt ; but in the following year he was unfortunately lost in the Sound between Ulva and Mull ; and this imperfect memorial, joined to the high honour of being tenderly and respectfully mentioned by Dr. Johnson, is the only return which the uncertainty of human events has permitted us to make to this deserving young man.

Sir Allan, who obligingly undertook to accompany us to Icolmkill, had a strong good boat, with four stout rowers. We coasted along Mull till we reached Gribon, where is what is called Mackinnon's cave, compared with which that at Ulinish is inconsiderable. It is in a rock of a great height, close to the sea. Upon the left of its entrance there is a cascade, almost perpendicular from the top to the bottom of the rock. There is a tradition that it was conducted thither artificially, to supply the inhabitants of the cave with water. Dr. Johnson gave no credit to this tradition. As, on the one hand, his faith in the Christian religion is firmly founded upon good grounds; so, on the other, he is incredulous when there is no sufficient reason for belief; being in this respect just the reverse of modern infidels, who, however nice and scrupulous in weighing the evidences of religion, are yet often so ready to believe the most absurd and improbable tales of another nature, that Lord Hailes well observed, a good essay might be written *Sur la credulité des Incredules.*

The height of this cave I cannot tell with any tolerable exactness: but it seemed to be very lofty, and to be a pretty regular arch. We penetrated, by candlelight, a great way; by our measurement, no less than four hundred and eighty-five feet. Tradition says, that a piper and twelve men once advanced into this cave, nobody can tell how far; and never returned. At the distance to which we proceeded the air was quite pure; for the candle burned freely, without the least appearance of the flame growing globular; but as we had only one, we thought it dangerous to venture farther, lest, should it have been extinguished, we should have had no means of ascertaining whether we could remain without danger. Dr. Johnson said, this was the greatest natural curiosity he had ever seen.

We saw the island of Staffa, at no very great distance, but could not land upon it, the surge was so high on its rocky coast.

Sir Allan, anxious for the honour of Mull, was still talking of its *woods*, and pointing them out to Dr. Johnson, as appearing at a distance on the skirts of that island, as we sailed along.—JOHNSON. " Sir, I saw at Tobermorie what they called a wood, which I un-

luckily took for *heath.* If you shew me what I shall
take for *furze,* it will be something.''

In the afternoon we went ashore on the coast of
Mull, and partook of a cold repast, which we carried
with us. We hoped to have procured some rum or
brandy for our boatmen and servants, from a publick-
house near where we landed ; but unfortunately a funeral
a few days before had exhausted all their store. Mr.
Campbell however, one of the Duke of Argyle's tacksmen, who lived in the neighbourhood, on receiving a
message from Sir Allan, sent us a liberal supply.

We continued to coast along Mull, and passed by
Nuns' Island, which, it is said, belonged to the nuns
of Icolmkill, and from which, we were told, the stone
for the buildings there was taken. As we sailed along
by moon-light, in a sea somewhat rough, and often
between black and gloomy rocks, Dr. Johnson said,
" If this be not *roving among the Hebrides,* nothing
is.''—The repetition of words which he had so often
previously used, made a strong impression on my imagination ; and, by a natural course of thinking, led me
to consider how our present adventures would appear
to me at a future period.

I have often experienced, that scenes through which
a man has passed, improve by lying in the memory :
they grow mellow. *Acti labores sunt jucundi.* This
may be owing to comparing them with present listless
ease. Even harsh scenes acquire a softness by length
of time ; and some are like very loud sounds, which
do not please, or at least do not please so much, till
you are removed to a certain distance. They may be
compared to strong coarse pictures, which will not
bear to be viewed near. Even pleasing scenes improve by time, and seem more exquisite in recollection,
than when they were present ; if they have not faded
to dimness in the memory. Perhaps, there is so much
evil in every human enjoyment, when present,—so much

dross mixed with it, that it requires to be refined by time ; and yet I do not see why time should not melt away the good and the evil in equal proportions ;—why the shade should decay, and the light remain in preservation.

After a tedious sail, which, by our following various turnings of the coast of Mull, was extended to about forty miles, it gave us no small pleasure to perceive a light in the village at Icolmkill, in which almost all the inhabitants of the island live, close to where the ancient building stood. As we approached the shore, the tower of the cathedral, just discernible in the air, was a picturesque object.

When we had landed upon the sacred place, which, as long as I can remember, I had thought on with veneration, Dr. Johnson and I cordially embraced. We had long talked of visiting Icolmkill ; and, from the lateness of the season, were at times very doubtful whether we should be able to effect our purpose. To have seen it, even alone, would have given me great satisfaction ; but the venerable scene was rendered much more pleasing by the company of my great and pious friend, who was no less affected by it than I was ; and who has described the impressions it should make on the mind, with such strength of thought, and energy of language, that I shall quote his words, as conveying my own sensations much more forcibly than I am capable of doing :

" We were now treading that illustrious Island, which was once the luminary of the Caledonian regions, whence savage clans and roving barbarians derived the benefits of knowledge, and the blessings of religion. To abstract the mind from all local emotion would be impossible, if it were endeavoured, and would be foolish if it were possible. Whatever withdraws us from the power of our senses, whatever makes the past, the distant, or the future, predominate over the present, advances us in the dignity of thinking beings. Far from me, and from my friends, be such frigid philosophy as may conduct us indifferent and unmoved over any ground which has been dignified by wisdom, bravery or virtue. That man is little to be envied, whose patriotism would not gain force upon the plain of *Marathon*, or whose piety would not grow warmer among the ruins of *Iona !* ''

Upon hearing that Sir Allan M'Lean was arrived, the inhabitants, who still consider themselves as the people of M'Lean, to whom the island formerly belonged, though the Duke of Argyle has at present possession of it, ran eagerly to him.

We were accommodated this night in a large barn, the island affording no lodging that we should have liked so well. Some good hay was strewed at one end of it, to form a bed for us, upon which we lay with our clothes on ; and we were furnished with blankets from the village. Each of us had a portmanteau for a pillow. When I awaked in the morning, and looked round me, I could not help smiling at the idea of the chief of the M'Leans, the great English Moralist, and myself, lying thus extended in such a situation.

Wednesday, 20th October

Early in the morning we surveyed the remains of antiquity at this place, accompanied by an illiterate fellow, as *Cicerone*, who called himself a descendant of a cousin of Saint Columba, the founder of the religious establishment here. As I knew that many persons had already examined them, and as I saw Dr. Johnson inspecting and measuring several of the ruins of which he has since given so full an account, my mind was quiescent ; and I resolved to stroll among them at my ease, to take no trouble to investigate

minutely, and only receive the general impression of
solemn antiquity, and the particular ideas of such objects as should of themselves strike my attention.

We walked from the monastery of Nuns to the great
church or cathedral, as they call it, along an old broken
causeway. They told us, that this had been a street;
and that there were good houses built on each side.
Dr. Johnson doubted if it was any thing more than a
paved road for the nuns. The convent of Monks, the
great church, Oran's chapel, and four other chapels,
are still to be discerned. But I must own that Icolmkill did not answer my expectations; for they were
high, from what I had read of it, and still more from
what I had heard and thought of it, from my earliest
years. Dr. Johnson said, it came up to his expectations,
because he had taken his impression from an account
of it subjoined to Sacheverel's *History of the Isle of
Man*, where it is said, there is not much to be seen here.
We were both disappointed, when we were shewn what
are called the monuments of the kings of Scotland,
Ireland, and Denmark, and of a King of France. There
are only some grave-stones flat on the earth, and we
could see no inscriptions. How far short was this of
marble monuments, like those in Westminster-Abbey,
which I had imagined here! The grave-stones of Sir
Allan M'Lean's family, and of that of M'Quarrie, had
as good an appearance as the royal grave-stones; if
they were royal, we doubted.

My easiness to give credit to what I heard in the
course of our Tour was too great. Dr. Johnson's
peculiar accuracy of investigation detected much traditional fiction, and many gross mistakes. It is not to
be wondered at, that he was provoked by people care-
lessly telling him, with the utmost readiness and confidence, what he found, on questioning them a little
more, was erroneous. Of this there were innumerable
instances.

I left him and Sir Allan at breakfast in our barn, and stole back again to the cathedral, to indulge in solitude and devout meditation. While contemplating the venerable ruins, I reflected with much satisfaction, that the solemn scenes of piety never lose their sanctity and influence, though the cares and follies of life may prevent us from visiting them, or may even make us fancy that their effects are only " as yesterday, when it is past," and never again to be perceived. I hoped, that, ever after having been in this holy place, I should maintain an exemplary conduct. One has a strange propensity to fix upon some point of time from whence a better course of life may begin.

Being desirous to visit the opposite shore of the island, where Saint Columba is said to have landed, I procured a horse from one M'Ginnis, who ran along as my guide. The M'Ginnises are said to be a branch of the clan of M'Lean. Sir Allan had been told that this man had refused to send him some rum, at which the knight was in great indignation. " You rascal ! (said he,) don't you know that I can hang you, if I please ? "—Not adverting to the Chieftain's power over his clan, I imagined that Sir Allan had known of some capital crime that the fellow had committed, which he could discover, and so get him condemned ; and said, " How so ? "—" Why, (said Sir Allan,) are they not all my people ? "—Sensible of my inadvertency, and most willing to contribute what I could towards the continuation of feudal authority, " Very true," said I.—Sir Allan went on : " Refuse to send rum to me, you rascal ! Don't you know that, if I order you to go and cut a man's throat, you are to do it ? "—" Yes, an't please your honour ! and my own too, and hang myself too."—The poor fellow denied that he had refused to send the rum. His making these professions was not merely a pretence in presence of his Chief ; for after he and I were out of Sir Allan's hearing, he told me, "Had he sent his dog for the rum, I would have given it : I would cut my bones for him."—It was very remarkable to find such an attachment to a Chief, though he had then no connection with the island, and had not been there for fourteen years.—Sir Allan, by way of upbraiding the fellow, said, " I believe you are a *Campbell*."

The place which I went to see is about two miles from the village. They call it *Portawherry*, from the wherry in which Columba came ; though, when they shew the length of his vessel, as marked on the beach by two heaps of stones, they say, " Here is the length of the *Currach*," using the Erse word.

Icolmkill is a fertile island. The inhabitants export some cattle and grain ; and I was told, they import nothing but iron and salt. They are industrious, and make their own woollen and linen cloth ; and they brew a good deal of beer, which we did not find in any of the other islands.

We set sail again about mid-day, and in the evening landed on Mull, near the house of the Reverend Mr. Neal M'Leod, who having been informed of our coming, by a message from Sir Allan, came out to meet us. We were this night very agreeably entertained at his house. Dr. Johnson observed to me, that he was the cleanest-headed man that he had met with in the Western islands. He seemed to be well acquainted with Dr. Johnson's writings, and courteously said, " I have been often obliged to you, though I never had the pleasure of seeing you before."

He told us, he had lived for some time in St. Kilda, under the tuition of the minister or catechist there, and had there first read Horace and Virgil. The scenes which they describe must have been a strong contrast to the dreary waste around him.

Thursday, 21st October

This morning the subject of politicks was introduced. —JOHNSON. " Pulteney was as paltry a fellow as could be. He was a Whig, who pretended to be honest ; and you know it is ridiculous for a Whig to pretend to be honest. He cannot hold it out." He called Mr. Pitt a meteor ; Sir Robert Walpole a fixed star.— He said, " It is wonderful to think that all the force of government was required to prevent Wilkes from being chosen the chief magistrate of London, though the liverymen knew he would rob their shops,—knew he would debauch their daughters."

BOSWELL. " The History of England is so strange, that, if it were not so well vouched as it is, it would hardly be credible."—JOHNSON. " Sir, if it were told as shortly, and with as little preparation for introducing the different events, as the History of the Jewish Kings, it would be equally liable to objections of improbability." —Mr. M'Leod was much pleased with the justice and novelty of the thought.—Dr. Johnson illustrated what he had said, as follows : " Take, as an instance, Charles the First's concessions to his parliament, which were greater and greater, in proportion as the parliament grew more insolent, and less deserving of trust. Had these concessions been related nakedly, without any detail of the circumstances which generally led to them, they would not have been believed."

Sir Allan M'Lean bragged, that Scotland had the advantage of England, by its having more water. JOHNSON. " Sir, we would not have your water, to take the vile bogs which produce it. You have too much ! A man who is drowned has more water than either of us ; "—and then he laughed.—(But this was surely robust sophistry : for the people of taste in England, who have seen Scotland, own that its variety of rivers and lakes makes it naturally more beautiful than England, in that respect.)—Pursuing his victory over Sir Allan, he proceeded: " Your country consists of two things, stone and water. There is, indeed, a little earth above the stone in some places, but a very little ; and the stone is always appearing. It is like a man in rags ; the naked skin is still peeping out."

He took leave of Mr. M'Leod, saying, " Sir, I thank you for your entertainment, and your conversation."

Mr. Campbell, who had been so polite yesterday, came this morning on purpose to breakfast with us, and very obligingly furnished us with horses to proceed on our journey to Mr. M'Lean's of Lochbuy, where we were to pass the night. We dined at the house of Dr. Alexander M'Lean, another physician in Mull, who was so much struck with the uncommon conversation of Dr. Johnson, that he observed to me, " This man is just a *hogshead* of sense."

Dr. Johnson said of the *Turkish Spy*, which lay in the room, that it told nothing but what every body might have known at that time ; and that what was good in it, did not pay you for the trouble of reading to find it.

After a very tedious ride, through what appeared to me the most gloomy and desolate country I had ever beheld, we arrived, between seven and eight o'clock, at Moy, the seat of the Laird of Lochbuy.—*Buy*, in Erse, signifies yellow, and I at first imagined that the loch or branch of the sea here, was thus denominated, in the same manner as the Red Sea ; but I afterwards learned that it derived its name from a hill above it, which being of a yellowish hue, has the epithet of Buy.

We had heard much of Lochbuy's being a great roaring braggadocio, a kind of Sir John Falstaff, both in size and manners ; but we found that they had swelled him up to a fictitious size, and clothed him with imaginary qualities.—Col's idea of him was equally ex-

travagant, though very different : he told us, he was
quite a Don Quixote ; and said, he would give a great
deal to see him and Dr. Johnson together. The truth
is, that Lochbuy proved to be only a bluff, comely,
noisy old gentleman, proud of his hereditary consequence, and a very hearty and hospitable landlord.
Lady Lochbuy was sister to Sir Allan M'Lean, but
much older. He said to me, " They are quite *Ante-
diluvians.*" Being told that Dr. Johnson did not hear
well, Lochbuy bawled out to him, " Are you of the
Johnstons of Glencro, or of Ardnamurchan ? "—Dr.
Johnson gave him a significant look, but made no
answer ; and I told Lochbuy that he was not Johns*ton*
but Johns*on*, and that he was an Englishman.

Lochbuy some years ago tried to prove himself a
weak man, liable to imposition, or, as we term it in
Scotland, a *facile* man, in order to set aside a lease which
he had granted ; but failed in the attempt. On my
mentioning this circumstance to Dr. Johnson, he seemed
much surprised that such a suit was admitted by the
Scottish law, and observed, that " in England no man
is allowed to *stultify* himself."

Sir Allan, Lochbuy, and I, had the conversation
chiefly to ourselves to-night : Dr. Johnson, being extremely weary, went to bed soon after supper.

Friday, 22nd October

Before Dr. Johnson came to breakfast, Lady Lochbuy said, " he was a *dungeon* of wit ; " a very common
phrase in Scotland to express a profoundness of intellect,
though he afterwards told me, that he never had heard
it. She proposed that he should have some cold sheep's-
head for breakfast. Sir Allan seemed displeased at his
sister's vulgarity, and wondered how such a thought
should come into her head. From a mischievous love

of sport, I took the lady's part; and very gravely said, "I think it is but fair to give him an offer of it. If he does not choose it, he may let it alone."—"I think so," said the lady, looking at her brother with an air of victory. Sir Allan, finding the matter desperate, strutted about the room, and took snuff. When Dr. Johnson came in, she called to him, "Do you choose any cold sheep's-head, sir?"—"No, madam," said he, with a tone of surprise and anger.—"It is here, sir," said she, supposing he had refused it to save the trouble of bringing it in. They thus went on at cross purposes, till he confirmed his refusal in a manner not to be misunderstood; while I sat quietly by, and enjoyed my success.

After breakfast, we surveyed the old castle, in the pit or dungeon of which Lochbuy had some years before taken upon him to imprison several persons; and though he had been fined in a considerable sum by the Court of Justiciary, he was so little affected by it, that while we were examining the dungeon, he said to me, with a smile, "Your father knows something of this;" (alluding to my father's having sat as one of the judges on his trial.) Sir Allan whispered me, that the laird could not be persuaded, that he had lost his heritable jurisdiction.

We then set out for the ferry, by which we were to cross to the main land of Argyleshire. Lochbuy and Sir Allan accompanied us. We were told much of a war-saddle, on which this reputed Don Quixote used to be mounted; but we did not see it, for the young laird had applied it to a less noble purpose, having taken it to Falkirk fair *with a drove of black cattle*.

We bade adieu to Lochbuy, and to our very kind conductor, Sir Allan M'Lean, on the shore of Mull, and then got into the ferry-boat, the bottom of which was strewed with branches of trees or bushes, upon which we sat. We had a good day and a fine passage, and in the evening landed at Oban, where we found a tolerable inn. After having been so long confined at different times in islands, from which it was always uncertain when we could get away, it was comfortable to be now on the main land, and to know that, if in health, we might get to any place in Scotland or England in a certain number of days.

Here we discovered from the conjectures which were formed, that the people on the main land were intirely ignorant of our motions ; for in a Glasgow news-paper we found a paragraph, which, as it contains a just and well-turned compliment to my illustrious friend, I shall here insert :

" We are well assured that Dr. Johnson is confined by tempestuous weather to the isle of Sky ; it being unsafe to venture, in a small boat upon such a stormy surge as is very common there at this time of the year. Such a philosopher, detained on an almost barren island, resembles a whale left upon the strand. The latter will be welcome to every body, on account of his oil, his bone, &c. and the other will charm his companions, and the rude inhabitants, with his superior knowledge and wisdom, calm resignation, and unbounded benevolence."

Saturday, 23rd October

After a good night's rest, we breakfasted at our leisure. We talked of Goldsmith's *Traveller*, of which Dr. Johnson spoke highly ; and, while I was helping him on with his great coat, he repeated from it the character of the British nation, which he did with such energy, that the tear started into his eye :

> " Stern o'er each bosom reason holds her state.
> With daring aims irregularly great,
> Pride in their port, defiance in their eye,
> I see the lords of humankind pass by,
> Intent on high designs, a thoughtful band,
> By forms unfashion'd, fresh from nature's hand ;

Fierce in their native hardiness of soul,
True to imagin'd right, above control,
While ev'n the peasant boasts these rights to scan,
And learns to venerate himself as man."

We could get but one bridle here, which, according to the maxim *detur digniori*, was appropriated to Dr. Johnson's sheltie. I and Joseph rode with halters. We crossed in a ferry-boat a pretty wide lake, and on the farther side of it, close by the shore, found a hut for our inn. We were much wet. I changed my clothes in part, and was at pains to get myself well dried. Dr. Johnson resolutely kept on all his clothes, wet as they were, letting them steam before the smoky turf fire. I thought him in the wrong; but his firmness was, perhaps, a species of heroism.

I remember but little of our conversation. I mentioned Shenstone's saying of Pope, that he had the art of condensing sense more than any body. Dr. Johnson said, " It is not true, sir. There is more sense in a line of Cowley than in a page (or a sentence, or ten lines,—I am not quite certain of the very phrase) of Pope." He maintained that Archibald, Duke of Argyle, was a narrow man. I wondered at this ; and observed that his building so great a house at Inveraray was not like a narrow man. " Sir, (said he,) when a narrow man has resolved to build a house, he builds it like another man. But Archibald, Duke of Argyle, was narrow in his ordinary expences, in his quotidian expences."

The distinction is very just. It is in the ordinary expences of life that a man's liberality or narrowness is to be discovered.—I never heard the word *quotidian* in this sense, and I imagined it to be a word of Dr. Johnson's own fabrication ; but I have since found it in *Young's Night Thoughts*, (Night fifth,)

" Death's a destroyer of quotidian prey."

and in my friend's Dictionary, supported by the authorities of Charles I. and Dr. Donne.

It rained very hard as we journied on after dinner. The roar of torrents from the mountains, as we passed along in the dusk, and the other circumstances attending our ride this evening, have been mentioned with so much animation by Dr. Johnson, that I shall not attempt to say any thing on the subject.

We got at night to Inveraray, where we found an excellent inn. Even here, Dr. Johnson would not change his wet clothes.

The prospect of good accommodation cheered us much. We supped well; and after supper, Dr. Johnson, whom I had not seen taste any fermented liquor during all our travels, called for a gill of whisky. "Come, (said he,) let me know what it is that makes a Scotchman happy!" He drank it all but a drop, which I begged leave to pour into my glass, that I might say we had drunk whisky together. I proposed Mrs. Thrale should be our toast. He would not have *her* drunk in whisky, but rather "some insular lady;" so we drank one of the ladies whom we had lately left.—He owned to-night, that he got as good a room and bed as at an English inn.

I had here the pleasure of finding a letter from home, which relieved me from the anxiety I had suffered, in consequence of not having received any account of my family for many weeks. I also found a letter from Mr. Garrick, which was a regale as agreeable as a pine-apple would be in a desert. He had favoured me with his correspondence for many years; and when Dr. Johnson and I were at Inverness, I had written to him as follows:

"INVERNESS, *Sunday*, 29 *August*, 1773.

"MY DEAR SIR,

"HERE I am, and Mr. Samuel Johnson actually with me. We were a night at Fores, in coming to which, in the dusk of the evening, we passed over the bleak and blasted heath where Macbeth met the witches.

Your old preceptor repeated, with much solemnity, the speech—

> " ' How far is't called to Fores ?   What are these,
>   So wither'd and so wild in their attire,' &c.

This day we visited the ruins of Macbeth's castle at Inverness.   I have had great romantick satisfaction in seeing Johnson upon the classical scenes of Shakspeare in Scotland ; which I really looked upon as almost as improbable as that ' Birnam wood should come to Dunsinane.'   Indeed, as I have always been accustomed to view him as a permanent London object, it would not be much more wonderful to me to see St. Paul's church moving along where we now are.   As yet we have travelled in post-chaises ; but to-morrow we are to mount on horseback, and ascend into the mountains by Fort Augustus, and so on to the ferry, where we are to cross to Sky.   We shall see that Island fully, and then visit some more of the Hebrides ; after which we are to land in Argyleshire, proceed by Glasgow to Auchinleck, repose there a competent time, and then return to Edinburgh, from whence the Rambler will depart for old England again, as soon as he finds it convenient. Hitherto we have had a very prosperous expedition. I flatter myself, *servetur ad imum, qualis ab incepto processerit.*   He is in excellent spirits, and I have a rich journal of his conversation.   Look back, *Davy,* to Litchfield ;—run up through the time that has elapsed since you first knew Mr. Johnson,—and enjoy with me his present extraordinary Tour.   I could not resist the impulse of writing to you from this place.   The situation of the old castle corresponds exactly to Shakspeare's description.   While we were there to-day, it happened oddly, that a raven perched upon one of the chimney-tops, and croaked.   Then I in my turn repeated—

> " ' The raven himself is hoarse,
>   That croaks the fatal entrance of Duncan,
>   Under my battlements.'

" I wish you had been with us. Think what enthusiastick happiness I shall have to see Mr. Samuel Johnson walking among the romantick rocks and woods of my ancestors at Auchinleck ! Write to me at Edinburgh. You owe me his verses on great George and tuneful Cibber, and the bad verses which led him to make his fine ones on Philips the musician. Keep your promise, and let me have them. I offer my very best compliments to Mrs. Garrick, and ever am

" Your warm admirer and friend,

" JAMES BOSWELL."

" To David Garrick, Esq. London."

His answer was as follows ;

" HAMPTON, *September* 14, 1773.

" DEAR SIR,

" You stole away from London, and left us all in the lurch ; for we expected you one night at the club, and knew nothing of your departure. Had I payed you what I owed you, for the book you bought for me, I should only have grieved for the loss of your company, and slept with a quiet conscience ; but, wounded as it is, it must remain so till I see you again, though I am sure our good friend Mr. Johnson will discharge the debt for me, if you will let him.—Your account of your journey to Fores, the raven, old castle, &c. &c. made me half mad. Are you not rather too late in the year for fine weather, which is the life and soul of seeing places ? —I hope your pleasure will continue *qualis ab incepto*, &c.

" Your friend —— threatens me much. I only wish that he would put his threats in execution, and, if he prints his play, I will forgive him. I remember he complained to you, that his bookseller called for the money for some copies of his ——, which I subscribed for, and that I desired him to call again.—The truth is, that my wife was not at home, and that for weeks together I have not ten shillings in my pocket.—However, had it been otherwise, it was not so great a crime to draw his poetical vengeance upon me.—I despise all that he can do, and am glad that I can so easily get rid of him and his ingratitude.—I am hardened both to abuse and ingratitude.

" You, I am sure, will no more recommend your poetasters to my civility and good offices.

" Shall I recommend to you a play of Eschylus, (the Prometheus,) published and translated by poor old Morell, who is a good scholar, and an acquaintance of mine ? It will be but half a guinea, and your name shall be put in the list I am making for him. You will be in very good company.

" Now for the Epitaphs !

[These, together with the verses on George the Second, and Colley Cibber, as his Poet Laureat, of which imperfect copies are gone about, will appear in my Life of Dr. Johnson.]

" I have no more paper, or I should have said more to you. My love and respects to Mr. Johnson.
" Yours ever,
" D. GARRICK."

" I can't write. I have the gout in my hand."

" To James Boswell, Esq. Edinburgh."

Sunday, 24th October

We passed the forenoon calmly and placidly. I prevailed on Dr. Johnson to read aloud Ogden's sixth Sermon on Prayer, which he did with a distinct expression, and pleasing solemnity. He praised my favourite preacher, his elegant language, and remarkable acuteness ; and said, he fought infidels with their own weapons.

As a specimen of Ogden's manner, I insert the following passage from the sermon which Dr. Johnson now read. The preacher, after arguing against that vain philosophy which maintains, in conformity with the hard principle of eternal necessity, or unchangeable predetermination, that the only effect of prayer for others, although we are exhorted to pray for them, is to produce good dispositions in ourselves towards them ; thus expresses himself :

" A plain man may be apt to ask, But if this then, though enjoined in the holy scriptures, is to be my real aim and intention, when I am taught to pray for other persons, why is it that I do not plainly so express it ? Why is not the form of the petition brought nearer to the meaning ? Give them, say I to our heavenly father, what is good. But this, I am to understand, will be as it will be, and is not for me to alter. What is it then that I am doing ? I am desiring to become charitable myself ; and why may I not plainly say so ? Is there shame in it, or impiety ? The wish is laudable : why should I form designs to hide it ?

" Or is it, perhaps, better to be brought about by indirect means, and in this artful manner ? Alas ! who is it that I would impose on ? From whom can it be, in this commerce, that I desire to hide any thing ? When, as my Saviour commands me, I have *entered into my closet, and shut my door*, there are but two parties privy to my devotions, GOD and my own heart : which of the two am I deceiving ? "

He wished to have more books, and, upon inquiring if there were any in the house, was told that a waiter had some, which were brought to him ; but I recollect none of them, except Hervey's *Meditations*. He thought slightingly of this admired book. He treated it with ridicule, and would not allow even the scene of the dying Husband and Father to be pathetick. I am not an impartial judge ; for Hervey's *Meditations* engaged my affections in my early years.——He read a passage concerning the moon, ludicrously, and shewed how easily he could, in the same style, make reflections on that planet, the very reverse of Hervey's, representing her as treacherous to mankind. He did this with much humour ; but I have not preserved the particulars. He then indulged a playful fancy, in making a *Meditation on a Pudding*, of which I hastily wrote down, in his presence, the following note ; which, though imperfect, may serve to give my readers some idea of it.

MEDITATION ON A PUDDING

" Let us seriously reflect of what a pudding is composed. It is composed of flour that once waved in the golden grain, and drank the dews of the morning ; of milk pressed from the swelling udder by the gentle hand of the beauteous milkmaid, whose beauty and innocence might have recommended a worse draught ; who, while she stroked the udder, indulged no ambitious thoughts of wandering in palaces, formed no plans for the destruction of her fellow-creatures ; milk, which is drawn from the cow, that useful animal, that eats the grass of the field, and supplies us with that which made the greatest part of the food of mankind in the age which the poets have agreed to call golden. It is made with an egg, that miracle of nature, which the theoretical Burnet has compared to creation. An egg contains water within its beautiful smooth surface ; and an unformed mass, by the incubation of the parent, becomes a regular animal, furnished with bones and sinews, and covered with feathers.——Let us consider ; can there be more wanting to complete the Meditation on a Pudding ? If more is wanting, more may be found. It contains salt, which keeps the sea from putrefaction : salt, which is made the image of intellectual excellence, contributes to the formation of a pudding."

In a Magazine I found a saying of Dr. Johnson's, something to this purpose ; that the happiest part of a man's life is what he passes lying awake in bed in the morning. I read it to him. He said, " I may, perhaps, have said this ; for nobody, at times, talks more laxly than I do." I ventured to suggest to him, that this was dangerous from one of his authority.

I spoke of living in the country, and upon what footing one should be with neighbours. I observed that some people were afraid of being on too easy a footing with them, from an apprehension that their time would not be their own. He made the obvious remark, that it depended much on what kind of neighbours one has, whether it was desirable to be on an easy footing with them, or not. I mentioned a certain baronet, who told me, he never was happy in the country, till he was not on speaking terms with his neighbours, which he contrived in different ways to bring about. " Lord —— (said he) stuck long ; but at last the fellow pounded my pigs, and then I got rid of him."—JOHNSON. " Nay, sir, My Lord got rid of Sir John, and shewed how little he valued him, by putting his pigs in the pound."

I told Dr. Johnson I was in some difficulty how to act at Inveraray. I had reason to think that the Duchess of Argyle disliked me, on account of my zeal in the Douglas cause ; but the Duke of Argyle had always been pleased to treat me with great civility. They were now at the castle, which is a very short walk from our inn ; and the question was, whether I should go and pay my respects there. Dr. Johnson, to whom I had stated the case, was clear that I ought ; but, in his usual way, he was very shy of discovering a desire to be invited there himself. Though from a conviction of the benefit of subordination to society, he has always shewn great respect to persons of high rank, when he happened to be in their company, yet his pride of character has ever made him guard against any appearance of courting the great. Besides, he was impatient to go to Glasgow, where he expected letters. At the same time he was, I believe, secretly not unwilling to have attention paid him by so great a Chieftain, and so exalted a nobleman. He insisted that I should not go to the castle this day before dinner, as it would look like seeking an invitation. " But, (said I,) if the duke invites us to dine with him to-morrow, shall we accept ? "—" Yes, sir ; " I think he said, " to be sure." But, he added, " He won't ask us ! "—I mentioned, that I was afraid my company might be disagreeable to the duchess. He treated this objection with a manly disdain : " *That*, sir, he must settle with his wife."— We dined well. I went to the castle just about the time when I supposed the ladies would be retired from dinner. I sent in my name ; and, being shewn in, found the amiable duke sitting at the head of his table with several gentlemen. I was most politely received, and gave his grace some particulars of the curious journey which I had been making with Dr. Johnson. When we rose from table, the duke said to me, " I hope you and Dr. Johnson will dine with us to-morrow." I thanked his grace ; but told him, my friend was in a great hurry to get back to London. The duke, with a kind complacency, said, " He will stay one day ; and I will take care he shall see this place to advantage." I said, I should be sure to let him know his grace's invitation.—As I was going away, the duke said, " Mr. Boswell, won't you have some tea ? "—I thought it best to get over the meeting with the duchess this night ; so respectfully agreed. I was conducted to the drawing-room by the duke, who announced my name ; but the duchess, who was sitting with her daughter, Lady Betty Hamilton, and some other ladies, took not the least notice of me. I should have been mortified at being thus coldly received by a lady of whom I, with the rest of the world, have always entertained a very high admiration, had I not been consoled by the obliging attention of the duke.

When I returned to the inn, I informed Dr. Johnson of the Duke of Argyle's invitation, with which he was much pleased, and readily accepted of it.—We talked of a violent contest which was then carrying on, with a view to the next general election for Ayrshire ; where one of the candidates, in order to undermine the old and established interest, had artfully held himself out as a champion for the independency of the county against aristocratic influence, and had persuaded several gentlemen into a resolution to oppose every candidate who was supported by peers.—" Foolish fellows ! (said Dr. Johnson,) don't they see that they are as much dependent upon the peers one way as the other. The peers have but to *oppose* a candidate, to ensure him success. It is said, the only way to make a pig go forward, is to pull him back by the tail. These people must be treated like pigs."

Monday, 25th October

My acquaintance, the Reverend Mr. John M'Aulay, one of the Ministers of Inveraray, and brother to our good friend at Calder, came to us this morning, and accompanied us to the castle, where I presented Dr. Johnson to the Duke of Argyle. We were shewn through the house ; and I never shall forget the impression made upon my fancy by some of the ladies' maids tripping about in neat morning dresses. After seeing for a long time little but rusticity, their lively manner, and gay inviting appearance, pleased me so

much, that I thought, for the moment, I could have
been a knight-errant for them.

We then got into a low one-horse chair, ordered for
us by the duke, in which we drove about the place.   Dr.
Johnson was much struck by the grandeur and elegance
of this princely seat.   He thought, however, the castle
too low, and wished it had been a story higher.——He
said, " What I admire here, is the total defiance of
expence."   I had a particular pride in shewing him
a great number of fine old trees, to compensate for
the nakedness which had made such an impression on
him on the eastern coast of Scotland.

When we came in, before dinner, we found the duke
and some gentlemen in the hall.   Dr. Johnson took much
notice of the large collection of arms, which are excel-
lently disposed there.   I told what he had said to Sir
Alexander M'Donald, of his ancestors not suffering their
arms to rust.   " Well, (said the doctor,) but let us be
glad we live in times when arms *may* rust.   We can
sit to-day at his grace's table, without any risk of being
attacked, and perhaps sitting down again wounded or
maimed."   The duke placed Dr. Johnson next himself at table.   I was in fine spirits ; and though sensible
that I had the misfortune of not being in favour with the
duchess, I was not in the least disconcerted, and offered
her grace some of the dish that was before me.   It must
be owned that I was in the right to be quite unconcerned,
if I could.   I was the Duke of Argyle's guest ; and I had
no reason to suppose that he adopted the prejudices and
resentments of the Duchess of Hamilton.

I knew it was the rule of modern high life not to
drink to any body ; but, that I might have the satisfaction for once to look the duchess in the face, with a glass
in my hand, I with a respectful air addressed her,——" My
Lady Duchess, I have the honour to drink your grace's
good health."——I repeated the words audibly, and with
a steady countenance.   This was, perhaps, rather too

much; but some allowance must be made for human feelings.

The duchess was very attentive to Dr. Johnson. I know not how a *middle state* came to be mentioned. Her grace wished to hear him on that point. "Madam, (said he,) your own relation, Mr. Archibald Campbell, can tell you better about it than I can. He was a bishop of the nonjuring communion, and wrote a book upon the subject."—He engaged to get it for her grace. He afterwards gave a full history of Mr. Archibald Campbell, which I am sorry I do not recollect particularly. He said, Mr. Campbell had been bred a violent Whig, but afterwards "kept *better company*, and became a Tory." He said this with a smile, in pleasant allusion, as I thought, to the opposition between his own political principles and those of the duke's clan. He added that Mr. Campbell, after the Revolution, was thrown into gaol on account of his tenets; but, on application by letter to the old Lord Townshend, was released: that he always spoke of his Lordship with great gratitude, saying, "though a *Whig*, he had humanity."

Dr. Johnson and I passed some time together, in June 1784, at Pembroke College, Oxford, with the Reverend Dr. Adams, the master; and I having expressed a regret that my note relative to Mr. Archibald Campbell was imperfect, he was then so good as to write with his own hand, on the blank page of my Journal, opposite to that which contains what I have now mentioned, the following paragraph; which, however, is not quite so full as the narrative he gave at Inveraray:

"The Honourable Archibald Campbell was, I believe, the nephew of the Marquis of Argyle. He began life by engaging in Monmouth's rebellion, and, to escape the law, lived some time in Surinam. When he returned, he became zealous for episcopacy and monarchy; and

at the Revolution adhered not only to the Nonjurors,
but to those who refused to communicate with the Church
of England, or to be present at any worship where the
usurper was mentioned as king. He was, I believe,
more than once apprehended in the reign of King
William, and once at the accession of George. He was
the familiar friend of Hicks and Nelson ; a man of
letters, but injudicious ; and very curious and inquisi-
tive, but credulous. He lived in 1743, or 44, about
75 years old.''

The subject of luxury having been introduced, Dr.
Johnson defended it. " We have now (said he) a
splendid dinner before us ; Which of all these dishes is
unwholsome ? " The duke asserted, that he had observed the grandees of Spain diminished in their size
by luxury. Dr. Johnson politely refrained from
opposing directly an observation which the duke himself had made ; but said, " Man must be very different
from other animals, if he is diminished by good living ;
for the size of all other animals is increased by it." I
made some remark that seemed to imply a belief in
second sight. The duchess said, " I fancy you will be
a *Methodist*."—This was the only sentence her grace
deigned to utter to me ; and I take it for granted, she
thought it a good hit on my *credulity* in the Douglas
cause.

A gentleman in company, after dinner, was desired
by the duke to go to another room, for a specimen of
curious marble, which his grace wished to shew us. He
brought a wrong piece, upon which the duke sent him
back again. He could not refuse ; but, to avoid any
appearance of servility, he whistled as he walked out
of the room, to show his independency. On my mentioning this afterwards to Dr. Johnson, he said, it was a nice
trait of character.

Dr. Johnson talked a great deal, and was so entertaining, that Lady Betty Hamilton, after dinner, went and placed her chair close to his, leaned upon the back of it, and listened eagerly. It would have made a fine picture to have drawn the Sage and her at this time in their several attitudes. He did not know, all the while, how much he was honoured. I told him afterwards. I never saw him so gentle and complaisant as this day.

We went to tea. The duke and I walked up and down the drawing-room, conversing. The duchess still continued to show the same marked coldness for me; for which, though I suffered from it, I made every allowance, considering the very warm part that I had taken for Douglas, in the cause in which she thought her son deeply interested. Had not her grace discovered some displeasure towards me, I should have suspected her of insensibility or dissimulation.

Her grace made Dr. Johnson come and sit by her, and asked him why he made his journey so late in the year. "Why, madam (said he), you know Mr. Boswell must attend the Court of Session, and it does not rise till the twelfth of August."—She said, with some sharpness, "I *know nothing* of Mr. Boswell." Poor Lady Lucy Douglas, to whom I mentioned this, observed, "She knew *too much* of Mr. Boswell." I shall make no remark on her grace's speech. I indeed felt it as rather too severe; but when I recollected that my punishment was inflicted by so dignified a beauty, I had that kind of consolation which a man would feel who is strangled by a *silken cord*. Dr. Johnson was all attention to her grace. He used afterwards a droll expression, upon her enjoying the three titles of Hamilton, Brandon, and Argyle. Borrowing an image from the Turkish empire, he called her a *Duchess* with *three tails*.

He was much pleased with our visit at the castle of Inveraray. The Duke of Argyle was exceedingly polite to him, and, upon his complaining of the shelties which he had hitherto ridden being too small for him, his grace told him he should be provided with a good horse to carry him next day.

Mr. John M'Aulay passed the evening with us at our inn. When Dr. Johnson spoke of people whose principles were good, but whose practice was faulty, Mr. M'Aulay said, he had no notion of people being in earnest in their good professions, whose practice was not suitable to them. The Doctor grew warm, and said, " Sir, are you so grossly ignorant of human nature, as not to know that a man may be very sincere in good principles, without having good practice ? "

Dr. Johnson was unquestionably in the right ; and whoever examines himself candidly, will be satisfied of it, though the inconsistency between principles and practice is greater in some men than in others.

I recollect very little of this night's conversation. I am sorry that indolence came upon me towards the conclusion of our journey, so that I did not write down what passed with the same assiduity as during the greatest part of it.

Tuesday, 26th October

Mr. M'Aulay breakfasted with us, nothing hurt or dismayed by his last night's correction. Being a man of good sense, he had a just admiration of Dr. Johnson.

Either yesterday morning, or this, I communicated to Dr. Johnson, from Mr. M'Aulay's information, the news that Dr. Beattie had got a pension of two hundred pounds a year. He sat up in his bed, clapped his hands, and cried, " O brave we ! "—a peculiar exclamation of his when he rejoices.

As we sat over our tea, Mr. Home's Tragedy of *Douglas* was mentioned. I put Dr. Johnson in mind, that once, in a coffee-house at Oxford, he called to old Mr. Sheridan, " How came you, sir, to give Home a

gold medal for writing that foolish play ? " and defied
Mr. Sheridan to shew ten good lines in it. He did not
insist they should be together ; but that there were
not ten good lines in the whole play. He now persisted
in this. I endeavoured to defend that pathetick and
beautiful tragedy, and repeated the following passage :

> " Sincerity,
> Thou first of virtues ! let no mortal leave
> Thy onward path, although the earth should gape,
> And from the gulph of hell destruction cry,
> To take dissimulation's winding way."

JOHNSON. " That will not do, sir. Nothing is good
but what is consistent with truth or probability, which
this is not. Juvenal, indeed, gives us a noble picture of
inflexible virtue :

> " ' *Esto bonus miles, tutor bonus, arbiter idem*
> *Integer : ambiguæ si quando citabere testis,*
> *Incertæque rei, Phalaris licet imperet, ut sis*
> *Falsus, et admoto dictet perjuria tauro,*
> *Summum crede nefas animam præferre pudori,*
> *Et propter vitam vivendi perdere causas.*' "

He repeated the lines with great force and dignity ;
then added, " And, after this, comes Johnny Home,
with his *earth gaping*, and his *destruction crying* :—
Pooh ! "

While we were lamenting the number of ruined
religious buildings which we had lately seen, I spoke
with peculiar feeling of the miserable neglect of the
chapel belonging to the palace of Holyrood-house, in
which are deposited the remains of many of the Kings
of Scotland, and of many of our nobility. I said, it
was a disgrace to the country that it was not repaired :
and particularly complained that my friend Douglas,
the representative of a great house, and proprietor of
a vast estate, should suffer the sacred spot where his
mother lies interred, to be unroofed, and exposed to all

the inclemencies of the weather. Dr. Johnson, who, I
know not how, had formed an opinion on the Hamilton
side, in the Douglas cause, slily answered, " Sir, sir,
don't be too severe upon the gentleman ; don't accuse
him of want of filial piety ! Lady Jane Douglas was
not *his* mother."—He roused my zeal so much that I
took the liberty to tell him he knew nothing of the
cause ; which I do most seriously believe was the case.

We were now " in a country of bridles and saddles,"
and set out fully equipped. The Duke of Argyle was
obliging enough to mount Dr. Johnson on a stately steed
from his grace's stable. My friend was highly pleased,
and Joseph said, " He now looks like a bishop."

We dined at the inn at Tarbat, and at night came
to Rosedow, the beautiful seat of Sir James Colquhoun,
on the banks of Lochlomond, where I, and any friends
whom I have introduced, have ever been received with
kind and elegant hospitality.

Wednesday, 27th October

When I went into Dr. Johnson's room this morning,
I observed to him how wonderfully courteous he had
been at Inveraray, and said, " You were quite a fine
gentleman, when with the duchess." He answered, in
good humour, " Sir, I look upon myself as a very polite
man : " and he was right, in a proper manly sense of
the word. As an immediate proof of it, let me observe,
that he would not send back the Duke of Argyle's horse
without a letter of thanks, which I copied.

" To his Grace the Duke of Argyle.

" My Lord,

" That kindness which disposed your grace to
supply me with the horse, which I have now returned,

will make you pleased to hear that he has carried me
well.

"By my diligence in the little commission with
which I was honoured by the duchess, I will endeavour
to shew how highly I value the favours which I have
received, and how much I desire to be thought,

"My lord,

"Your grace's most obedient,

"and most humble servant,

"SAM. JOHNSON."

"ROSEDOW, *Oct.* 29, 1773."

The duke was so attentive to his respectable guest,
that on the same day, he wrote him an answer, which
was received at Auchinleck :

"To DR. JOHNSON, Auchinleck, Ayrshire.

"SIR,

"I AM glad to hear your journey from this place
was not unpleasant, in regard to your horse. I wish I
could have supplied you with good weather, which I
am afraid you felt the want of.

"The Duchess of Argyle desires her compliments to
you, and is much obliged to you for remembering her
commission.

"I am, sir,

"Your most obedient humble servant,

"ARGYLE."

"INVERARAY, *Oct.* 29, 1773."

I am happy to insert every memorial of the honour
done to my great friend. Indeed, I was at all times
desirous to preserve the letters which he received from
eminent persons, of which, as of all other papers, he
was very negligent ; and I once proposed to him, that
they should be committed to my care, as his *Custos
Rotulorum.* I wish he had complied with my request,

as by that means many valuable writings might have been preserved, that are now lost.

After breakfast, Dr. Johnson and I were furnished with a boat, and sailed about upon Lochlomond, and landed on some of the islands which are interspersed. He was much pleased with the scene, which is so well known by the accounts of various travellers, that it is unnecessary for me to attempt any description of it.

I recollect none of his conversation, except that, when talking of dress, he said, " Sir, were I to have any thing fine, it should be very fine. Were I to wear a ring, it should not be a bauble, but a stone of great value. Were I to wear a laced or embroidered waistcoat, it should be very rich. I had once a very rich laced waistcoat, which I wore the first night of my tragedy."

Lady Helen Colquhoun being a very pious woman, the conversation, after dinner, took a religious turn. Her ladyship defended the presbyterian mode of publick worship ; upon which Dr. Johnson delivered those excellent arguments for a form of prayer which he has introduced into his *Journey*. I am myself fully convinced that a form of prayer for publick worship is in general most decent and edifying. *Solennia verba* have a kind of prescriptive sanctity, and make a deeper impression on the mind than extemporaneous effusions, in which, as we know not what they are to be, we cannot readily acquiesce. Yet I would allow also of a certain portion of extempore address, as occasion may require. This is the practice of the French Protestant churches. And although the office of forming supplications to the throne of Heaven is, in my mind, too great a trust to be indiscriminately committed to the discretion of every minister, I do not mean to deny that sincere devotion may be experienced when joining in prayer with those who use no Liturgy.

We were favoured with Sir James Colquhoun's coach to convey us in the evening to Cameron, the seat of

Commissary Smollet. Our satisfaction of finding ourselves again in a comfortable carriage was very great. We had a pleasing conviction of the commodiousness of civilization, and heartily laughed at the ravings of those absurd visionaries who have attempted to persuade us of the superior advantages of a *state of nature*.

Mr. Smollet was a man of considerable learning, with abundance of animal spirits ; so that he was a very good companion for Dr. Johnson, who said to me, " We have had more solid talk here than at any place where we have been."

I remember Dr. Johnson gave us this evening an able and eloquent discourse on the *Origin of Evil*, and on the consistency of moral evil with the power and goodness of GOD. He shewed us how it arose from our free agency, an extinction of which would be a still greater evil than any we experience. I know not that he said anything absolutely new, but he said a great deal wonderfully well ; and perceiving us to be delighted and satisfied, he concluded his harangue with an air of benevolent triumph over an objection which has distressed many worthy minds : " This then is the answer to the question, Πόθεν το Κακον ? "—Mrs. Smollet whispered me, that it was the best sermon she had ever heard. Much do I upbraid myself for having neglected to preserve it.

Thursday, 28th October

Mr. Smollet pleased Dr. Johnson, by producing a collection of news-papers in the time of the Usurpation, from which it appeared that all sorts of crimes were very frequent during that horrible anarchy. By the side of the high road to Glasgow, at some distance from his house, he had erected a pillar to the memory of his ingenious kinsman, Dr. Smollet ; and he consulted Dr. Johnson as to an inscription for it. Lord Kames, who, though he had a great store of knowledge, with much ingenuity, and uncommon activity of mind, was no profound scholar, had it seems recommended an English inscription. Dr. Johnson treated this with great contempt, saying, " An English inscription would be a disgrace to Dr Smollet ; " and, in answer to what Lord Kames had urged, as to the advantage of its being in English, because it would be generally understood, I observed, that all to whom Dr. Smollet's merit could be an object of respect and imitation, would understand it as well in Latin ; and that surely it was not meant for the Highland drovers, or other such people, who pass and repass that way.

We were then shewn a Latin inscription, proposed for this monument. Dr. Johnson sat down with an ardent and liberal earnestness to revise it, and greatly improved it by several additions and variations. I unfortunately did not take a copy of it, as it originally stood ; but I have happily preserved every fragment of what Dr. Johnson wrote :

> *Quisquis ades, viator,*
> *Vel mente felix, vel studiis cultus,*
> *Immorare paululum memoriæ*
> T O B I Æ   S M O L L E T   M.D.
> *Viri iis virtutibus*
> *Quas in homine et cive*
> *Et laudes, et imiteris,*
> *   *   *   *   *
> *Postquam mira* * * * .
> *Se* * * * * * * * * *
> *   *   *   *
> *Tali tantoque viro, suo patrueli,*
> *   *   *   *   *   *
> *Hanc columnam,*
> *Amoris eheu ! inane monumentum,*
> *In ipsis Leviniæ ripis,*
> *Quas primis infans vagitibus personuit,*
> *Versiculisque jam fere moriturus illustravit,*
> *Ponendam curavit*
> *   *   *   *   *   *

We had this morning a singular proof of Dr. Johnson's quick and retentive memory. Hay's translation of Martial was lying in a window. I said, I thought it was pretty well done, and shewed him a particular epigram, I think of ten, but am certain of eight, lines. He read it, and tossed away the book, saying—" No, it is *not* pretty well." As I persisted in my opinion, he said, " Why, sir, the original is thus,"—(and he repeated it ;) " and this man's translation is thus,"— and then he repeated that also, exactly, though he had never seen it before, and read it over only once, and that too, without any intention of getting it by heart.

Here a post-chaise, which I had ordered from Glasgow, came for us, and we drove on in high spirits. We stopped at Dunbarton, and though the approach to the castle there is very steep, Dr. Johnson ascended it with alacrity, and surveyed all that was to be seen. During the whole of our Tour he shewed uncommon spirit, could not bear to be treated like an old or infirm man, and was very unwilling to accept of any assistance, insomuch that, at our landing at Icolmkill, when Sir Allan M'Lean and I submitted to be carried on men's shoulders from the boat to the shore, as it could not be brought quite close to land, he sprang into the sea, and waded vigorously out.

On our arrival at the Saracen's Head Inn, at Glasgow, I was made happy by good accounts from home ; and Dr. Johnson, who had not received a single letter since we left Aberdeen, found here a great many, the perusal of which entertained him much. He enjoyed in imagination the comforts which we could now command, and seemed to be in high glee. I remember, he put a leg up on each side of the grate, and said, with a mock solemnity, by way of soliloquy, but loud enough for me to here it, " Here am I, an ENGLISH man, sitting by a *coal* fire."

Friday, 29th October

The professors of the university being informed of
our arrival, Dr. Stevenson, Dr. Reid, and Mr. Anderson, breakfasted with us. Mr. Anderson accompanied
us while Dr. Johnson viewed this beautiful city. He
had told me, that one day in London, when Dr. Adam
Smith was boasting of it, he turned to him and said,
" Pray, sir, have you ever seen Brentford ? "—This
was surely a strong instance of his impatience, and spirit
of contradiction. I put him in mind of it to-day, while
he expressed his admiration of the elegant buildings, and
whispered him, " Don't you feel some remorse ? "

We were received in the college by a number of the
professors, who shewed all due respect to Dr. Johnson ;
and then we paid a visit to the principal, Dr. Leechman, at his own house, where Dr. Johnson had the
satisfaction of being told that his name had been gratefully celebrated in one of the parochial congregations in
the Highlands, as the person to whose influence it was
chiefly owing, that the New Testament was allowed to
be translated into the Erse language. It seems some
political members of the Society in Scotland for pro-
pagating Christian Knowledge, had opposed this pious
undertaking, as tending to preserve the distinction between the Highlanders and Lowlanders. Dr. Johnson
wrote a long letter upon the subject to a friend, which
being shewn to them, made them ashamed, and afraid
of being publickly exposed ; so they were forced to a
compliance. It is now in my possession, and is, perhaps, one of the best productions of his masterly pen.

Professors Reid and Anderson, and the two Messieurs
Foulis, the Elzevirs of Glasgow, dined and drank tea
with us at our inn, after which the professors went
away ; and I, having a letter to write, left my fellow-
traveller with Messieurs Foulis. Though good and

ingenious men, they had that unsettled speculative mode of conversation which is offensive to a man regularly taught at an English school and university. I found that, instead of listening to the dictates of the Sage, they had teazed him with questions and doubtful disputations. He came in a flutter to me, and desired I might come back again, for he could not bear these men. " O ho ! sir, (said I,) you are flying to me for refuge ! " He never, in any situation, was at a loss for a ready repartee. He answered, with quick vivacity, " It is of two evils choosing the least." I was delighted with this flash bursting from the cloud which hung upon his mind, closed my letter directly, and joined the company.

We supped at Professor Anderson's. The general impression upon my memory is, that we had not much conversation at Glasgow, where the professors, like their brethren at Aberdeen, did not venture to expose themselves much to the battery of cannon which they knew might play upon them. Dr. Johnson, who was fully conscious of his own superior powers, afterwards praised Principal Robertson for his caution in this respect. He said to me, " Robertson, sir, was in the right. Robertson is a man of eminence, and the head of a college at Edinburgh. He had a character to maintain, and did well not to risk its being lessened."

Saturday, 30th October

We set out towards Ayrshire. I sent Joseph on to Loudoun, with a message, that, if the earl was at home, Dr. Johnson and I would have the honour to dine with him. Joseph met us on the road, and reported that the earl " jumped for joy," and said, " I shall be very happy to see them."—We were received with a most pleasing courtesy by his lordship, and by the countess his mother, who, in her ninety-fifth year, had all her faculties quite unimpaired. This was a very cheering sight to Dr. Johnson, who had an extraordinary desire for long life. Her ladyship was sensible and well-informed, and had seen a great deal of the world. Her lord had held several high offices, and she was sister to the great Earl of Stair.

I cannot here refrain from paying a just tribute to the character of John Earl of Loudoun, who did more service to the county of Ayr in general, as well as to individuals in it, than any man we have ever had. It is painful to think that he met with much ingratitude from persons both in high and low rank : but such was his temper, such his knowledge of " base mankind," that, as if he had expected no other return, his mind was never soured, and he retained his good-humour and benevolence to the last. The tenderness of his heart was proved in 1745–6, when he had an important command in the Highlands, and behaved with a generous humanity to the unfortunate. I cannot figure a more honest politician ; for, though his interest in our county was great, and generally successful, he not only did not deceive by fallacious promises, but was anxious that people should not deceive themselves by too sanguine expectations. His kind and dutiful attention to his mother was unremitted. At his house was true hospitality ; a plain but a plentiful table ; and every guest, being left at perfect freedom, felt himself quite easy and happy. While I live, I shall honour the memory of this amiable man.

At night, we advanced a few miles farther, to the house of Mr. Campbell of Treesbank, who was married to one of my wife's sisters, and were entertained very agreeably by a worthy couple.

Sunday, 31st October

We reposed here in tranquillity. Dr. Johnson was pleased to find a numerous and excellent collection of books, which had mostly belonged to the Reverend Mr. John Campbell, brother of our host. I was desirous to have procured for my fellow-traveller, to-day, the company of Sir John Cuninghame, of Caprington, whose castle was but two miles from us. He was a very distinguished scholar, was long abroad, and during part of the time lived much with the learned Cuninghame, the opponent of Bentley as a critick upon Horace. He wrote Latin with great elegance, and, what is very remarkable, read Homer and Ariosto through every year. I wrote to him to request he would come to us ; but unfortunately he was prevented by indisposition.

Monday, 1st November

Though Dr. Johnson was lazy, and averse to move, I insisted that he should go with me, and pay a visit to the Countess of Eglintoune, mother of the late and present earl. I assured him, he would find himself amply recompensed for the trouble ; and he yielded to my solicitations, though with some unwillingness. We were well mounted, and had not many miles to ride. He talked of the attention that is necessary in order to distribute our charity judiciously. " If thoughtlessly done, we may neglect the most deserving objects : and, as every man has but a certain proportion to give, if it is lavished upon those who first present themselves, there may be nothing left for such as have a better claim. A man should first relieve those who are nearly connected with him, by whatever tie ; and then, if he has any thing to spare, may extend his bounty to a wider circle."

As we passed very near the castle of Dundonald, which was one of the many residences of the kings of Scotland, and in which Robert the Second lived and died, Dr. Johnson wished to survey it particularly. It stands on a beautiful rising ground, which is seen at a great distance on several quarters, and from whence there is an extensive prospect of the rich district of Cuninghame, the western sea, the isle of Arran, and a part of the northern coast of Ireland. It has long been unroofed ; and, though of considerable size, we could not, by any power of imagination, figure it as having been a suitable habitation for majesty. Dr. Johnson, to irritate my *old Scottish* enthusiasm, was very jocular on the homely accommodation of " King *Bob*," and roared and laughed till the ruins echoed.

Lady Eglintoune, though she was now in her eighty-fifth year, and had lived in the retirement of the country for almost half a century, was still a very agreeable woman. She was of the noble house of Kennedy, and had all the elevation which the consciousness of such birth inspires. Her figure was majestick, her manners high-bred, her reading extensive, and her conversation elegant. She had been the admiration of the gay circles of life, and the patroness of poets. Dr. Johnson was delighted with his reception here. Her principles in church and state were congenial with his. She knew all his merit, and had heard much of him from her son, Earl Alexander, who loved to cultivate the acquaintance of men of talents, in every department.

All who knew his lordship, will allow that his understanding and accomplishments were of no ordinary rate. From the gay habits which he had early acquired, he spent too much of his time with men, and in pursuits far beneath such a mind as his. He afterwards became sensible of it, and turned his thoughts to objects of importance ; but was cut off in the prime of his life. I cannot speak, but with emotions of the most affectionate regret, of one, in whose company many of my early days were passed, and to whose kindness I was much indebted.

Often must I have occasion to upbraid myself, that soon after our return to the main land, I allowed indolence to prevail over me so much, as to shrink from the labour of continuing my Journal with the same minuteness as before ; sheltering myself in the thought, that we had done with the *Hebrides* ; and not considering, that Dr. Johnson's *Memorabilia* were likely to be more valuable when we were restored to a more polished society. Much has thus been irrecoverably lost.

In the course of our conversation this day, it came out, that Lady Eglintoune was married the year before Dr. Johnson was born ; upon which she graciously said to him, that she might have been his mother ; and that she now adopted him ; and when we were going away, she embraced him, saying, " My dear son, farewell ! "—My friend was much pleased with this day's entertainment, and owned that I had done well to force him out.

Tuesday, 2nd November

We were now in a country not only " of saddles and bridles," but of post-chaises ; and having ordered one from Kilmarnock, we got to Auchinleck before dinner.

My father was not quite a year and a half older than Dr. Johnson ; but his conscientious discharge of his laborious duty as a judge in Scotland, where the law proceedings are almost all in writing,—a severe complaint which ended in his death,—and the loss of my mother, a woman of almost unexampled piety and goodness,—had before this time in some degree affected his spirits, and rendered him less disposed to exert his faculties : for he had originally a very strong mind, and cheerful temper. He assured me, he never had felt one moment of what is called low spirits, or uneasiness, without a real cause. He had a great many good stories, which he told uncommonly well, and he was remarkable for " humour, *incolumi gravitate*," as Lord Monboddo used to characterise it. His age, his office, and his character, had long given him an acknowledged claim to great attention, in whatever company he was ; and he could ill brook any diminution of it. He was as sanguine a Whig and Presbyterian, as Dr. Johnson was a Tory and church of England man : and as he had not much leisure to be informed of Dr. Johnson's great merits by reading his works, he had a partial and un-favourable notion of him, founded on his supposed political tenets ; which were so discordant to his own, that, instead of speaking of him with that respect to which he was entitled, he used to call him " a Jacobite fellow." Knowing all this, I should not have ventured to bring them together, had not my father, out of kind-ness to me, desired me to invite Dr. Johnson to his house.

I was very anxious that all should be well ; and begged of my friend to avoid three topicks, as to which they differed very widely ; Whiggism, Presbyterianism, and—Sir John Pringle. He said courteously, " I shall certainly not talk on subjects which I am told are dis-agreeable to a gentleman under whose roof I am ; especially, I shall not do so to *your father*."

Our first day went off very smoothly. It rained, and we could not get out ; but my father shewed Dr. Johnson his library, which, in curious editions of the Greek and Roman classicks, is, I suppose, not excelled by any private collection in Great Britain. My father had studied at Leyden, and been very intimate with the Gronovii, and other learned men there. He was a sound scholar, and, in particular, had collated manu-scripts and different editions of Anacreon, and others of the Greek Lyrick poets, with great care; so that my friend and he had much matter for conversation, without touching on the fatal topicks of difference.

Dr. Johnson found here Baxter's *Anacreon*, which he told me he had long enquired for in vain, and began to suspect there was no such book. Baxter was the keen antagonist of Barnes. His life is in the *Biographia Britannica*. My father has written many notes on this book, and Dr. Johnson and I talked of having it reprinted.

Wednesday, 3rd November

It rained all day, and gave Dr. Johnson an impression of that incommodiousness of climate in the west, of which he has taken notice in his *Journey*; but, being well accommodated, and furnished with variety of books, he was not dissatisfied.

Some gentlemen of the neighbourhood came to visit my father; but there was little conversation. One of them asked Dr. Johnson how he liked the Highlands. The question seemed to irritate him, for he answered, " How, sir, can you ask me what obliges me to speak unfavourably of a country where I have been hospitably entertained? Who *can* like the Highlands?— I like the inhabitants very well."—The gentleman asked no more questions.

Let me now make up for the present neglect, by again gleaning from the past. At Lord Monboddo's, after the conversation upon the decrease of learning in England, his Lordship mentioned *Hermes* by Mr. Harris of Salisbury, as the work of a living authour, for whom he had a great respect. Dr. Johnson said nothing at the time; but when we were in our post-chaise, told me, he thought Harris " a coxcomb." This he said of him, not as a man, but as an authour;

and I give his opinions of men and books, faithfully, whether they agree with my own, or not. I do admit, that there always appeared to me something of affectation in Mr. Harris's manner of writing; something of a habit of clothing plain thoughts in analytick and categorical formality. But all his writings are imbued with learning; and all breathe that philanthropy and amiable disposition, which distinguished him as a man.

At another time, during our Tour, he drew the character of a rapacious Highland Chief with the strength of Theophrastus or La Bruyere; concluding with these words: " Sir, he has no more the soul of a Chief, than an attorney who has twenty houses in a street, and considers how much he can make by them."

He this day, when we were by ourselves, observed, how common it was for people to talk from books; to retail the sentiments of others, and not their own; in short, to converse without any originality of thinking. He was pleased to say, " You and I do not talk from books."

Thursday, 4th November

I was glad to have at length a very fine day, on which I could shew Dr. Johnson the Place of my family, which he has honoured with so much attention in his *Journey*. He is, however, mistaken in thinking that the Celtick name, *Auchinleck*, has no relation to the natural appearance of it. I believe every Celtick name of a place will be found very descriptive. *Auchinleck* does not signify a stony field, as he has said, but a *field of flag stones*; and this place has a number of rocks, which abound in strata of that kind. The " sullen dignity of the old castle," as he has forcibly expressed it, delighted him exceedingly. On one side of the rock on which its ruins stand, runs the river Lugar, which is here of considerable breadth, and is bordered by other high rocks, shaded with wood. On the other side runs a brook, skirted in the same manner, but on a smaller scale. I cannot figure a more romantick scene.

I felt myself elated here, and expatiated to my illustrious Mentor on the antiquity and honourable alliances of my family, and on the merits of its founder, Thomas Boswell, who was highly favoured by his sovereign, James IV. of Scotland, and fell with him at the battle of Flodden-field; and in the glow of what, I am sensible, will, in a commercial age, be considered as genealogical enthusiasm, did not omit to mention what I was sure my friend would not think lightly of, my relation to the Royal Personage, whose liberality, on his accession to the throne, had given him comfort and independence. I have, in a former page, acknowledged my pride of ancient blood, in which I was encouraged by Dr. Johnson : my readers therefore will not be surprised at my having indulged it on this occasion.

Not far from the old castle is a spot of consecrated earth, on which may be traced the foundations of an ancient chapel, dedicated to St. Vincent, and where in old times " was the place of graves " for the family. It grieves me to think that the remains of sanctity here, which were considerable, were dragged away, and employed in building a part of the house of Auchinleck, of the middle age ; which was the family residence, till my father erected that " elegant modern mansion," of which Dr. Johnson speaks so handsomely. Perhaps this chapel may one day be restored.

Dr. Johnson was pleased, when I shewed him some venerable old trees, under the shade of which my ancestors had walked. He exhorted me to plant assiduously, as my father had done to a great extent.

As I wandered with my reverend friend in the groves

of Auchinleck, I told him, that, if I survived him, it
was my intention to erect a monument to him here,
among scenes which, in my mind, were all classical;
for in my youth I had appropriated to them many of
the descriptions of the Roman poets. He could not
bear to have death presented to him in any shape; for
his constitutional melancholy made the king of terrours
more frightful. He turned off the subject, saying,
" Sir, I hope to see your grand-children ! "

This forenoon he observed some cattle without
horns, of which he has taken notice in his *Journey*,
and seems undecided whether they be of a particular
race. His doubts appear to have had no foundation;
for my respectable neighbour, Mr. Fairlie, who, with
all his attention to agriculture, finds time both for the
classicks and his friends, assures me they are a distinct
species, and that, when any of their calves have horns,
a mixture of breed can be traced. In confirmation of
his opinion, he pointed out to me the following passage
in Tacitus,—" *Ne armentis quidem suus honor, aut gloria
frontis;*" (De mor. Germ. § 5.) which he wondered
had escaped Dr. Johnson.

On the front of the house of Auchinleck is this
inscription :

> *Quod petis, hic est ;*
> *Est Ulubris ; animus si te non deficit æquus.*

It is characteristick of the founder; but the *animus
æquus* is, alas ! not inheritable, nor the subject of devise.
He always talked to me as if it were in a man's own
power to attain it; but Dr. Johnson told me that he
owned to him, when they were alone, his persuasion
that it was in a great measure constitutional, or the
effect of causes which do not depend on ourselves, and
that Horace boasts too much, when he says, *æquum mi
animum ipse parabo.*

Friday, 5th November

The Reverend Mr. Dun, our parish minister, who
had dined with us yesterday, with some other company,
insisted that Dr. Johnson and I should dine with him
to-day. This gave me an opportunity to shew my
friend the road to the church, made by my father at a
great expence, for above three miles, on his own estate,
through a range of well enclosed farms, with a row of
trees on each side of it. He called it the *Via sacra,*
and was very fond of it. Dr. Johnson, though he held
notions far distant from those of the Presbyterian clergy,
yet could associate on good terms with them. He indeed
occasionally attacked them. One of them discovered a
narrowness of information concerning the dignitaries of
the church of England, among whom may be found men
of the greatest learning, virtue, and piety, and of a truly
apostolic character. He talked before Dr. Johnson, of
fat bishops and drowsy deans ; and, in short, seemed to
believe the illiberal and profane scoffings of professed
satyrists, or vulgar railers. Dr. Johnson was so highly
offended, that he said to him, " Sir, you know no more
of our church than a Hottentot."—I was sorry that
he brought this upon himself.

Saturday, 6th November

I cannot be certain, whether it was on this day, or a
former, that Dr. Johnson and my father came in col-
lision. If I recollect right, the contest began while my
father was shewing him his collection of medals ; and
Oliver Cromwell's coin unfortunately introduced Charles
the First, and Toryism. They became exceedingly
warm, and violent, and I was very much distressed by
being present at such an altercation between two men,

both of whom I reverenced ; yet I durst not interfere. It would certainly be very unbecoming in me to exhibit my honoured father, and my respected friend, as intellectual gladiators, for the entertainment of the publick ; and therefore I suppress what would, I dare say, make an interesting scene in this dramatick sketch,— this account of the transit of Johnson over the Caledonian Hemisphere.

Yet I think I may, without impropriety, mention one circumstance, as an instance of my father's address. Dr. Johnson challenged him, as he did us all at Talisker, to point out any theological works of merit written by Presbyterian ministers in Scotland. My father, whose studies did not lie much in that way, owned to me afterwards, that he was somewhat at a loss how to answer, but that luckily he recollected having read in catalogues the title of *Durham on the Galatians* ; upon which he boldly said, " Pray, sir, have you read Mr. Durham's excellent commentary on the Galatians ? " —" No, sir," said Dr. Johnson. By this lucky thought my father kept him at bay, and for some time enjoyed his triumph ; but his antagonist soon made a retort, which I forbear to mention.

In the course of their altercation, Whiggism and Presbyterianism, Toryism and Episcopacy, were terribly buffeted. My worthy hereditary friend, Sir John Pringle, never having been mentioned, happily escaped without a bruise.

My father's opinion of Dr. Johnson may be conjectured from the name he afterwards gave him, which was URSA MAJOR. But it is not true, as has been reported, that it was in consequence of my saying that he was a *constellation* of genius and literature. It was a sly abrupt expression to one of his brethren on the bench of the Court of Session, in which Dr. Johnson was then standing ; but it was not said in his hearing.

Sunday, 7th November

My father and I went to publick worship in our parish-church, in which I regretted that Dr. Johnson would not join us ; for, though we have there no form of prayer, nor magnificent solemnity, yet, as GOD is worshipped in spirit and in truth, and the same doctrines preached as in the church of England, my friend would certainly have shewn more liberality, had he attended. I doubt not, however, but he employed his time in private to very good purpose. His uniform and fervent piety was manifested on many occasions during our Tour, which I have not mentioned.—His reason for not joining in Presbyterian worship has been recorded in a former page.

Monday, 8th November

Notwithstanding the altercation that had passed, my father, who had the dignified courtesy of an old Baron, was very civil to Dr. Johnson, and politely attended him to the post-chaise, which was to convey us to Edinburgh.

Thus they parted.—They are now in another, and a higher, state of existence : and as they were both worthy christian men, I trust they have met in happiness. But I must observe, in justice to my friend's political principles, and my own, that they have met in a place where there is no room for *Whiggism*.

We came at night to a good inn at Hamilton.—I recollect no more.

Tuesday, 9th November

I wished to have shewn Dr. Johnson the Duke of Hamilton's house, commonly called the Palace of Hamilton, which is close by the town. It is an object which, having been pointed out to me as a splendid edifice, from my earliest years, in travelling between Auchinleck and Edinburgh, has still great grandeur in my imagination. My friend consented to stop, and view the outside of it, but could not be persuaded to go into it.

We arrived this night at Edinburgh, after an absence of eighty-three days. For five weeks together, of the tempestuous season, there had been no account received of us. I cannot express how happy I was on finding myself again at home.

Wednesday, 10th November

Old Mr. Drummond, the bookseller, came to breakfast. Dr. Johnson and he had not met for ten years. There was respect on his side, and kindness on Dr. Johnson's. Soon afterwards Lord Elibank came in, and was much pleased at seeing Dr. Johnson in Scotland. His lordship said, " hardly any thing seemed to him more improbable." Dr. Johnson had a very high opinion of him. Speaking of him to me, he characterized him thus : " Lord Elibank has read a great deal. It is true, I can find in books all that he has read ; but he has a great deal of what is in books, proved by the test of real life."—Indeed, there have been few men whose conversation discovered more knowledge enlivened by fancy. He published several small pieces of distinguished merit ; and has left some in manuscript, in particular an account of the expedition against Carthagena, in which he served as an officer in the army. His writings deserve to be collected. He was the early patron of Dr. Robertson, the historian, and Mr. Home, the tragick poet ; who, when they were ministers of country parishes, lived near his seat. He told me, " I saw these lads had talents, and they were much with me."—I hope they will pay a grateful tribute to his memory.

The morning was chiefly taken up by Dr. Johnson's giving him an account of our Tour.—The subject of difference in political principles was introduced.—JOHNSON. " It is much increased by opposition. There was a violent Whig, with whom I used to contend with great eagerness. After his death I felt my Toryism much abated."—I suppose he meant Mr. Walmsley of Lichfield, whose character he has drawn so well in his life of Edmund Smith.

Mr. Nairne came in, and he and I accompanied Dr. Johnson to Edinburgh castle, which he owned was " a great place." But I must mention, as a striking instance of that spirit of contradiction to which he had a strong propensity, when Lord Elibank was some days after talking of it with the natural elation of a Scotchman, or of any man who is proud of a stately fortress in his own country, Dr. Johnson affected to despise it, observing that, " it would make a good *prison* in ENGLAND."

Lest it should be supposed that I have suppressed one of his sallies against my country, it may not be improper here to correct a mistaken account that has been circulated, as to his conversation this day. It has been said, that being desired to attend to the noble prospect from the Castle-hill, he replied, " Sir, the noblest prospect that a Scotchman ever sees, is the high road that leads him to London."—This lively sarcasm was thrown out at a tavern in London, in my presence, many years before.

We had with us to day at dinner, at my house, the Lady Dowager Colvill, and Lady Anne Erskine, sisters of the Earl of Kelly; the Honourable Archibald Erskine, who has now succeeded to that title; Lord Elibank; the Reverend Dr. Blair; Mr. Tytler, the acute vindicator of Mary Queen of Scots, and some other friends.

Fingal being talked of, Dr. Johnson, who used to

boast that he had, from the first, resisted both Ossian and the Giants of Patagonia, averred his positive disbelief of its authenticity. Lord Elibank said, " I am sure it is not M'Pherson's. Mr. Johnson, I keep company a great deal with you ; it is known I do. I may borrow from you better things than I can say myself, and give them as my own ; but, if I should, every body will know whose they are."—The Doctor was not softened by this compliment. He denied merit to *Fingal*, supposing it to be the production of a man who has had the advantages that the present age affords ; and said, " nothing is more easy than to write enough in that style if once you begin."—One gentleman in company expressing his opinion " that *Fingal* was certainly genuine, for that he had heard a great part of it repeated in the original," Dr. Johnson indignantly asked him, whether he understood the original ; to which an answer being given in the negative, " Why then, (said Dr. Johnson,) we see to what *this* testimony comes :—thus it is."

I mentioned this as a remarkable proof how liable the mind of man is to credulity, when not guarded by such strict examination as that which Dr. Johnson habitually practised. The talents and integrity of the gentleman who made the remark are unquestionable ; yet, had not Dr. Johnson made him advert to the consideration, that he who does not understand a language, cannot know that something which is recited to him is in that language, he might have believed, and reported to this hour, that he had " heard a great part of *Fingal* repeated in the original."

For the satisfaction of those on the north of the Tweed, who may think Dr. Johnson's account of Caledonian credulity and inaccuracy too strong, it is but fair to add, that he admitted the same kind of ready belief might be found in his own country. " He would undertake, (he said) to write an epick poem on the story of Robin Hood, and half England, to whom the names and places he should mention in it are familiar, would believe and declare they had heard it from their earliest years."

One of his objections to the authenticity of *Fingal*, during the conversation at Ulinish, is omitted in my Journal, but I perfectly recollect it.—" Why is not the original deposited in some publick library, instead of exhibiting attestations of its existence ? Suppose there were a question in a court of justice, whether a man be dead or alive : You aver he is alive, and you bring fifty witnesses to swear it : I answer, ' Why do you not produce the man ? ' "—This is an argument founded on one of the first principles of the law of evidence which Gilbert would have held to be irrefragable.

I do not think it incumbent on me to give any precise decided opinion upon this question, as to which I believe more than some, and less than others. The subject appears to have now become very uninteresting to the publick. That *Fingal* is not from beginning to end a translation from the Gallick, but that *some* passages have been supplied by the editor to connect the whole, I have heard admitted by very warm advocates for its authenticity. If this be the case, why are not these distinctly ascertained ? Antiquaries, and admirers of the work, may complain, that they are in a situation similar to that of the unhappy gentleman whose wife informed him, on her death-bed, that one of their reputed children was not his ; and, when he eagerly begged her to declare which of them it was, she answered, " *That* you shall never know ; " and expired, leaving him in irremediable doubt as to them all.

I beg leave now to say something upon second sight, of which I have related two instances, as they impressed my mind at the time. I own, I returned from the Hebrides with a considerable degree of faith in the many stories of that kind which I heard with a too easy acquiescence, without any close examination of the evidence : but, since that time, my belief in those stories has been much weakened, by reflecting on the careless inaccuracy of narrative in common matters, from which we may certainly conclude that there may be the same in what is more extraordinary.—It is but just, however, to add, that the belief in second sight is not peculiar to the Highlands and Isles.

Some years after our Tour, a cause was tried in the Court of Session, where the principal fact to be ascertained was, whether a ship-master, who used to frequent the Western Highlands and Isles, was drowned in one particular year, or in the year after. A great number of witnesses from those parts were examined on each side, and swore directly contrary to each other, upon this simple question. One of them, a very respectable Chieftain, who told me a story of second sight, which I have not mentioned, but which I too implicitly believed, had in this case, previous to this publick examination, not only said, but attested under his hand, that he had seen the ship-master in the year subsequent to that in which the court was finally satisfied he was drowned. When interrogated with the strictness of judicial inquiry, and under the awe of an oath, he recollected himself better, and retracted what he had formerly asserted, apologising for his inaccuracy, by telling the judges, "A man will *say* what he will not *swear*."—By many he was much censured, and it was maintained that every gentleman would be as attentive to truth without the sanction of an oath, as with it. Dr. Johnson, though he himself was distinguished at all times by a scrupulous adherence to truth, controverted this proposition ; and, as a proof that this was not, though it ought to be, the case, urged the very different decisions of elections under Mr. Grenville's Act, from those formerly made. " Gentlemen will not pronounce upon oath, what they would have said, and voted in the house, without that sanction."

However difficult it may be for men who believe in preternatural communications, in modern times, to satisfy those who are of a different opinion, they may easily refute the doctrine of their opponents, who impute a belief in second sight to superstition. To entertain a visionary notion that one sees a distant or future event, may be called superstition; but the correspondence of the fact or event with such an impression on the fancy, though certainly very wonderful, *if proved*, has no more connection with superstition, than magnetism or electricity.

After dinner, various topicks were discussed; but I recollect only one particular. Dr. Johnson compared the different talents of Garrick and Foote, as companions, and gave Garrick greatly the preference for elegance, though he allowed Foote extraordinary powers of entertainment. He said, " Garrick is restrained by some principle; but Foote has the advantage of an unlimited range. Garrick has some delicacy of feeling; it is possible to put him out; you may get the better of him; but Foote is the most incompressible fellow that I ever knew: when you have driven him into a corner, and think you are sure of him, he runs through between your legs, or jumps over your head, and makes his escape."

Dr. Erskine and Mr. Robert Walker, two very respectable ministers of Edinburgh, supped with us, as did the Reverend Dr. Webster.—The conversation turned on the Moravian missions, and on the Methodists. Dr. Johnson observed in general, that missionaries were too sanguine in their accounts of their success among savages, and that much of what they tell is not to be believed. He owned that the Methodists had done good; had spread religious impressions among the vulgar part of mankind: but, he said, they had great bitterness against other Christians, and that he never could get a Methodist to explain in what he excelled others; that it always ended in the indispensable necessity of hearing one of their preachers.

Thursday, 11th November

Principal Robertson came to us as we sat at breakfast ; he advanced to Dr. Johnson, repeating a line of Virgil, which I forget. I suppose, either

or

Post varios casus, per tot discrimina rerum,

—multum ille et terris jactatus, et alto.

Every body had accosted us with some studied compliment on our return. Dr. Johnson said, " I am really ashamed of the congratulations which we receive. We are addressed as if we had made a voyage to Nova Zembla, and suffered five persecutions in Japan." And he afterwards remarked, that, " to see a man come up with a formal air, and a Latin line, when we had no fatigue and no danger, was provoking."—I told him, he was not sensible of the danger, having lain under cover in the boat during the storm : he was like the chicken, that hides its head under its wing, and then thinks itself safe.

Lord Elibank came to us, as did Sir William Forbes. The rash attempt in 1745 being mentioned, I observed, that it would make a fine piece of History. Dr. Johnson said it would. Lord Elibank doubted whether any man of this age could give it impartially.—JOHNSON. " A man, by talking with those of different sides, who were actors in it, and putting down all that he hears, may in time collect the materials of a good narrative. You are to consider, all history was at first oral. I suppose Voltaire was fifty years in collecting his *Louis XIV.*, which he did in the way that I am proposing."—

ROBERTSON. " He did so. He lived much with all the great people who were concerned in that reign, and heard them talk of every thing ; and then either took Mr. Boswell's way, of writing down what he heard, or, which is as good, preserved it in his memory ; for he has a wonderful memory."—With the leave, how-ever, of this elegant historian, no man's memory can preserve facts or sayings with such fidelity as may be done by writing them down when they are recent.— Dr. Robertson said, " it was now full time to make such a collection as Dr. Johnson suggested ; for many of the people who were then in arms, were dropping off ; and both Whigs and Jacobites were now come to talk with moderation."—Lord Elibank said to him, " Mr. Robertson, the first thing that gave me a high opinion of you, was your saying in the Select Society, while parties ran high, soon after the year 1745, that you did not think worse of a man's moral character for his having been in rebellion. This was venturing to utter a liberal sentiment, while both sides had a detesta-tion of each other."

Dr. Johnson observed, that being in rebellion from a notion of another's right, was not connected with depravity ; and that we had this proof of it, that all mankind applauded the pardoning of rebels ; which they would not do in the case of robbers and murderers. He said, with a smile, that, " he wondered that the phrase of *unnatural* rebellion should be so much used, for that all rebellion was natural to man."

As I kept no Journal of any thing that passed after this morning, I shall, from memory, group together this and the other days, till that on which Dr. Johnson departed for London. They were in all nine days ; on which he dined at Lady Colvill's, Lord Hailes's, Sir Adolphus Oughton's, Sir Alexander Dick's, Principal Robertson's, Mr. M'Laurin's, and thrice at Lord Elibank's seat in the country, where we also passed two nights. He supped at the Honourable Alexander Gordon's, now one of our judges, by the title of Lord Rockville ; at Mr. Nairne's, now also one of our judges, by the title of Lord Dunsinan ; at Dr. Blair's, and Mr. Tytler's ; and at my house thrice, one evening with a numerous company, chiefly gentlemen of the law ; another with Mr. Menzies of Culdares, and Lord Monboddo, who disengaged himself on purpose to meet him ; and the evening on which we returned from Lord Elibank's, he supped with my wife and me by ourselves.

He breakfasted at Dr. Webster's, at old Mr. Drummond's, and at Dr. Blacklock's ; and spent one forenoon at my uncle Dr. Boswell's, who shewed him his curious museum ; and, as he was an elegant scholar, and a physician bred in the school of Boerhaave, Dr. Johnson was pleased with his company.

On the mornings when he breakfasted at my house, he had, from ten o'clock till one or two, a constant levee of various persons, of very different characters and descriptions. I could not attend him, being obliged to be in the Court of Session ; but my wife was so good as to devote the greater part of the morning to the endless task of pouring out tea for my friend and his visitors.

Such was the disposition of his time at Edinburgh. He said one evening to me, in a fit of languor, " Sir, we have been harassed by invitations." I acquiesced. " Ay, sir," he replied ; " but how much worse would it have been, if we had been neglected ? "

From what has been recorded in this Journal, it may well be supposed that a variety of admirable conversation has been lost, by my neglect to preserve it.—I shall endeavour to recollect some of it, as well as I can.

At Lady Colvill's, to whom I am proud to introduce any stranger of eminence, that he may see what dignity and grace is to be found in Scotland, an officer observed, that he had heard Lord Mansfield was not a great English lawyer.—JOHNSON. " Why, sir, supposing Lord Mansfield not to have the splendid talents which he possesses, he must be a great English lawyer, from having been so long at the bar, and having passed through so many of the great offices of the law. Sir, you may as well maintain that a carrier, who has driven a packhorse between Edinburgh and Berwick for thirty years, does not know the road, as that Lord Mansfield does not know the law of England."

At Mr. Nairne's, he drew the character of Richardson, the author of *Clarissa*, with a strong yet delicate pencil. I lament much that I have not preserved it : I only remember that he expressed a high opinion of his talents and virtues ; but observed, that " his perpetual study was to ward off petty inconveniencies, and procure petty pleasures ; that his love of continual superiority was such, that he took care to be always surrounded by women, who listened to him implicitly, and did not venture to controvert his opinions ; and that his desire of distinction was so great, that he used to give large vails to the Speaker Onslow's servants, that they might treat him with respect."

On the same evening, he would not allow that the private life of a judge, in England, was required to be so strictly decorous as I supposed. " Why then, sir, (said I,) according to your account, an English judge may just live like a gentleman."—JOHNSON." Yes, sir, —if he *can*."

At Mr. Tytler's, I happened to tell that one evening, a great many years ago, when Dr. Hugh Blair and I were sitting together in the pit of Drury-lane playhouse, in a wild freak of youthful extravagance, I entertained the audience prodigiously, by imitating the lowing of a cow. A little while after I had told this story, I differed from Dr. Johnson, I suppose too confidently, upon some point, which I now forget. He

I2

did not spare me. "Nay, sir, (said he,) if you cannot talk better as a man, I'd have you bellow like a cow."

At Dr. Webster's, he said, that he believed hardly any man died without affectation. This remark appears to me to be well founded, and will account for many of the celebrated death-bed sayings which are recorded.

On one of the evenings at my house, when he told that Lord Lovat boasted to an English nobleman, that though he had not his wealth, he had two thousand men whom he could at any time call into the field, the Honourable Alexander Gordon observed, that those two thousand men brought him to the block.—"True, sir, (said Dr. Johnson :) but you may just as well argue, concerning a man who has fallen over a precipice to which he has walked too near,—' His two legs brought him to that,' is he not the better for having two legs ? "

At Dr. Blair's I left him, in order to attend a consultation, during which he and his amiable host were by themselves. I returned to supper, at which were Principal Robertson, Mr. Nairne, and some other gentlemen. Dr. Robertson and Dr. Blair, I remember, talked well upon subordination and government ; and, as my friend and I were walking home, he said to me, "Sir, these two doctors are good men, and wise men."—I begged of Dr. Blair to recollect what he could of the long conversation that passed between Dr. Johnson and him alone, this evening, and he obligingly wrote to me as follows :

" *March* 3, 1785.

" DEAR SIR,

" As so many years have intervened, since I chanced to have that conversation with Dr. Johnson in my house, to which you refer, I have forgotten most of what then passed, but remember that I was both instructed and entertained by it. Among other subjects, the discourse happening to turn on modern Latin poets, the Doctor expressed a very favourable opinion of Buchanan, and instantly repeated, from beginning to end, an ode of his, intituled *Calendæ Maiæ*, (the eleventh in his *Miscellaneorum Liber*,) beginning with these words, ' *Salvete sacris deliciis sacræ*,' with which I had formerly been unacquainted ; but upon perusing it, the praise which he bestowed upon it, as one of the happiest of Buchanan's poetical compositions, appeared to me very just. He also repeated to me a Latin ode he had composed in one of the western islands, from which he had lately returned. We had much discourse concerning his excursion to those islands, with which he expressed himself as having been highly pleased ; talked in a favourable manner of the hospitality of the inhabitants ; and particularly spoke much of his happiness in having you for his companion ; and said, that the longer he knew you, he loved and esteemed you the more. This conversation passed in the interval between tea and supper, when we were by ourselves. You, and the rest of the company who were with us at supper, have often taken notice that he was uncommonly bland and gay that evening, and gave much pleasure to all who were present.—This is all that I can recollect distinctly of that long conversation.

> " Yours sincerely,
> " HUGH BLAIR."

At Lord Hailes's, we spent a most agreeable day ; but again I must lament that I was so indolent as to let almost all that passed evaporate into oblivion. Dr. Johnson observed there, that " it is wonderful how ignorant many officers of the army are, considering how much leisure they have for study, and the acquisition of knowledge." I hope he was mistaken ; for he maintained that many of them were ignorant of things belonging immediately to their own profession ; " for instance, many cannot tell how far a musket will carry

a bullet ; " in proof of which, I suppose, he mentioned
some particular person, for Lord Hailes, from whom I
solicited what he could recollect of that day, writes to
me as follows :

" As to Dr. Johnson's observation about the ignorance
of officers, in the length that a musket will carry, my
brother, Colonel Dalrymple, was present, and he thought
that the doctor was either mistaken, by putting the
question wrong, or that he had conversed on the subject
with some person out of service.

" Was it upon that occasion that he expressed no
curiosity to see the room at Dumfermline, where Charles
I. was born ? ' I know that he was born, (said he ;)
no matter where.'—Did he envy us the birth-place of
the king ? "

Near the end of his *Journey*, Dr. Johnson has
given liberal praise to Mr. Braidwood's academy for
the deaf and dumb.   When he visited it, a circumstance
occurred which was truly characteristical of our great
Lexicographer.   " Pray, (said he,) can they pronounce
any *long* words ? "—Mr. Braidwood informed him they
could.   Upon which Dr. Johnson wrote one of his
sesquipedalia verba, which was pronounced by the
scholars, and he was satisfied.—My readers may perhaps wish to know what the word was ; but I cannot
gratify their curiosity.   Mr. Braidwood told me, it
remained long in his school, but had been lost before I
made my inquiry.

Dr. Johnson one day visited the Court of Session.
He thought the mode of pleading there too vehement,
and too much addressed to the passions of the judges.
" This (said he) is not the Areopagus."

At old Mr. Drummond's, Sir John Dalrymple quaintly
said, the two noblest animals in the world were, a Scotch
Highlander and an English Sailor.   " Why, sir, (said

Dr. Johnson,) I shall say nothing as to the Scotch Highlander ; but as to the English Sailor, I cannot agree
with you."—Sir John said, he was generous in giving
away his money.—JOHNSON. " Sir, he throws away his
money, without thought, and without merit. I do not
call a tree generous, that sheds its fruit at every breeze."
—Sir John having affected to complain of the attacks
made upon his *Memoirs*, Dr. Johnson said, " Nay, sir,
do not complain. It is advantageous to an authour,
that his book should be attacked as well as praised.
Fame is a shuttlecock. If it be struck only at one end
of the room, it will soon fall to the ground. To keep
it up, it must be struck at both ends."—Often have I
reflected on this since ; and, instead of being angry at
many of those who have written against me, have smiled
to think that they were unintentionally subservient to
my fame, by using a battledoor to make me *virum
volitare per ora.*

At Sir Alexander Dick's, from that absence of mind
to which every man is at times subject, I told, in a
blundering manner, Lady Eglintoune's complimentary
adoption of Dr. Johnson as her son ; for I unfortunately
stated that her ladyship adopted him as her son, in
consequence of her having been married the year *after*
he was born. Dr. Johnson instantly corrected me.
" Sir, don't you perceive that you are defaming the
countess ? For, supposing me to be her son, and that
she was not married till the year after my birth, I must
have been her *natural* son." A young lady of quality,
who was present, very handsomely said, " Might not
the son have justified the fault."—My friend was much
flattered by this compliment, which he never forgot.
When in more than ordinary spirits, and talking of his
journey in Scotland, he has called to me, " Boswell,
what was it that the young lady of quality said of me
at Sir Alexander Dick's ? " Nobody will doubt that I
was happy in repeating it.

My illustrious friend, being now desirous to be again in the great theatre of life and animated exertion, took a place in the coach, which was to set out for London on Monday the 22nd of November. Sir John Dalrymple pressed him to come on the Saturday before, to his house at Cranston, which being twelve miles from Edinburgh, upon the middle road to Newcastle, (Dr. Johnson had come to Edinburgh by Berwick, and along the naked coast,) it would make his journey easier, as the coach would take him up at a more seasonable hour than that at which it sets out. Sir John, I perceived, was ambitious of having such a guest ; but, as I was well assured, that at this very time he had joined with some of his prejudiced countrymen in railing at Dr. Johnson, and had said, " he wondered how any gentleman of Scotland could keep company with him," I thought he did not deserve the honour : yet, as it might be a convenience to Dr. Johnson, I contrived that he should accept the invitation, and engaged to conduct him. I resolved that, on our way to Sir John's, we should make a little circuit by Roslin Castle, and Hawthornden, and wished to set out soon after breakfast ; but young Mr. Tytler came to shew Dr. Johnson some essays which he had written ; and my great friend, who was exceedingly obliging when thus consulted, was detained so long that it was, I believe, one o'clock before we got into our post-chaise. I found that we should be too late for dinner at Sir John Dalrymple's, to which we were engaged : but I would by no means lose the pleasure of seeing my friend at Hawthornden,—of seeing *Sam Johnson* at the very spot where *Ben Jonson* visited the learned and poetical Drummond.

We surveyed Roslin Castle, the romantick scene around it, and the beautiful Gothick chapel, and dined and drank tea at the inn ; after which we proceeded to Hawthornden, and viewed the caves ; and I all the while had *Rare Ben* in my mind, and was pleased to think that this place was now visited by another celebrated wit of England.

By this time " the waning night was growing old," and we were yet several miles from Sir John Dalrymple's. Dr. Johnson did not seem much troubled at our having treated the baronet with so little attention to politeness; but when I talked of the grievous disappointment it must have been to him that we did not come to the *feast* that he had prepared for us, (for he told us he had killed a seven-year-old sheep on purpose,) my friend got into a merry mood, and jocularly said, " I dare say, sir, he has been very sadly distressed : Nay, we do not know but the consequence may have been fatal. Let me try to describe his situation in his own historical style. I have as good a right to make him think and talk, as he has to tell us how people thought and talked a hundred years ago, of which he has no evidence. All history, so far as it is not supported by contemporary evidence, is romance.—Stay now.—Let us consider ! " —He then (heartily laughing all the while) proceeded in his imitation, I am sure to the following effect, though now, at the distance of almost twelve years, I cannot pretend to recollect all the precise words :

" Dinner being ready, he wondered that his guests were not yet come. His wonder was soon succeeded by impatience. He walked about the room in anxious agitation ; sometimes he looked at his watch, sometimes he looked out at the window with an eager gaze of expectation, and revolved in his mind the various accidents of human life. His family beheld him with mute concern. ' Surely (said he, with a sigh,) they will not fail me.'—The mind of man can bear a certain pressure ; but there is a point when it can bear no more. A rope was in his view, and he died a Roman death."

It was very late before we reached the seat of Sir John Dalrymple, who, certainly with some reason, was not in very good humour. Our conversation was not brilliant. We supped, and went to bed in ancient rooms, which would have better suited the climate of Italy in summer, than that of Scotland in the month of November.

I recollect no conversation of the next day, worth preserving, except one saying of Dr. Johnson, which will be a valuable text for many decent old dowagers, and other good company, in various circles to descant upon.—He said, " I am sorry I have not learned to play at cards. It is very useful in life : it generates kindness, and consolidates society."—He certainly could not mean deep play.

My friend and I thought we should be more comfortable at the inn at Blackshields, two miles farther on. We therefore went thither in the evening, and he was very entertaining ; but I have preserved nothing but the pleasing remembrance, and his verses on George the Second and Cibber, and his epitaph on Parnell, which he was then so good as to dictate to me. We breakfasted together next morning, and then the coach came, and took him up. He had, as one of his companions in it, as far as Newcastle, the worthy and ingenious Dr. Hope, botanical professor at Edinburgh. Both Dr. Johnson and he used to speak of their good fortune in thus accidentally meeting ; for they had much instructive conversation, which is always a most valuable enjoyment, and, when found where it is not expected, is peculiarly relished.

I have now completed my account of our Tour to the Hebrides. I have brought Dr. Johnson down to Scotland, and seen him into the coach which in a few hours carried him back into England. He said to me often, that the time he spent in this Tour was the pleasantest part of his life, and asked me if I would lose the recollection of it for five hundred pounds. I answered I would not ; and he applauded my setting such a value on an accession of new images in my mind.

Had it not been for me, I am persuaded Dr. Johnson never would have undertaken such a journey ; and I must be allowed to assume some merit from having been the cause that our language has been enriched with such a book as that which he published on his return ; a book which I never read but with the utmost admiration, as I had such opportunities of knowing from what very meagre materials it was composed.

But my praise may be supposed partial ; and therefore I shall insert two testimonies, not liable to that objection, both written by gentlemen of Scotland, to whose opinions I am confident the highest respect will be paid, Lord Hailes, and Mr. Dempster.

" To James Boswell, Esq.

" Sir,

" I have received much pleasure and much instruction, from perusing *The Journey to the Hebrides*.

" I admire the elegance and variety of description, and the lively picture of men and manners. I always approve of the moral, often of the political, reflections. I love the benevolence of the authour.

" They who search for faults, may possibly find them in this, as well as in every other work of literature.

" For example, the friends of the old family say that *the æra of planting* is placed too late, at the Union of the two kingdoms. I am known to be no friend of the old family ; yet I would place the æra of planting at the Restoration ; after the murder of Charles I. had been expiated in the anarchy which succeeded it.

" Before the Restoration, few trees were planted, unless by the monastick drones : their successors, (and worthy patriots they were,) the barons, first cut down the trees, and then sold the estates. The gentlemen at St. Andrews, who said that there were but two trees in Fife, ought to have added, that the Elms of Balmerino

were sold within these twenty years, to make pumps
for the fire-engines.

"In J. Major *de Gestis Scotorum*, L. i. C. 2. last edition,
there is a singular passage :

"'Davidi Cranstoneo conterraneo, dum de prima
theologiæ licentia foret, duo ei consocii et familiares,
et mei cum eo in artibus auditores, scilicet Jacobus
Almain Senonensis, et Petrus Bruxcellensis, Prædica-
toris ordinis, in Sorbonæ curia die Sorbonico commili-
tonibus suis publice objecerunt, *quod pane avenaceo
plebeii Scoti,* sicut a quodam religioso intellexerant,
*vescebantur, ut virum, quem cholericum noverant, honestis
salibus tentarent, qui hoc inficiari tanquam patriæ dedecus
nisus est.*'

"Pray introduce our countryman, Mr. Licentiate
David Cranston, to the acquaintance of Mr. Johnson.

"The syllogism seems to have been this :

> "They who feed on oatmeal are barbarians ;
> But the Scots feed on oatmeal :
> Ergo—

"The licentiate denied the *minor.*
            "I am, Sir,
                    "Your most obedient servant,
                                "DAV. DALRYMPLE.'
"NEWHAILES, *6th Feb.* 1775."

TO JAMES BOSWELL, ESQ. Edinburgh.

"DUNNICHEN, 16*th February,* 1775.

"MY DEAR BOSWELL,

"I CANNOT omit a moment to return you my best
thanks for the entertainment you have furnished me,
my family, and guests, by the perusal of Dr. Johnson's
Journey to the Western Islands ;—and now for my
sentiments of it.—I was well entertained. His descriptions are accurate and vivid. He carried me on the

Tour along with him. I am pleased with the justice
he has done to your humour and vivacity. 'The noise
of the wind being all its own,' is a *bon-mot*, that it would
have been a pity to have omitted, and a robbery not
to have ascribed to its author.

" There is nothing in the book, from beginning to
end, that a Scotchman need to take amiss. What he
says of the country is true, and his observations on the
people are what must naturally occur to a sensible,
observing, and reflecting inhabitant of a *convenient*
Metropolis, where a man on thirty pounds a year may
be better accommodated with all the little wants of
life, than Col or Sir Allan. He reasons candidly about
the second sight ; but I wish he had enquired more,
before he ventured to say he even doubted of the possibility of such an unusual and useless deviation from
all the known laws of nature. The notion of the second
sight I consider as a remnant of superstitious ignorance
and credulity, which a philosopher will set down as
such, till the contrary is clearly proved, and then it will
be classed among the other certain, though unaccountable, parts of our nature, like dreams, and—I do not
know what.

" In regard to the language, it has the merit of being
all his own. Many words of foreign extraction are
used, where, I believe, common ones would do as well,
especially on familiar occasions. Yet I believe he
could not express himself so forcibly in any other stile.
I am charmed with his researches concerning the Erse
language, and the antiquity of their manuscripts. I
am quite convinced ; and I shall rank *Ossian*, and his
Fingals and *Oscars*, amongst the Nursery Tales, not
the true history of our country, in all time to come.

" Upon the whole, the book cannot displease, for
it has no pretensions. The author neither says he is
a Geographer, nor an Antiquarian, nor very learned
in the History of Scotland, nor a Naturalist, nor a

Fossilist. The manners of the people, and the face of the country, are all he attempts to describe, or seems to have thought of. Much were it to be wished, that they who have travelled into more remote, and of course more curious, regions, had all possessed his good sense. Of the state of learning, his observations on Glasgow university shew he has formed a very sound judgement. He understands our climate too, and he has accurately observed the changes, however slow and imperceptible to us, which Scotland has undergone, in consequence of the blessings of liberty and internal peace. I could have drawn my pen through the story of the old woman at St. Andrews, being the only silly thing in the book. He has taken the opportunity of ingrafting into the work several good observations, which I dare say he had made upon men and things, before he set foot on Scotch ground, by which it is considerably enriched. A long journey, like a tall may-pole, though not very beautiful itself, yet is pretty enough, when ornamented with flowers and garlands : it furnishes a sort of cloak-pins for hanging the furniture of your mind upon ; and whoever sets out upon a journey, without furnishing his mind previously with much study and useful knowledge, erects a may-pole in December, and puts up very useless cloak-pins.

" I hope the book will induce many of his countrymen to make the same jaunt, and help to intermix the more liberal part of them still more with us, and perhaps abate somewhat of that virulent antipathy which many of them entertain against the Scotch ; who certainly would never have formed those *combinations* which he takes notice of, more than their ancestors, had they not been necessary for their mutual safety, at least for their success, in a country where they are treated as foreigners. They would find us not deficient, at least in point of hospitality, and they would be ashamed ever after to abuse us in the mass.

"So much for the Tour.—I have now, for the first time in my life, passed a winter in the country; and never did three months roll on with more swiftness and satisfaction. I used not only to wonder at, but pity, those whose lot condemned them to winter any where but in either of the capitals. But every place has its charms to a cheerful mind. I am busy planting and taking measures for opening the summer campaign in farming; and I find I have an excellent resource, when revolutions in politicks perhaps, and revolutions of the sun for certain, will make it decent for me to retreat behind the ranks of the more forward in life.

"I am glad to hear the last was a very busy week with you. I see you as counsel in some causes which must have opened a charming field for your humourous vein. As it is more uncommon, so I verily believe it is more useful than the more serious exercise of reason; and, to a man who is to appear in publick, more eclat is to be gained, sometimes more money too, by a *bon-mot*, than a learned speech. It is the fund of natural humour which Lord North possesses, that makes him so much the favourite of the house, and so able, because so amiable, a leader of a party.

"I have now finished *my* Tour of *Seven Pages*. In what remains, I beg leave to offer my compliments, and those of *ma tres chere femme*, to you and Mrs. Boswell. Pray unbend the busy brow, and frolick a little in a letter to,

      "My dear Boswell,
          "Your affectionate friend,
              "GEORGE DEMPSTER."

I shall also present the publick with a correspondence with the Laird of Rasay, concerning a passage in the *Journey to the Western Islands*, which shews Dr. Johnson in a very amiable light.

" To James Boswell, Esq.

" Dear Sir,   " Rasay, *April* 10th, 1775.

" I take this occasion of returning you my most hearty thanks for the civilities shown to my daughter by you and Mrs. Boswell. Yet, though she has informed me that I am under this obligation, I should very probably have deferred troubling you with making my acknowledgments at present, if I had not seen Dr. Johnson's *Journey to the Western Isles*, in which he has been pleased to make a very friendly mention of my family, for which I am surely obliged to him, as being more than an equivalent for the reception you and he met with. Yet there is one paragraph I should have been glad he had omitted, which I am sure was owing to misinformation ; that is, that I had acknowledged M'Leod to be my chief, though my ancestors disputed the pre-eminence for a long tract of time.

" I never had occasion to enter seriously on this argument with the present laird or his grandfather, nor could I have any temptation to such a renunciation from either of them. I acknowledge, the benefit of being chief of a clan is in our days of very little significancy, and to trace out the progress of this honour to the founder of a family, of any standing, would perhaps be a matter of some difficulty.

" The true state of the present case is this : the M'Leod family consists of two different branches ; the M'Leods of Lewis, of which I am descended, and the M'Leods of Harris. And though the former have lost a very extensive estate by forfeiture in King James the Sixth's time, there are still several respectable families of it existing, who would justly blame me for such an unmeaning cession, when they all acknowledge me head of that family ; which though in fact it be but an ideal point of honour, is not hitherto so far disregarded in our country, but it would determine

some of my friends to look on me as a much smaller
man than either they or myself judge me at present to
be. I will, therefore, ask it as a favour of you to acquaint
the Doctor with the difficulty he has brought me to. In
travelling among rival clans, such a silly tale as this
might easily be whispered into the ear of a passing
stranger; but as it has no foundation in fact, I hope
the Doctor will be so good as to take his own way in
undeceiving the publick, I principally mean my friends
and connections, who will be first angry at me, and
next sorry to find such an instance of my littleness
recorded in a book which has a very fair chance of being
much read. I expect you will let me know what he
will write you in return, and we here beg to make
offer to you and Mrs. Boswell of our most respectful
compliments. I am,

"Dear sir,
"Your most obedient humble servant,
"JOHN M'LEOD."

"TO THE LAIRD OF RASAY

"LONDON, *May* 8, 1775.

"DEAR SIR,
"THE day before yesterday I had the honour to
receive your letter, and I immediately communicated
it to Dr. Johnson. He said he loved your spirit, and
was exceedingly sorry that he had been the cause of
the smallest uneasiness to you. There is not a more
candid man in the world than he is, when properly
addressed, as you will see from his letter to you, which
I now enclose. He has allowed me to take a copy of it,
and he says you may read it to your clan, or publish it
if you please. Be assured, sir, that I shall take care
of what he has entrusted to me, which is to have an
acknowledgment of his errour inserted in the Edinburgh
newspapers. You will, I dare say, be fully satisfied

with Dr. Johnson's behaviour. He is desirous to know that you are ; and therefore when you have read his acknowledgement in the papers, I beg you may write to me ; and if you choose it, I am persuaded a letter from you to the Doctor also will be taken kind. I shall be at Edinburgh the week after next.

" Any civilities which my wife and I had in our power to shew to your daughter, Miss M'Leod, were due to her own merit, and were well repaid by her agreeable company. But I am sure I should be a very unworthy man if I did not wish to shew a grateful sense of the hospitable and genteel manner in which you were pleased to treat me. Be assured, my dear sir, that I shall never forget your goodness, and the happy hours which I spent in Rasay.

" You and Dr. M'Leod were both so obliging as to promise me an account in writing, of all the particulars which each of you remember, concerning the transactions of 1745-6. Pray do not forget this, and be as minute and full as you can ; put down every thing ; I have a great curiosity to know as much as I can, authentically.

" I beg that you may present my best respects to Lady Rasay, my compliments to your young family, and to Dr. M'Leod ; and my hearty good wishes to Malcolm, with whom I hope again to shake hands cordially. I have the honour to be,

" Dear sir,
" Your obliged and faithful humble servant,
" JAMES BOSWELL."

ADVERTISEMENT, written by Dr. Johnson, and inserted by his desire in the Edinburgh newspapers :—Referred to in the foregoing letter.

" THE author of the *Journey to the Western Islands*, having related that the M'Leods of Rasay acknowledge the chieftainship or superiority of the M'Leods of Sky, finds that he has been misinformed or mistaken. He

means in a future edition to correct his errour, and wishes
to be told of more, if more have been discovered.''

Dr. Johnson's letter was as follows :

" To the Laird of Rasay.

" Dear Sir,

" Mr. Boswell has this day shewn me a letter,
in which you complain of a passage in the *Journey to
the Hebrides*. My meaning is mistaken. I did not
intend to say that you had personally made any cession
of the rights of your house, or any acknowledgement
of the superiority of M'Leod of Dunvegan. I only
designed to express what I thought generally admitted,
—that the house of Rasay allowed the superiority of
the house of Dunvegan. Even this I now find to be
erroneous, and will therefore omit or retract it in the
next edition.

" Though what I had said had been true, if it had
been disagreeable to you, I should have wished it un-
said ; for it is not my business to adjust precedence.
As it is mistaken, I find myself disposed to correct,
both by my respect for you, and my reverence for
truth.

" As I know not when the book will be reprinted,
I have desired Mr. Boswell to anticipate the correction
in the Edinburgh papers. This is all that can be done.

" I hope I may now venture to desire that my compliments may be made, and my gratitude expressed,
to Lady Rasay, Mr. Malcolm M'Leod, Mr. Donald
M'Queen, and all the gentlemen and all the ladies
whom I saw in the island of Rasay ; a place which I
remember with too much pleasure and too much kindness, not to be sorry that my ignorance, or hasty persuasion, should, for a single moment, have violated its
tranquillity.

"I beg you all to forgive an undesigned and involuntary injury, and to consider me as,

"Sir, your most obliged,

"and most humble servant,

"SAM. JOHNSON."

'LONDON *May 6*, 1775."

It would be improper for me to boast of my own labours ; but I cannot refrain from publishing such praise as I received from such a man as Sir William Forbes, of Pitsligo, after the perusal of the original manuscript of my Journal.

"To JAMES BOSWELL, ESQ.

"EDINBURGH, *March* 7, 1777.

"MY DEAR SIR,

"I OUGHT to have thanked you sooner, for your very obliging letter, and for the singular confidence you are pleased to place in me, when you trust me with such a curious and valuable deposit as the papers you have sent me. Be assured I have a due sense of this favour, and shall faithfully and carefully return them to you. You may rely that I shall neither copy any part, nor permit the papers to be seen.

"They contain a curious picture of society, and form a journal on the most instructive plan that can possibly be thought of ; for I am not sure that an ordinary observer would become so well acquainted either with Dr. Johnson, or with the manners of the Hebrides, by a personal intercourse, as by a perusal of your Journal.

"I am very truly, Dear Sir,

"Your most obedient,

"And affectionate humble servant,

"WILLIAM FORBES."

When I consider how many of the persons mentioned in this Tour are now gone to " that undiscovered country, from whose bourne no traveller returns," I feel an impression at once awful and tender.—*Requiescant in pace!*

It may be objected by some persons, as it has been by one of my friends, that he who has the power of thus exhibiting an exact transcript of conversations is not a desirable member of society. I repeat the answer which I made to that friend:— " Few, very few, need be afraid that their sayings will be recorded. Can it be imagined that I would take the trouble to gather what grows on every hedge, because I have collected such fruits as the *Nonpareil* and the BON CHRETIEN ? "

On the other hand, how useful is such a faculty, if well exercised ! To it we owe all those interesting apothegms and *memorabilia* of the ancients, which Plutarch, Xenophon, and Valerius Maximus, have transmitted to us. To it we owe all those instructive and entertaining collections which the French have made under the title of *Ana,* affixed to some celebrated name. To it we owe the *Table-talk* of Selden, the *Conversation* between Ben Jonson and Drummond of Hawthornden, Spence's *Anecdotes* of Pope, and other valuable remains in our own language. How delighted should we have been, if thus introduced into the company of Shakspeare and of Dryden, of whom we know scarcely anything but their admirable writings ! What pleasure would it have given us, to have known their petty habits, their characteristick manners, their modes of composition, and their genuine opinion of preceding writers and of their contemporaries ! All these are now irrecoverably lost.—Considering how many of the strongest and most brilliant effusions of exalted intellect must have perished, how much is it to be regretted that all men of distinguished wisdom and wit have not been attended by friends, of taste enough to relish, and abilities enough to register their conversation ;

Vixere fortes ante Agamemnona
Multi, sed omnes illacrymabiles
Urgentur, ignotique longa
Nocte, carent quia vate sacro.

They whose inferiour exertions are recorded, as serving to explain or illustrate the sayings of such men, may be proud of being thus associated, and of their names being transmitted to posterity, by being appended to an illustrious character.

Before I conclude, I think it proper to say, that I have suppressed every thing which I thought could *really* hurt any one now living. Vanity and self-conceit indeed may sometimes suffer. With respect to what *is* related, I considered it my duty to " extenuate nothing, nor set down aught in malice ; " and with those lighter strokes of Dr. Johnson's satire, proceeding from a warmth and quickness of imagination, not from any malevolence of heart, and which, on account of their excellence, could not be omitted, I trust that they who are the subject of them have good sense and good temper enough not to be displeased.

I have only to add, that I shall ever reflect with great pleasure on a Tour, which has been the means of preserving so much of the enlightened and instructive conversation of one whose virtues will, I hope, ever be an object of imitation, and whose powers of mind were so extraordinary, that ages may revolve before such a man shall again appear.

APPENDIX

No. I

In justice to the ingenious DR. BLACKLOCK, I publish the following letter from him, relative to a passage in p. 42 :—

" To JAMES BOSWELL, ESQ.

" DEAR SIR,
" HAVING lately had the pleasure of reading your account of the journey which you took with Dr. Samuel Johnson to the Western Isles, I take the liberty of transmitting my ideas of the conversation which happened between the doctor and myself concerning Lexicography and Poetry, which, as it is a little different from the delineation exhibited in the former edition of your Journal, cannot, I hope, be unacceptable ; particularly since I have been informed that a second edition of that work is now in contemplation, if not in execution : and I am still more strongly tempted to encourage that hope, from considering that, if every one concerned in the conversations related, were to send you what they can recollect of these colloquial entertainments, many curious and interesting particulars might be recovered, which the most assiduous attention could not observe, nor the most tenacious memory retain. A little reflection, sir, will convince you, that there is not an axiom in Euclid more intuitive nor more evident than the doctor's assertion that poetry was of much easier

execution than lexicography. Any mind therefore endowed with common sense, must have been extremely absent from itself, if it discovered the least astonishment from hearing that a poem might be written with much more facility than the same quantity of a dictionary.

" The real cause of my surprise was what appeared to me much more paradoxical, that he could write a sheet of dictionary *with as much pleasure* as a sheet of poetry. He acknowledged, indeed, that the latter was much easier than the former. For in the one case, books and a desk were requisite ; in the other, you might compose when lying in bed, or walking in the fields, &c. He did not, however, descend to explain, nor to this moment can I comprehend, how the labours of a mere Philologist, in the most refined sense of that term, could give equal pleasure with the exercise of a mind replete with elevated conceptions and pathetic ideas, while taste, fancy, and intellect were deeply enamoured of nature, and in full exertion. You may likewise, perhaps, remember, that when I complained of the ground which Scepticism in religion and morals was continually gaining, it did not appear to be on my own account, as my private opinions upon these important subjects had long been inflexibly determined. What I then deplored, and still deplore, was the unhappy influence which that gloomy hesitation had, not only upon particular characters, but even upon life in general ; as being equally the bane of action in our present state, and of such consolations as we might derive from the hopes of a future.

" I have the pleasure of remaining with sincere esteem and respect,

" Dear Sir,

" Your most obedient humble servant,

" THOMAS BLACKLOCK."

" EDINBURGH, *Nov.* 12, 1785."

I am very happy to find that Dr. Blacklock's apparent uneasiness on the subject of Scepticism was not on his own account, (as I supposed,) but from a benevolent concern for the happiness of mankind. With respect, however, to the question concerning poetry, and composing a dictionary, I am confident that my state of Dr. Johnson's position is accurate. One may misconceive the motive by which a person is induced to discuss a particular topick (as in the case of Dr. Blacklock's speaking of Scepticism) ; but an assertion, like that made by Dr. Johnson, cannot be easily mistaken. And indeed it seems not very probable, that he who so pathetically laments the *drudgery* to which the unhappy lexicographer is doomed, and is known to have written his splendid imitation of Juvenal with astonishing rapidity, should have had " as much pleasure in writing a sheet of a dictionary as a sheet of poetry." Nor can I concur with the ingenious writer of the foregoing letter, in thinking it an axiom as evident as any in Euclid, that " poetry is of easier execution than lexicography." I have no doubt that Bailey, and the " mighty blunderbuss of law," Jacob, wrote ten pages of their respective Dictionaries with more ease than they could have written five pages of poetry.

If this book should again be reprinted, I shall, with the utmost readiness, correct any errours I may have committed, in stating conversations, provided it can be clearly shewn to me that I have been inaccurate. But I am slow to believe, (as I have elsewhere observed,) that any man's memory, at the distance of several years, can preserve facts or sayings with such fidelity as may be done by writing them down when they are recent : and I beg it may be remembered, that it is not upon *memory*, but upon what was *written at the time*, that the authenticity of my Journal rests.

No. II

VERSES WRITTEN BY SIR ALEXANDER (NOW LORD) MACDONALD;

ADDRESSED AND PRESENTED TO DR. JOHNSON, AT ARMIDALE IN THE ISLE OF SKY.

Viator, o qui nostra per æquora
Visurus agros Skiaticos venis,
  En te salutantes tributim
    Undique conglomerantur oris.

Donaldiani,—quotquot in insulis
Compescit arctis limitibus mare ;
  Alitque jamdudum, ac alendos
    Piscibus indigenas fovebit.

Ciere fluctus siste, Procelliger,
Nec tu laborans perge, precor, ratis
  Ne conjugem plangat marita,
    Ne doleat soboles parentem.

Nec te vicissim pœniteat virum
Luxisse ;—vestro scimus ut æstuant
  In corde luctantes dolores,
    Cum feriant inopina corpus.

Quidni ! peremptum clade tuentibus
Plus semper illo qui moritur pati
  Datur, doloris dum profundos
    Pervia mens aperit recessus.

Valete luctus ;—hinc lacrymabiles
Arcete visus :—ibimus, ibimus
   Superbienti qua theatro
     Fingaliæ memorantur aule.

Illustris hospes ! mox spatiabere
Qua mens ruinæ ducta meatibus
   Gaudebit explorare cœtus,
     Buccina qua cecinit triumphos ;

Audin ? resurgens spirat anhelita
Dux usitato, suscitat efficax
   Poeta manes, ingruitque
     Vi solitâ redivivus horror.

Ahæna quassans tela gravi manu
Sic ibat atrox Ossiani pater :
   Quiescat urnâ, stet fidelis
     " Phersonius vigil ad favillam."

THE END

PRINTED IN GREAT BRITAIN AT
THE PRESS OF THE PUBLISHERS

NELSON CLASSICS

Cloth gilt. 1s. 6d. *net.*

This famous series has been completely rejuvenated; it is far more attractive in every way than it has ever been before, and it offers value absolutely unequalled in the world of books. Its range and appeal are apparent from a mere glance through the list, but the books themselves have to be seen to be appreciated. Ask your bookseller to show them to you. They are being reissued in striking new wrappers, with new bindings (fadeless and washable, ten attractive colours blocked in real gold), tinted tops, and fresh title-pages.

Recent additions include classics of modern fiction, by Conrad, Hugh Walpole, Walter de la Mare, E. C. Bentley, John Buchan, etc., and authoritative works for the more studious reader—*The Atom*, by Professor Andrade, for example; *The English Novel*, by J. B. Priestley; *Money*, by Hartley Withers; and *Protestantism*, by Dean Inge.

New volumes are added every month. If you would like notices of them, send a card to-day to Nelsons, 35–36 Paternoster Row, London, E.C.4; Parkside Works, Edinburgh; 25 rue Denfert-Rochereau, Paris; 91–93 Wellington Street West, Toronto; 381–385 Fourth Avenue, New York; 312 Flinders Street, Melbourne.

HARRISON AINSWORTH : Old St. Paul's ; The Tower of London ; Windsor Castle.

LOUISA ALCOTT : Little Women.

HANS ANDERSEN : Fairy Tales.

E. N. DA C. ANDRADE : The Atom.

ANONYMOUS : Tales from the Arabian Nights.

MATTHEW ARNOLD : Poems. Introduction by John Buchan.

JANE AUSTEN : Emma ; Mansfield Park ; Northanger Abbey ; Persuasion ; Pride & Prejudice ; Sense & Sensibility.

FRANCIS BACON : Essays.

WALTER BAGEHOT : Selected Essays.

JOHN BAILEY (Editor) : A Shorter Boswell. *Illustrated.*

R. M. BALLANTYNE : Martin Rattler, *Illustrated* ; The Coral Island, *Illustrated* ; Ungava, *Illustrated.*

H. DE BALZAC : Eugénie Grandet.

R. H. BARHAM : The Ingoldsby Legends.

R. R. DU BATY : 15,000 Miles in a Ketch.

CUTHBERT BEDE : Mr. Verdant Green.

E. C. BENTLEY : Trent's Last Case.

R. D. BLACKMORE : Lorna Doone.

GEORGE BORROW : The Bible in Spain ; Lavengro ; The Romany Rye ; Wild Wales.

JAMES BOSWELL : A Tour in the Hebrides with Dr. Johnson ; A Shorter Boswell, edited by John Bailey. *Illustrated.*

ANNE BRONTË : Agnes Grey (with the Poems of Charlotte, Emily, and Anne Brontë, and The Brontës, by Flora Masson).

CHARLOTTE BRONTË : Jane Eyre ; The Professor ; Shirley ; Villette.

EMILY BRONTË : Wuthering Heights, *Illustrated.*

DR. JOHN BROWN : Horæ Subsecivæ.

ROBERT BROWNING : Poems. Intro. by John Buchan.

JOHN BUCHAN : Greenmantle.

JOHN BUNYAN : The Pilgrim's Progress, *Illustrated.*

EDMUND BURKE : Selections.

ROBERT BURNS : Complete Poems. (2s.)

THOMAS CARLYLE : Sartor Resartus ; Selected Essays.

WILLIAM COBBETT : Rural Rides.

S. T. COLERIDGE : Poems. Intro. by Sir Henry Newbolt.

WILKIE COLLINS : The Moonstone ; The Woman in White.

A. COMPTON-RICKETT : A Primer of English Literature. (*With 56 illustrations.*)

JOSEPH CONRAD : Romance.

FENIMORE COOPER : The Deerslayer ; The Last of the Mohicans ; The Pathfinder.

WILLIAM COWPER : Poems. Intro. by John Bailey.

G. W. COX : Tales of the Gods and Heroes.

MRS. CRAIK : John Halifax, Gentleman.

R. H. DANA : Two Years before the Mast, *Illustrated.*

CHARLES DARWIN : The Voyage of the " Beagle."

DANIEL DEFOE : Robinson Crusoe.

WALTER DE LA MARE : The Nap, and other Stories.

CHARLES DICKENS : American Notes *and* Master Humphrey's Clock ; Barnaby Rudge ; Bleak House ; A Child's History of England ; Christmas Books ; Christmas Stories ; David Copperfield (2s.) ; Dombey and Son (2s.) ; Great Expectations ; Hard Times ; Little Dorrit (2s.) ; Martin Chuzzlewit (2s.) ; The Mystery of Edwin Drood *and* Pictures from Italy ; Nicholas Nickleby (2s.) ; Pickwick Papers (2s.) ; Oliver Twist ; Our Mutual Friend (2s.) ; A Tale of Two Cities ; Sketches by Boz ; The Uncommercial Traveller.

BENJAMIN DISRAELI : Coningsby ; Lothair ; Sybil.

JOHN DRYDEN : Poems. Intro. by John St. Loe Strachey.

ALEXANDRE DUMAS : The Black Tulip, *Illustrated* ; The Count of Monte-Cristo (2 vols.) ; Marguerite de Valois ; The Queen's Necklace ; The Three Musketeers, *Illustrated.*

GEORGE ELIOT : Adam Bede ; The Mill on the Floss, *Illustrated* ; Romola ; Scenes of Clerical Life ; Silas Marner.

R. W. EMERSON : Selected Essays.

JOHN GALT : Annals of the Parish.

MRS. GASKELL : Cranford ; Mary Barton ; Sylvia's Lovers.

MRS. GATTY : Parables from Nature.

OLIVER GOLDSMITH : Essays and Tales, selected by Rosalind Vallance, with Thackeray's Essay on Goldsmith ; Poems and Plays, Introduction by Professor Garrod ; The Vicar of Wakefield, *Illustrated*, with Sir Walter Scott's Life of Goldsmith.

KENNETH GRAHAME : The Golden Age (*April* 1936).

JAMES GRANT : The Yellow Frigate.

J. L. and W. K. GRIMM : Fairy Tales.

E. S. GROGAN : From the Cape to Cairo.

JOHN HAMPDEN (Editor) : Sea Stories (by John Buchan,
H. G. Wells, John Masefield, W. W. Jacobs, etc.).

BRET HARTE : Tales of the West *and* Condensed Novels.

NATHANIEL HAWTHORNE : The Scarlet Letter ;
Tanglewood Tales.

ROBERT HERRICK : Poems. Intro. by Sir John Squire.

THOMAS HUGHES : Tom Brown's Schooldays, *Illustrated* ; Tom Brown at Oxford.

VICTOR HUGO : The Laughing Man ; Les Misérables
(2 vols.) ; 'Ninety-Three ; Notre Dame ; Toilers of the
Sea.

W. R. INGE : Protestantism.

W. W. JACOBS : Many Cargoes.

JOHN KEATS : Poems. Intro. by Sir Henry Newbolt.

THOMAS À KEMPIS : Of the Imitation of Christ.

A. W. KINGLAKE : Eothen.

CHARLES KINGSLEY : Alton Locke ; Hereward the
Wake ; The Heroes ; Hypatia, *Illustrated* ; Westward Ho !
Illustrated ; Yeast.

HENRY KINGSLEY : Geoffrey Hamlyn ; Ravenshoe.

CHARLES LAMB : Essays of Elia ; Tales from Shakespeare.

LORD LYTTON : Last Days of Pompeii.

LORD MACAULAY : Historical Essays ; Literary Essays ;
Lays of Ancient Rome.

CAPTAIN MARRYAT : The Children of the New Forest,
Illustrated ; Masterman Ready, *Illustrated*; Midshipman
Easy.

JOHN MASEFIELD : Lost Endeavour.

JOHN MILTON : Poems. Intro. by Sir Henry Newbolt.

WILLIAM MORRIS : Poems *and* Two Prose Romances.

SIR HENRY NEWBOLT : The New June.

SIR HENRY NEWBOLT (Editor) : Seventeenth-century
Devotional Poetry (Donne, Herbert, Crashaw, Herrick,
Vaughan, Traherne).

F. T. PALGRAVE (Editor) : The Golden Treasury.

EDGAR ALLAN POE : Tales of Mystery and Imagination,
Illustrated. Introduction by John Buchan.

ALEXANDER POPE : Poems. Intro. by John Bailey.

J. B. PRIESTLEY : The English Novel (18 *portraits*).

SIR ROBERT S. RAIT : British History (to 1924).

ARTHUR RANSOME : Old Peter's Russian Tales, *Illustrated* by Dmitri Mitrokhin.

A. J. J. RATCLIFF (Editor) : Prose of Our Time (by famous modern writers).

CHARLES READE : The Cloister and the Hearth ; Peg Woffington.

LORD ROSEBERY : Napoleon—The Last Phase.

D. G. ROSSETTI : Poems. Introduction by John Buchan.

JOHN RUSKIN : Modern Painters (Selections) ; Sesame and Lilies.

SIR WALTER SCOTT : The Abbot ; The Antiquary ; The Betrothed ; The Bride of Lammermoor ; Chronicles of the Canongate *and* The Highland Widow ; The Fair Maid of Perth ; The Fortunes of Nigel ; Guy Mannering ; The Heart of Midlothian ; Ivanhoe, *Illustrated* ; Journal (2 vols.) ; Kenilworth ; A Legend of Montrose ; The Monastery ; Old Mortality ; The Pirate ; Quentin Durward ; Redgauntlet ; Rob Roy ; St. Ronan's Well ; The Talisman ; Waverley ; Woodstock.

WILLIAM SHAKESPEARE : Complete Works—Comedies (2 vols.) ; Histories, Poems (2 vols.) ; Tragedies (2 vols.). —Plays for Community Players (*Julius Cæsar, As You Like It, Romeo and Juliet*).

P. B. SHELLEY : Poems. Introduction by Sir Henry Newbolt.

H. SIENKIEWICZ : Quo Vadis ?

SOMERVILLE and ROSS : Some Experiences of an Irish R.M. (*April* 1936).

R. L. STEVENSON : Across the Plains ; The Black Arrow, *Illustrated* ; Catriona ; Poems—A Child's Garden of Verses, Underwoods, Songs of Travel (1 vol.) ; Dr. Jekyll and Mr. Hyde *and* The Story of a Lie ; The Dynamiter ; Familiar Studies of Men and Books ; An Inland Voyage ; In the South Seas ; Island Nights' Entertainments ; Kidnapped ; The Master of Ballantrae ; Memories and Portraits ; The Merry Men and other tales ; New Arabian

Nights ; Prince Otto ; The Silverado Squatters *and* The Amateur Emigrant ; Travels with a Donkey in the Cevennes ; Treasure Island, *Illustrated* ; Vailima Letters ; Virginibus Puerisque ; Weir of Hermiston.

MRS. BEECHER STOWE : Uncle Tom's Cabin, *Illustrated*.

JONATHAN SWIFT : Gulliver's Travels, *Illustrated*.

LORD TENNYSON : Poems.

W. M. THACKERAY : The Book of Snobs *and* Barry Lyndon ; Henry Esmond ; Pendennis (2s.) ; The New-comes (2s.) ; Vanity Fair (2s.).

TOLSTOY : Anna Karenina (2 vols.).

G. M. TREVELYAN : Garibaldi and the Thousand.

ANTHONY TROLLOPE : Barchester Towers, *Illustrated* ; Framley Parsonage ; The Last Chronicle of Barset (2s.) ; The Warden.

HUGH WALPOLE : Fortitude.

IZAAK WALTON and C. COTTON : The Compleat Angler.

IZAAK WALTON : Lives of Donne, Walton, Hooker, Herbert, and Sanderson.

ELIZABETH WETHERELL : The Wide, Wide World.

HARTLEY WITHERS : Money.

MRS. HENRY WOOD : East Lynne ; Mrs. Haliburton's Troubles ; Roland Yorke.

WILLIAM WORDSWORTH : Poems. Introduction by Viscount Grey of Fallodon.

J. R. WYSS : The Swiss Family Robinson, *Illustrated*.

CHARLOTTE YONGE : A Book of Golden Deeds.

Many of the above volumes are issued also in the WINCHESTER CLASSICS, *at 2s. 6d. net (double volumes, 3s. 6d. net), in blue rexine binding, with gilt top and slip case. Complete list post free.*